Korea's Fight for Freedom

F.A. McKenzie

Contents

KOREA'S FIGHT
FOR FREEDOM

BY

F.A. McKenzie

KOREA'S FIGHT FOR FREEDOM

M r. F.A. McKenzie has been abused in the columns of the Japanese press with a violence which, in the absence of any reasoned controversy, indicated a last resource. In answer to his specific charges, only one word has been uttered--'lies!'

"Yet these charges embrace crimes of the first magnitude--murder, plunder, outrage, incendiarism, and in short all the horrors that make up tyranny of the worst description. It is difficult to see how Mr. McKenzie's sincerity could be called into question, for he, too, like many other critics of the new Administration, was once a warm friend and supporter of Japan. "In those days, his contributions were quoted at great length in the newspapers of Tokyo, while the editorial columns expressed their appreciation of his marked capacity. So soon, however, as he found fault with the conditions prevailing in Korea, he was contemptuously termed a 'yellow journalist' and a 'sensation monger.'"-- From "Empires of the Far East" by F. Lancelot Lawson. London. Grant Richards . "Mr. McKenzie was perhaps the only foreigner outside the ranks of missionaries who ever took the trouble to elude the vigilance of the Japanese, escape from Seoul into the interior, and there see with his own eyes what the Japanese were really doing. And yet when men of this kind, who write of things which come within scope of personal observation and enquiry, have the presumption to tell the world that all is not well in Korea, and that the Japanese cannot be acquitted of guilt in this context, grave pundits in Tokyo, London and New York gravely rebuke them for following their own senses in preference to the official returns of the Residency General. It is a poor joke at the best! Nor is it the symptom of a powerful cause that the failure of the Japanese authorities to 'pacify' the interior is ascribed to 'anti-Japanese' writers like Mr. McKenzie."-- From "Peace and War in the Far East," by E.J. Harrison. Yokohama. Kelly and Walsh .

Preface

The peaceful uprising of the people of Korea against Japan in the spring of 1919 came as a world surprise. Here was a nation that had been ticketed and docketed by world statesmen as degenerate and cowardly, revealing heroism of a very high order.

The soldier facing the enemy in the open is inspired by the atmosphere of war, and knows that he has at least a fighting chance against his foe. The Koreans took their stand--their women and children by their side--without weapons and without means of defense. They pledged themselves ahead to show no violence. They had all too good reason to anticipate that their lot would be the same as that of others who had preceded them--torture as ingenious and varied as Torquemada and his familiars ever practiced.

They were not disappointed. They were called on to endure all that they had anticipated, in good measure, pressed down and running over. When they were dragged to prison, others stepped into their place. When these were taken, still others were ready to succeed them. And more are even now waiting to join in the dreadful procession, if the protests of the civilized world do not induce Japan to call a halt.

It seems evident that either the world made a mistake in its first estimate of Korean character, or these people have experienced a new birth. Which is the right explanation? Maybe both.

To understand what has happened, and what, as I write, is still happening, one has to go back for a few years. When Japan, in face of her repeated pledges, annexed Korea, her statesmen adopted an avowed policy of assimilation. They attempted to turn the people of Korea into Japanese--an inferior brand of Japanese, a serf race, speaking the language and following the customs of their overlords, and serving them.

To accomplish this better, the Koreans were isolated, not allowed to mix freely with the outer world, and deprived of liberty of speech, person and press. The Japanese brought certain material reforms. They forgot to supply one thing--justice. Men of progressive ideas were seized and imprisoned in such numbers that a new series of prisons had to be built. In six years the total of prisoners convicted or awaiting trial doubled. The rule of the big stick was instituted, and the Japanese police were given the right to flog without trial any Korean they pleased. The bamboo was employed on scores of thousands of people each year, employed so vigorously as to leave a train of cripples and corpses behind. The old tyranny of the yang-ban was replaced by a more terrible, because more scientifically cruel, tyranny of an uncontrolled police.

The Japanese struck an unexpected strain of hardness in the Korean character. They found, underneath the surface apathy, a spirit as determined as their own. They succeeded, not in assimilating the people, but in reviving their sense of nationality.

Before Japan acquired the country, large numbers of Koreans had adopted Christianity. Under the influence of the teachers from America, they became clean in person, they brought their women out from the "anpang" (zenana) into the light of day, and they absorbed Western ideas and ideals. The mission schools taught modern history, with its tales of the heroes and heroines of liberty, women like Joan of Arc, men like Hampden and George Washington. And the missionaries circulated and taught the Bible--the most dynamic and disturbing book in the world. When a people saturated in the Bible comes into touch with tyranny, either one of two things happens, the people are exterminated or tyranny ceases.

The Japanese realized their danger. They tried, in vain, to bring the Churches under Japanese control. They confiscated or forbade missionary textbooks, substituting their own. Failing to win the support of the Christians, they instituted a widespread persecution of the Christian leaders of the north. Many were arrested and tortured on charges which the Japanese Courts themselves afterwards found to be false. The Koreans endured until they could endure no more. Not the Christians alone, but men of all faiths and all classes acted as one. The story of their great protest, of what led up to it, and the way in which it was met, is told in this book.

To the outsider, one of the most repulsive features of the Japanese method of government of Korea is the wholesale torture of untried prisoners, particularly political prisoners. Were this torture an isolated occurrence, I would not mention it. There are always occasional men who, invested with authority and not properly controlled, abuse their position. But here torture is employed in many centres and on thousands of people. The Imperial Japanese Government, while enacting paper regulations against the employment of torture, in effect condones it. When details of the inhuman treatment of Christian Korean prisoners have been given in open court, and the victims have been found innocent, the higher authorities have taken no steps to bring the torturers to justice.

The forms of torture freely employed include, among others:--

1. The stripping, beating, kicking, flogging, and outraging of schoolgirls and young women.

2. Flogging schoolboys to death.

3. Burning--the burning of young girls by pressing lighted cigarettes against their tender parts, and the burning of men, women and children by searing their bodies with hot irons.

4. Stringing men up by their thumbs, beating them with bamboos and iron rods until unconscious, restoring them and repeating the process, sometimes several times in one day, sometimes until death.

5. Contraction--tying men up in such fashion as to cause intense suffering.

6. Confinement for long periods under torturing conditions, as, e.g., where men and women are packed so tightly in a room that they cannot lie or sit down for days at a stretch.

In the latter chapters of this book I supply details of many cases where such methods have been employed. Where it can safely be done, I give full names and places. In many instances this is impossible, for it would expose the victims to further ill treatment. Sworn statements have been made before the American Consular authorities covering many of the worst events that followed the 1919 uprising. These are now, I understand, with the State Department at Washington. It is to be hoped that in due course they will be published in full.

*   *   *   *   *

When my book, "The Tragedy of Korea," was published in 1908, it seemed a thankless and hopeless task to plead for a stricken and forsaken nation. The book, however, aroused a wide-spread and growing interest. It has been more widely quoted and discussed in 1919 than in any previous year. Lawyers have argued over it in open court; statesmen have debated parts of it in secret conferences, Senates and Parliaments. At a famous political trial, one question was put to the prisoner, "Have you read the 'Tragedy of Korea'?" It has been translated into Chinese.

At first I was accused of exaggeration and worse. Subsequent events have amply borne out my statements and warnings. The book has been for a long time out of print, and even second-hand copies have been difficult to obtain. I was strongly urged to publish a new edition, bringing my narrative up to date, but I found that it would be better to write a new book, including in it, however, some of the most debated passages and chapters of the old. This I have done.

Some critics have sought to charge me with being "anti-Japanese." No man has written more appreciatively of certain phases of Japanese character and accomplishments than myself. My personal relations with the Japanese, more especially with the Japanese Army, left me with no sense of personal grievance but with many pleasant and cordial memories. My Japanese friends were good enough to say, in the old days, that these agreeable recollections were mutual.

I have long been convinced, however, that the policy of Imperial expansion adopted by Japan, and the means employed in advancing it, are a grave menace to her own permanent well-being and to the future peace of the world. I am further convinced that the militarist party really controls Japanese policy, and that temporary modifications which have been recently announced do not imply any essential change of national plans and ambitions. If to believe and to proclaim this is "anti-Japanese," then I plead guilty to the charge. I share my guilt with many loyal and patriotic Japanese subjects, who see, as I see, the perils ahead.

In this book I describe the struggle of an ancient people towards liberty. I tell of a Mongol nation, roughly awakened from its long sleep, under conditions of tragic terror, that has seized hold of and is clinging fast to, things vital to civilization as we see it, freedom and free faith, the honour of their women, the development of their own souls.

I plead for Freedom and Justice. Will the world hear?

F.A. McKENZIE.

I
OPENING THE OYSTER

Up to the last quarter of the nineteenth century, Korea refused all intercourse with foreign nations. Peaceful ships that approached its uncharted and unlit shores were fired upon. Its only land approach, from the north, was bounded by an almost inaccessible mountain and forest region, and by a devastated "No Man's Land," infested by bandits and river pirates. When outside Governments made friendly approaches, and offered to show Korea the wonders of modern civilization, they received the haughty reply that Korea was quite satisfied with its own civilization, which had endured for four thousand years.

Even Korea, however, could not keep the world entirely in the dark about it. Chinese sources told something of its history. Its people were the descendants of Kitzse, a famous Chinese sage and statesman who, eleven hundred years before Christ, moved with his tribesmen over the river Yalu because he would not recognize or submit to a new dynasty that had usurped power in China. His followers doubtless absorbed and were influenced by still older settlers in Korea. The result was a people with strong national characteristics, different and distinct from the Chinese on the one side and the Japanese on the other.

We knew that, as Korea obtained much of its early knowledge from China, so it gave the younger nation of Japan its learning and industries. Its people reached a high stage of culture, and all records indicate that in the days when the early Briton painted himself with woad and when Rome was at her prime, Korea was a powerful, orderly and civilized kingdom. Unhappily it was placed as a buffer between two states, China, ready to absorb it, and Japan, keen to conquer its people as a preliminary to triumph over China.

In the course of centuries, it became an inbred tradition with the Japanese that they must seize Korea. Hideyoshi, the famous Japanese Regent, made a tremendous effort in 1582. Three hundred thousand troops swept over Korea, capturing city after city, and driving the Korean forces to the north. Korea appealed to China for aid, and after terrible fighting, the Japanese were driven back. They left a Korea in ruins, carrying off everything they could, and destroying all they could not carry off. They kidnapped, among others, the skilled workmen of Korea, and made them remain in Japan and carry on their industries there.

Hideyoshi's invasion is of more than historic interest Korea has never recovered the damage then done. The Japanese desire for Korea, thwarted for the moment, smouldered, waiting for the moment to burst afresh into flame. The memories of their terrible sufferings at the hands of the Japanese ground into the Koreans a hatred of their neighbour, handed down undiminished from generation to generation, to this day.

Korea might have recovered, but for another and even more serious handicap. A new dynasty, the House of Yi, succeeded to the Korean throne over five centuries ago, and established a rule fatal to all progress. The King was everything, and the nation lived solely for him. No man was allowed to become too rich or powerful. There must be no great nobles to come together and oppose these kings as the Norman Barons fought and checked the Norman Kings of England.

No man was allowed to build a house beyond a certain size, save the King. The only way to wealth or power was by enlisting in the King's service. The King's governors were free to plunder as they would, and even the village magistrate, representing the King, could freely work his will on those under him. The King had his eyes everywhere. His spies were all over the land. Let yang-ban (official or noble) however high show unhealthy ambition or seek to conceal anything from the royal knowledge and he would be called to Court and broken in an hour, and would count himself fortunate if he escaped with his life.

The Korean people are eminently pacific. Up to a point, they endure hard thing's uncomplainingly. It would have been better for them had they not suffered wrongs so tamely. The Yi method of government killed ambition--except for the King's service--killed enterprise and killed progress. The aim of the business man and the farmer was to escape notice and live quietly.

Foreigners attempted, time after time, to make their way into the country. French Catholic priests, as far back as the end of the eighteenth century, smuggled themselves in. Despite torture and death, they kept on, until the great persecution of 1866 wiped them and their converts out. This persecution arose because of fear of foreign aggression.

A Russian war vessel appeared off Broughton's Bay, demanding on behalf of Russians the right of commerce. The King at this time was a minor, adopted by the late King. His father, the Tai Won Kun, or Regent, ruled in his stead. He was a man of great force of character and no scruples. He slew in wholesale fashion those who dared oppose him. He had the idea that the Christians favoured the coming of the foreigner and so he turned his wrath on them. The native Catholics were wiped out, under every possible circumstance of brutality, and with them perished a number of French Catholic priests. By one of those contradictions which are constantly happening in real life, the crew of an American steamer, the Surprise, who were wrecked off the coast of Whang-hai that year were treated with all possible honour and consideration, and were returned home, through Manchuria, officials conducting them and the people coming out to greet them as they travelled through the land.

The French Minister at Peking determined on revenge for the death of the priests. A strong expedition was sent to the Han River, and attacked the forts on the Kangwha Island. The Korean troops met them bravely, and although the French obtained a temporary success, thanks to their modern weapons, they were in the end forced to retire.

An American ship, the General Sherman, set out for Korea in 1866, sailing from Tientsin for the purpose, it was rumoured, of plundering the royal tombs at Pyeng-yang. It entered the Tai-tong River, where it was ordered to stop. A fight opened between it and the Koreans, the latter in their dragon cloud armour, supposed to be impervious to bullets, sending their fire arrows against the invaders. The captain, not knowing the soundings of the river, ran his ship ashore. The Koreans sent fire boats drifting down the river towards the American ship. One of them set the General Sherman *in flames. Those of the crew who were not burned on the spot were soon slaughtered by the triumphant Korean soldiers. A more disreputable expedition, headed by a German Jew, Ernest Oppert and an American called Jenkins, left Shanghai in the following year, with a strong fighting crew of Chinese and Malays, and with a French missionary priest, M. Feron, as guide. They landed, and actually succeeded in reaching the royal tombs near the capital. Their shovels were useless, however, to remove the immense stones over the graves. A heavy fog enabled them to carry on their work for a time undisturbed. Soon an angry crowd gathered, and they had to return to their ship, the* China. They were fortunate to escape before the Korean troops came up. The American consular authorities in Shanghai placed Jenkins on trial, but there was not enough evidence to convict him.

The killing of the crew of the General Sherman **brought the American Government into action. Captain Shufeldt, commander of the** Wachusset, was ordered to go to Korea and obtain redress. He reached the mouth of the Han River, and sent a message to the King, asking an explanation of the matter. He had to retire, owing to weather conditions, before the reply arrived. The Korean reply, when eventually delivered, was in effect a plea of justification. The Americans, however, determined to inflict punishment, and a fleet was sent to destroy the forts on the Han River.

The American ships, the Monacacy **and the** Palos bombarded the forts. The Korean brass guns, of one and one-half inch bore, and their thirty pounders, could do nothing against the American howitzers, throwing eight and ten inch shells. The American Marines and sailors landed, and in capturing a hill fort, had a short, hot hand-to-hand battle with the defenders. The Koreans fought desperately, picking up handfuls of dust to fling in the eyes of the Americans when they had nothing else to fight with. Refusing to surrender they were wiped out. Having destroyed the forts and killed a number of the soldiers, there was nothing for the Americans to do but to retire. The "gobs" were the first to admit the real courage of the Korean soldiers.

Japan, which herself after considerable internal trouble, had accepted the coming of the Westerner as inevitable, tried on several occasions to renew relations with Korea. At first she was repulsed. In 1876 a Japanese ship, approaching the Korean coast, was fired on, as the Japanese a generation before had fired on foreign ships approaching their shore. There was a furious demand all over the country for revenge. Ito and other leaders with cool heads resisted the demand, but took such steps that Korea was compelled to conclude a treaty opening several ports to Japanese trade and giving Japan the right to send a minister to Seoul, the capital. The first clause of the first article of the treaty was in itself a warning of future trouble. "Chosen (Korea) being an independent state enjoys the same sovereign rights as does Japan." In other words Korea was virtually made to disown the slight Chinese protectorate which had been exercised for centuries.

The Chinese statesmen in Peking watched this undisturbed. They despised the Japanese too much to fear them, little dreaming that this small nation was within less than twenty years to humble them in the dust. Their real fear at this time was not Japan but Russia. Russia was stretching forth throughout Asia, and it looked as though she would try to seize Korea itself. And so Li Hung-chang advised the Korean rulers to guard themselves. "You must open your doors to other nations in order to keep out Russia," he told them. At the same time it was intimated to Ministers in Peking, particularly to the American Minister, that if he would approach the Koreans, they would be willing to listen. Commodore Shufeldt was made American Envoy, and an American-Korean Treaty was signed at Gensan on May 22, 1882. It was, truth to tell, a somewhat amateurish production, and had to be amended before it was finally ratified. It provided for the appointment of diplomatic and Consular officials, and for the opening of the country to commerce. A treaty with Britain was concluded in the following year, and other nations followed.

One clause in the American Treaty was afterwards regarded by the Korean ruler as the sheet anchor of his safety, until storm came and it was found that the sheet anchor did not hold.

> There shall be perpetual peace and friendship between the President of the United States and the King of Chosen and the citizens and subjects of their respective Governments. If other powers deal unjustly or oppressively with either Government, the other will exert their good offices, on being informed of the case, to bring about an amicable arrangement, thus showing their friendly feelings.

All of the treaties provided for extra-territoriality in Korea, that is to say that the foreigners charged with any offence there should be tried not by the Korean Courts but by their own, and punished by them.

Groups of adventurous foreigners soon entered the country. Foreign ministers and their staffs arrived first. Missionaries, concession hunters, traders and commercial travellers followed.

They found Seoul, the capital, beautifully placed in a valley surrounded by hills, a city of royal palaces and one-storied, mud-walled houses, roofed with thatch--a city guarded by great walls. Statesmen and nobles and generals, always surrounded by numerous retinues in glorious attire, ambled through the narrow streets in dignified procession. Closed palanquins, carried by sturdy bearers, bore yet other dignitaries.

The life of the city revolved round the King's Court, with its four thousand retainers, eunuchs, sorcerers, blind diviners, politicians and place hunters. The most prominent industry--outside of politics--was the making of brass ware, particularly of making fine brass mounted chests. The average citizen dressed in long flowing white robes, with a high, broad-brimmed, black gauze hat. Hundreds of women were ever busy at the river bank washing these white garments.

Women of good family remained at home, except for one hour after dark, when the men retired from the streets and the women came out. Working women went to and fro, with their faces shielded by green jackets thrown over their heads. Their usual dress was a white skirt coming high up and a very short jacket. The breasts and the flesh immediately below the breasts were often freely displayed. Fishing and farming supported ninety per cent of the population, and the Korean farmer was an expert. At sunset the gates of Seoul were closed, and belated wayfarers refused admission until morning. But there was no difficulty in climbing over the city walls. That was typical. Signal fires at night on the hills proclaimed that all was well.

The Koreans were mild, good natured, and full of contradictory characteristics. Despite their usual good nature, they were capable of great bursts of passion, particularly over public affairs. They often looked dirty, because their white clothes soiled easily; yet they probably spent more time and money over external cleanliness than any other Asiatic people. At first, they gave an impression of laziness. The visitor would note them sleeping in the streets of the cities at noon. But Europeans soon found that Korean labourers, properly handled, were capable of great effort. And young men of the cultured classes amazed their foreign teachers by the quickness with which they absorbed Western learning.

The land was torn, at the time of the entry of the foreigners, by the rivalry of two great families--the Yi's, the blood relatives of the King, and the Mins, the family of the Queen. The ex-Regent was leader of the Yi's. He had exercised absolute power for many years during the King's minority, and attempted to retain power even after he ceased to be Regent. But he reckoned without the Queen. She was as ambitious as the Regent. The birth of a son greatly improved and strengthened her authority, and she gradually edged the Regent's party out of high office. Her brother, Min Yeung-ho, became Prime Minister; her nephew, Min Yung-ik, was sent as Ambassador to the United States. The Regent was anti-foreign; the Queen advocated the admission of foreigners. The Regent tried to strengthen his hold by a very vigorous policy of murder, attempting the death of the Queen and her relatives. One little incident was an effort to blow up the Queen. But Queen Min was triumphant every time. The King, usually weak and easily moved, really loved the Queen, refused to be influenced away from her, and was dominated by her strong character.

In the summer of 1881 there was a famine in the land. The Regent's agents were busy everywhere whispering that the spirits were angry with the nation for admitting the foreigner, and that Queen Min had brought the wrath of the gods on them. The National Treasury failed, and many of the King's soldiers and retainers were ready for any trouble. A great mob gathered in the streets. It first attacked and murdered the King's Ministers, and destroyed their houses. Then it turned against the King's palace.

Word came to the Queen's quarters that the rioters were hammering at the gates and would soon be on her. The palace guards had weakened, and some had even joined the people. Queen Min was calm and collected. She quickly changed clothes with one of her serving women, who somewhat resembled her in appearance. The serving woman, dressed in the robes of the Queen, was given a draught of poison and died.

The Queen hurried out through a side way, in peasant woman's dress, guarded by a water carrier, Yi Yung-ik, who for his services that day rose till he finally became Prime Minister of the land. When the crowd broke into the Queen's private apartments, they were shown the corpse and told that it was the Queen, who had died rather than face them.

The crowd swept on and attacked the Japanese Legation. The Minister, Hanabusa, and his guard, with all the civilians who could reach the place--the rest were murdered--fought bravely, keeping the mob back until the Legation building was set afire. Then they battled their way through the city to the coast. The survivors--twenty-six out of forty--set to sea in a junk. They were picked up at sea by a British survey ship, the Flying Fish, and conveyed to Nagasaki.

There was, naturally, intense anger in Japan over this incident and loud demands for war. A little more than three weeks after, Hanabusa returned to Seoul with a strong military escort. He demanded and obtained punishment of the murderers, the honourable burial of the Japanese dead, an indemnity of 400,000 yen, and further privileges in trade for the Japanese.

Meanwhile China, Korea's usually apathetic suzerain power, took action. Li Hung-chang sent 4,000 troops to Seoul to maintain order. The Regent, now humble and conciliatory, attempted to put blame for the outbreak on others. But that did not save him. The Chinese, with elaborate courtesy, invited him to a banquet and to inspect their ships. There was one ship, in particular, to which they called his honourable attention. They begged him to go aboard and note the wonders of the apartments below. The Regent went. Once below, he found the door shut, and could hear the ropes being thrown off as the ship hastily departed. It was in vain for him to call for his attendants and warriors waiting on the shore.

They took him to China, and Li Hung-chang sent him into imprisonment and exile for three years, until it was deemed safe to allow him to return.

II
JAPAN MAKES A FALSE MOVE

For hundreds of years it was the ambition of Japan to replace China as the Protector of Korea. It was the more mortifying, therefore, that the Hanabusa incident served to strengthen China's authority. It gave Peking an excuse to despatch and maintain a considerable force at Seoul, for the first time for hundreds of years.

The Japanese tried to turn the affair to their advantage by demanding-still more concessions. The Korean rulers found it hard to refuse these determined little men. So they adopted a policy of procrastination, arguing endlessly. Now Japan was in a hurry, and could not wait.

The Japanese Minister at Seoul at this time was Takezoi, timid and hesitating constitutionally, but, like many timid folk, acting at times with great rashness. Under him was a subordinate of stronger and rougher type, Shumamura, Secretary to the Legation. Shumamura kept in touch with a group of Cabinet Ministers who had been to Japan and regarded Japan as their model. They mourned together over the growth of Chinese power, and agreed that it was threatening the independence of the country. They repeated the rumour that a secret treaty had actually been signed by the King, recognizing Chinese supremacy in more binding form than ever before. They felt that the Queen was against them. Her nephew, Min Yung-ik, had been on their side when he returned from America. Now, under her influence, he had taken the other side.

Kim Ok-kiun, leader of the malcontents, was an ambitious and restless politician, eager to have the control of money. One of his chief supporters was Pak Yung-hyo, relative of the King, twenty-three years old, and a sincere reformer. Hong Yung-sik, keen on foreign ways, was a third. He was hungry for power. He was the new Postmaster General, and a building now being erected in Seoul for a new post-office was to mark the entry of Korea into the world's postal service. So Kwang-pom, another Minister, was working with them.

Kim Ok-kiun and Shumamura had long conferences. They discussed ways and means. The reformers were to overthrow the reactionaries in the Cabinet by the only possible way, killing them; they were then in the King's name to grant Japan further commercial concessions, and the Japanese were to raise a considerable loan which should be handed over to Kim for necessary purposes.

Takezoi was on a visit to Tokyo when his deputy and the Korean came to an understanding. They were rather anxious to have the whole thing through before his return, for they knew, as every one knew, that Takezoi was not the best man for a crisis. But when the Minister returned from Tokyo there was none so bold as he. He boasted to his friends that Japan had at last resolved to make war on China, and that every Chinaman would soon be driven out of the land. He received Kim and heard of his plans with satisfaction. There would be no trouble about money. A few Japanese in Seoul itself would arrange all that was necessary. Let the thing be done quickly.

It had been customary for the Legations only to drill their soldiers in daytime, and to inform the Government before they were taken out to public places. But one night Takezoi had his Japanese troops turned out, marched up the great hill, Nam-zan, commanding the city, and drilled there. When asked why he did it, he cheerfully replied that he had just made an experiment to see how far he could startle the Chinese and Koreans; and he was quite satisfied with the result.

He sought an interview with the King. He had brought back the 400,000 yen which Japan had exacted as indemnity for the Hanabusa outrage. Japan desired Korea's friendship, he declared, not her money. He also brought a stand of Japanese-made rifles, a gift from the Emperor to the King, and a very significant gift, too. The Minister urged on the King the helpless condition of China, and the futility of expecting assistance from her, and begged the King to take up a bold position, announce Korea's independence and dare China's wrath. The King listened, but made no pledges.

Kim and the Japanese Secretary called in their allies, to discuss how to strike. One scheme proposed was that they should send two men, disguised as Chinese, to kill two of the Ministers they had marked as their victims. Then they would charge the other Ministers with the deed and kill them. Thus they would get rid of all their enemies at a blow. A second plan was that Kim should invite the Ministers to the fine new house he had built, should entertain them and then kill them. Unfortunately for Kim, the Ministers were not willing to come to his house. He had invited them all to a grand banquet shortly before, and only a few had accepted.

"Make haste!" urged Shumamura. "Japan is ready for anything." At last some one hit on a happy scheme. Twenty-two young Koreans had been sent to Japan to learn modern military ways, and had studied at the Toyama Military School at Tokyo. Returning home, they had given an exhibition of their physical drill and fencing before the King, who was as delighted with them as a child with a new toy. He had declared that he would have all his army trained this way. The leader of the students, So Jai-pil, nephew of one of the King's favourite generals, was made a Colonel of the Palace Guard, although only seventeen years old. But despite the King, the old military leaders, whose one idea of martial ardour was to be carried around from one point to another surrounded with bearers and warriors who made a loud noise to impress the crowd, shuddered at the idea of reform, and managed to block it. The students were kicking their heels idly around the palace. Here were the very lads for the job. Appeal to their patriotism. Let them do the killing, and their seniors take the glory. And so it was decided.

The Japanese were talking so boastingly that it would be surprising if the Chinese had learned nothing. At the head of the Chinese troops was Yuan Shih-kai, afterwards to prove himself the strongest man in the Middle Kingdom and to overthrow the Manchu dynasty. He said nothing, but it does not follow that he did nothing. At a dinner given to the Foreign Representatives, the Interpreter to the Japanese Legation delivered a speech in Korean on the shameless unscrupulousness and cowardice of the Chinese. He even went so far as to call them "sea slugs," giving a malicious glance at the Chinese Consul-General while he spoke. The Chinese official did not know Korean, but he could understand enough of the speech to follow its import.

The plans were now complete. Every victim had two assassins assigned to him. The occasion was to be the opening of the new post-office, when Hong Yung-sik would give an official banquet to which all must come. During the dinner, the detached palace was to be set on fire, a call was to be raised that the King was in danger, and the reactionary Ministers were to be killed as they rushed to his help. Two of the students were appointed sentries, two were to set fire to the palace, one group was to wait at the Golden Gate for other members of the Government who tried to escape that way. Four young Japanese, including one from the Legation, were to act as a reserve guard, to complete the killing in case the Koreans failed. The Commander of the Palace Guard, a strong sympathizer, posted his men in such a way as to give the conspirators a free hand. The Japanese Minister promised that his soldiers would be ready to cooperate at the right time.

On the afternoon of December 4th, the Japanese Legation people busied themselves with fetching ammunition and provisions from the barracks. In the afternoon a detachment of soldiers came over. They knew that the deed was to be done that night.

The dinner was held, according to plan. It was a singularly harmonious gathering--up to a point. Many were the jokes and pointed was the wit. The gesang (geisha), spurred by the merriment of their lords, did more than ever to amuse the guests. The drink was not stinted.

Then there came a call of "Fire!" It was the duty of Min Yung-ik, as General Commanding the right Guard Regiment, to keep the custody of the fire apparatus. Deploring his rough luck in being called to duty at such a time, he left the hall and, surrounded by his braves and attendants, who were waiting for him in the anteroom, made his way to his yungmun, or official residence. When he was near the post-office five young men, armed with sharp swords, suddenly broke through his guard, killed one of the soldiers and attacked the Minister. "He received seven sword slashes, all great ones, two all but taking his head off," wrote a contemporary chronicler. He staggered back into the banqueting hall, blood pouring from him. There was at once great confusion. The Ministers not in the plot, fearing that some ill was intended against them, threw away their hats of state, turned their coats, and concealed themselves amongst their coolies. Fortunately for Min, just as the palace doctors were about to attempt to stop his wounds by pouring boiling wax on them, a modern surgeon came hurrying up. He was Dr. Allen, an American Presbyterian missionary, the first to arrive in Korea. He did such good work on his patient that night that King and Court became friends of the missionaries for ever on.

Leaving the banqueting hall, Pak Yung-kyo and his companions at once hurried to the palace, informed the King that a Great Event had happened, and told him that he and the Queen must go with them for their safety. They took him to the Tai Palace, near at hand. Here they were at once surrounded by the Japanese troops, by the students, and some 800 Korean soldiers, under General Han Kiu-chik, who commanded one of the four regiments of the Palace Guard.

The King and Queen were of course accompanied by their own attendants. The Chief Eunuch, who was among them, took General Han on one side. "This is a very serious matter," he urged. "Let us send for General Yuan and the Chinese." General Han apparently weakened and agreed. There was no weakening on the part of the students. The Chief Eunuch and the General were "one by one withdrawn from the King's presence" and when outside were promptly despatched. Then the King was bidden to write notes to his chief anti-Progressive Ministers, summoning them to his presence. As they arrived, "one by one, each in his turn, was despatched by the students and his body thrown aside."

The King called for the Japanese Minister. At first he would not come. Finally he appeared. He had arranged that most of the work was to be done without his presence, in order to avoid diplomatic trouble. A number of edicts had been drawn up which the King was obliged to sign. All kinds of reforms were commanded, and the land was made on paper, in an hour, into a modern state. The reformers did not forget their own interests. Hong Yung-sik, the Postmaster General, was made Prime Minister, Kim Ok-kiun was made second officer of the Royal Treasury, and the lad So Jai-pil, on whom the chief command of the students and Korean soldiers now devolved, was made General Commanding a Guard Regiment.

In answer to his urgent entreaties, the King was allowed next morning to return to his palace, the Japanese and the Progressives accompanying him. It was soon clear, even to the reformers, that they had gone too far. As news of the affair became known, the people made their sentiments felt in unmistakable fashion. Odd Japanese in the streets were killed, others made their way to the Legation and shut themselves in there, while the Japanese Minister and the Progressives were hemmed in the palace by an angry mob.

They were short of ammunition. The Japanese had twenty-five rounds a man, the twenty-two students had fifteen rounds apiece, and the eight hundred Korean soldiers either had none or destroyed what they had. There was plenty in the Legation but the mob barred the way. General So Jai-pil (to give him his new title) was on the move day and night, going from outpost to outpost, threatening and encouraging weaklings, and arranging and inspiring his men.

The affair started on the evening of December 4th; the reformers remained in the palace until the afternoon of December 7th. Then General Yuan Shih-kai, the Chinese leader, approached the palace gates and sent in his card, demanding admission. The Queen had already smuggled a message out to him begging his aid. The Japanese soldiers on guard refused to allow him to enter. He gave warning that he would attack. He had 2,000 Chinese troops and behind them were fully 3,000 Korean soldiers and the mass of the population.

Takezoi weakened. He did not want to risk an engagement with the Chinese, and he declared that he would withdraw his Guard, and take them back to his Legation. Young General So drew his sword threateningly, and told him that they must stay and see it through. The Japanese captain in command of the troops was as eager for a fight as was So, and the Minister was for the time overruled.

A great fight followed. The Chinese sought to outflank the reformers, and to force an entry by climbing over the walls. One of the personal attendants of the King suddenly attacked the new Premier, Hong Yung-sik, and slew him. The Korean soldiers seemed to disappear from the scene as soon as the real fighting started, but the students and the Japanese did valiantly. They claimed that they shot fully three hundred Chinese. The great gate of the palace still held, in spite of all attacks. But the ammunition of the defenders had at last all gone.

"Let us charge the Chinese with our bayonets," cried So. The Japanese captain joyfully assented. But Takezoi now asserted his authority. He pulled from his pocket his Imperial warrants giving him supreme command of the Japanese in Korea and read them to the captain. "The Emperor has placed you under my command," he declared. "Refuse to obey me and you refuse to obey your Emperor. I command you to call your men together and let us all make our way back to the Legation." There was nothing to do but obey.

While the Chinese were still hammering at the front gate, the Japanese and reformers crept quietly around by the back wall towards the Legation. The people in the building, hearing this mass of men approach in the dark, unlit street, thought that they were the enemy, and opened fire on them. A Japanese sergeant and an interpreter were shot down on either side of General So. Not until a bugle was sounded did the Japanese inside the building recognize their friends. The party staggered in behind the barricades worn out. So, who had not closed his eyes for four days, dropped to the ground exhausted and slept.

He did not awake until the next afternoon. He heard a voice calling him, and started up to find that the Japanese were already leaving. They had resolved to fight their way to the sea. "I do not know who it was called me," said So, afterwards. "Certainly it was none of the men in the Legation. I sometimes believe that it must have been a voice from the other world." Had he wakened five minutes later, the mob would have caught him and torn him to bits.

The Japanese blew up a mine, and, with women and children in the centre, flung themselves into the maelstrom of the howling mob. The people of Seoul were ready for them. They had already burned the houses of the Progressive statesmen, Kim, Pak, So and Hong. They tried, time after time, to rush the Japanese circle. The escaping party marched all through the night, fighting as it marched. At one point it had to pass near a Chinese camp. A cannon opened fire on it. At Chemulpo, the coast port twenty-seven miles from Seoul, it found a small Japanese mail steamer, the Chidose Maru. The Koreans who had escaped with the party were hidden. Before the Chidose *could sail a deputation from the King arrived, disclaiming all enmity against the Japanese, but demanding the surrender of the Koreans. Takezoi seemed to hesitate, and the reformers feared for the moment that he was about to surrender them. But the pockmarked captain of the* Chidose drove the deputation from the side of his ship, in none too friendly fashion, and steamed away.

The reformers landed in Japan, expecting that they would be received like heroes, and that they would return with a strong army to fight the Chinese. They did not realize that the revolutionist who fails must look for no sympathy or aid.

The Japanese Foreign Minister at first refused even to see them. When at last they secured an audience, he told them bluntly that Japan was not going to war with China over the matter. "We are not ready yet," said he. He then demanded of the reformers what they were going to do with themselves. This was too much for So Jai-pil. His seniors tried to restrain him, but in vain, "What way is this for Samurai to treat Samurai?" he hotly demanded. "We trusted you, and now you betray and forsake us. I have had enough of you. I am going to a new world, where men stand by their bonds and deal fairly with one another. I shall go to America."

A few weeks later he landed in San Francisco, penniless. He knew scarcely any English. He sought work. His first job was to deliver circulars from door to door, and for this he was paid three dollars a day. He attended churches and meetings to learn how to pronounce the English tongue. He saved money enough to enter college, and graduated with honours. He became an American citizen, taking a new form of his name, Philip Jaisohn. He joined the United States Civil Service and in due course was made a doctor of medicine by Johns Hopkins University. He acquired a practice at Washington, and was lecturer for two medical schools. Later on, he was recalled to his native land.

The Korean reformers themselves saw, later on, the folly of their attempt. "We were very young," they say. They were the tools of the Japanese Minister, and they had inherited a tradition of political life which made revolt seem the natural weapon by which to overthrow your enemies. They learned wisdom in exile, and some of them were subsequently to reach high rank in their country's service.

There is a sequel to this story. The King and the Court regarded Kim Ok-kiun as the unpardonable offender. Other men might be forgiven, for after all attempted revolts were no novelties. But there was to be no forgiveness for Kim.

A price was put on his head. Assassins followed him to Japan, but could find no opportunity to kill him. Then a plot was planned and he was induced to visit Shanghai. He had taken great pains to conceal his visit, but everything had been arranged ahead for him. Arriving at Shanghai he was promptly slain, and his body was carried in a Chinese war-ship to Chemulpo. It was cut up, and exhibited in different parts of the land as the body of a traitor. The mortified Japanese could do nothing at the time.

Years passed. The Japanese now had control of Korea. One of the last things they did, in 1910, before contemptuously pushing the old Korean Government into limbo, was to make it issue an Imperial rescript, restoring Kim Ok-kiun, Hong Yung-sik and others--although long dead--to their offices and honours, and doing reverence to their memory.[1]

1　Curiosity may be felt about my authority for many of the particulars supplied in this chapter. Accounts published by foreigners living at Seoul at the time are of use as giving current impressions,

III

THE MURDER OF THE QUEEN

W e are not ready to fight China yet," said the Japanese Foreign Minister to the impetuous young Korean. It was ten years later before Japan was ready, ten years of steady preparation, and during that time the real focus of the Far Eastern drama was not Tokyo nor Peking, but Seoul. Here the Chinese and Japanese outposts were in contact. Here Japan when she was ready created her cause of war.

China despised Japan, and did not think it necessary to make any real preparations to meet her. The great majority of European experts and of European and American residents in the Far East were convinced that if it came to an actual contest, Japan would stand no chance. She might score some initial victories, but in the end the greater weight, numbers and staying power of her monster opponent must overwhelm her.

The development of Korea proceeded slowly. It seemed as though there were some powerful force behind all the efforts of more enlightened Koreans to prevent effective reforms from being carried out The Japanese were, as was natural the most numerous settlers in the land, and their conduct did not win them the popular affection. Takezoi's disastrous venture inflicted for a time a heavy blow on Japanese prestige. The Japanese dead lay unburied in the streets for the dogs to eat. China was momentarily supreme. "The whole mass of the people are violently pro-Chinese in

but are not wholly to be relied on for details. A very interesting official report, based on information supplied by the King, is to be found in the unpublished papers of Lieutenant George C. Foulk, U.S. Naval Attache at Seoul, which are stored in the New York Public Library. A valuable account from the Japanese point of view was found among the posthumous papers of Mr. Fukuzawa (in whose house several of the exiles lived for a time) and was published in part in the Japanese press in 1910. I learned the conspirators' side directly from one of the leading actors in the drama.

their sentiments," the American representative stated in a private despatch to his Government, "and so violently anti-Japanese that it is impossible to obtain other than a volume of execrations and vituperations against them when questioned," A semi-official Japanese statement that their Minister and his troops had gone to the palace at the King's request, to defend him, made the matter rather worse.

The affair would have been more quickly forgotten but for the overbearing attitude of Japanese settlers towards the Korean people, and of Japanese Ministers towards the Korean Government. Officially they advanced claims so unjust that they aroused the protest of other foreigners. The attitude of the Japanese settlers was summed up by Lord (then the Hon. G.N.) Curzon, the famous British statesman, after a visit in the early nineties. "The race hatred between Koreans and Japanese," he wrote, "is the most striking phenomenon in contemporary Chosen. Civil and obliging in their own country, the Japanese develop in Korea a faculty for bullying and bluster that is the result partly of nation vanity, partly of memories of the past. The lower orders ill-treat the Koreans on every possible opportunity, and are cordially detested by them in return."[2]

The old Regent returned from China in 1885, to find his power largely gone, at least so far as the Court was concerned. But he still had friends and adherents scattered all over the country. Furious with the Chinese for his arrest and imprisonment, he threw himself into the arms of the Japanese. They found in him a very useful instrument.

Korea has for centuries been a land of secret societies. A new society now sprang up, and spread with amazing rapidity, the Tong-haks. It was anti-foreign and anti-Christian, and Europeans were at first inclined to regard it in the same light as Europeans in China later on regarded the Boxers. But looking back at it to-day it is impossible to deny that there was much honest patriotism behind the movement. It was not unnatural that a new departure, such as the introduction of Europeans and European civilization should arouse some ferment. In a sense, it would not have been healthy if it had not done so. The people who would accept a vital revolution in their life and ways without critical examination would not be worth much.

Few of the Tong-haks had any idea that their movement was being organized under Japanese influences. It did not suit Japan that Korea should develop indepen-

---

2 "Problems of the Far East," London, 1894.

dently and too rapidly. Disturbances would help to keep her back.

When the moment was ripe, Japan set her puppets to work. The Tong-haks were suddenly found to be possessed of arms, and some of their units were trained and showed remarkable military efficiency. Their avowed purpose was to drive all foreigners, including the Japanese, out of the country; but this was mere camouflage. The real purpose was to provoke China to send troops to Korea, and so give Japan an excuse for war.

The Japanese had secured an agreement from China in 1885 that both countries should withdraw their troops from Korea and should send no more there without informing and giving notice to the other. When the Tong-haks, thirty thousand in number, came within a hundred miles of Seoul, and actually defeated a small Korean force led by Chinese, Yuan Shih-kai saw that something must be done. If the rebels were allowed to reach and capture the capital, Japan would have an excuse for intervention. He induced the King to ask for Chinese troops to come and put down the uprising; and as required by the regulations, due notice of their coming was sent to Japan.

This was what Japan wanted. She poured troops over the channel until there were 10,000 in the capital Then she showed her hand. The Japanese Minister, Mr. Otori, brusquely demanded of the King that he should renounce Chinese suzerainty. The Koreans tried evasion. The Japanese pressed their point, and further demanded wholesale concessions, railway rights and a monopoly of gold mining in Korea. A few days later, confident that Europe would not intervene, they commanded the King to accept their demand unconditionally, and to give the Chinese troops three days' notice to withdraw from the land. The King refused to do anything while the Japanese troops menaced his capital.

The declaration of war between Japan and China followed. The first incident was the blowing up by the Japanese of a Chinese transport carrying 1,200 men to Korea. The main naval battle was in the Yalu, between Korea and Manchuria, and the main land fight, in which the Chinese Army was destroyed, in Pyeng-yang, the main Korean city to the north. The war began on July 25, 1894; the Treaty of Peace, which made Japan the supreme power in the Extreme East, was signed at Shimonoseki on April 17, 1895.

Before fighting actually began, the Japanese took possession of Seoul, and seized the palace on some trumpery excuse that Korean soldiers had fired on them and they had therefore been obliged to enter and guard the royal apartments. They wanted to make their old friend and ally the ex-Regent, the actual ruler, as he had been in the King's minority but he did not care to take responsibility. Japanese soldiers turned the King out of his best rooms and occupied them themselves. Any hole was good enough for the King. Finally they compelled the King to yield and follow their directions. A new treaty was drawn up and signed. It provided

1. That the independence of Korea was declared, confirmed, and established, and in keeping with it the Chinese troops were to be driven out of the country.

2. That while war against China was being carried on by Japan, Korea was to facilitate the movements and to help in the food supplies of the Japanese troops in every possible way.

3. That this treaty should only last until the conclusion of peace with China.

Japan at once created an assembly, in the name of the King, for the "discussion of everything, great and small, that happened within the realm." This assembly at first met daily, and afterwards at longer intervals. There were soon no less than fifty Japanese advisers at work in Seoul. They were men of little experience and less responsibility, and they apparently thought that they were going to transform the land between the rising and setting of the sun. They produced endless ordinances, and scarce a day went by save that a number of new regulations were issued, some trivial, some striking at the oldest and most cherished institutions in the country. The Government was changed from an absolute monarchy to one where the King governed only by the advice of his Ministers. The power of direct address to the throne was denied to any one under the rank of Governor. One ordinance created a constitution, and the next dealt with the status of the ladies of the royal seraglio. At one hour a proclamation went forth that all men were to cut their hair, and the wearied runners on their return were again despatched hot haste with an edict altering the official language. Nothing was too small, nothing too great, and nothing too contradictory for these constitution-mongers. Their doings were the laugh and the amazement of every foreigner in the place.

Acting on the Japanese love of order and of defined rank, exact titles of honour were provided for the wives of officials. These were divided into nine grades: "Pure and Reverend Lady," "Pure Lady," "Chaste Lady," "Chaste Dame," "Worthy

Dame," "Courteous Dame," "Just Dame," "Peaceful Dame," and "Upright Dame." At the same time the King's concubines were equally divided, but here eight divisions were sufficient: "Mistress," "Noble Lady," "Resplendent Exemplar," "Chaste Exemplar," "Resplendent Demeanour," "Chaste Demeanour," "Resplendent Beauty," and "Chaste Beauty." The Japanese advisers instituted a number of sumptuary laws that stirred the country to its depths, relating to the length of pipes, style of dress, and the attiring of the hair of the people. Pipes were to be short, in place of the long bamboo churchwarden beloved by the Koreans. Sleeves were to be clipped. The topknot, worn by all Korean men, was at once to be cut off. Soldiers at the city gates proceeded to enforce this last regulation rigorously.

Japanese troops remained in the palace for a month, and the King was badly treated during that time. It did not suit the purpose of the Japanese Government just then to destroy the old Korean form of administration. It was doubtful how far the European Powers would permit Japan to extend her territory, and so the Japanese decided to allow Korea still to retain a nominal independence. The King and his Ministers implored Mr. Otori to withdraw his soldiers from the royal presence. Mr. Otori agreed to do so, at a price, and his price was the royal consent to a number of concessions that would give Japan almost a monopoly of industry in Korea. The Japanese guard marched out of the palace on August 25th, and was replaced by Korean soldiers armed with sticks. Later on the Korean soldiers were permitted to carry muskets, but were not served with any ammunition. Japanese troops still retained possession of the palace gates and adjoining buildings.

Another movement took place at this time as the result of Japanese supremacy. The Min family--the family of the Queen--was driven from power and the Mins, who a few months before held all the important offices in the kingdom, were wiped out of public life, so much so that there was not a single Min in one of the new departments of state.

Victory did not improve the attitude of the Japanese to the Koreans. While the war was on the Japanese soldiers had shown very strict discipline, save on certain unusual occasions. Now, however, they walked as conquerors. The Japanese Government presented further demands to the King that would have meant the entire trade of Korea being monopolized by their countrymen. These demands went so far that the foreign representatives protested.

The new Japanese Minister, Count Inouye, protested publicly and privately against the violent ways and rascalities of the new Japanese immigrants pouring into Korea. He denounced their lack of cooeperation, arrogance and extravagance. "If the Japanese continue in their arrogance and rudeness," he declared, "all respect and love due to them will be lost and there will remain hatred and enmity against them."

Several of the participants in the emeute of 1884 were brought back by the Japanese and Pak Yung-hyo became Home Minister. He was very different from the rash youth who had tried to promote reform by murder eleven years before. He had a moderate, sensible program, the reform and modernization of the army, the limitation of the powers of the monarchy and the promotion of education on Western lines. "What our people need," he declared, "is education and Christianization." Unfortunately he fell under suspicion. The Queen thought that his attempt to limit the power of the King was a plot against the throne. He received warning that his arrest had been ordered, and had to flee the country.

Count Inouye ranks with Prince Ito as the two best Japanese administrators sent to Korea. He was followed, in September, 1895, by Viscount General Miura, an old soldier, a Buddhist of the Zen school and an extreme ascetic.

The Queen continued to exercise her remarkable influence over the King, who took her advice in everything. She was the real ruler of the country. What if her family was, for a time, in disgrace? She quietly worked and brought them back in office again. Time after time she checked both the Japanese Minister and the Regent.

The Japanese Secretary of Legation, Fukashi Sugimura, had long since lost patience with the Queen and urged on Miura that the best thing was to get rid of her. Why should one woman be allowed to stand between them and their purpose? Every day she was interfering more and more in the affairs of state. She was proposing to disband a force of troops that had been created, the Kunrentai, and placed under Japanese officers. It was reported that she was contemplating a scheme for usurping all political power by degrading some and killing other Cabinet Ministers favourable to Japan. Miura agreed. She was ungrateful. Disorder and confusion would be introduced into the new Japanese organization for governing the country. She must be stopped.

While Miura was thinking in this fashion the Regent came to see him. He proposed to break into the palace, seize the King and assume real power. As a result of their conversation, a conference was held between the Japanese Minister and his two leading officials, Sugimura and Okamoto. "The decision arrived at on that occasion," states the report of the Japanese Court of Preliminary Enquiries, "was that assistance should be rendered to the Tai Won Kun's (Regent's) entry into the palace by making use of the Kunrentai, who, being hated by the Court, felt themselves in danger, and of the young men who deeply lamented the course of events, and also by causing the Japanese troops stationed in Seoul to offer support to the enterprise. It was further resolved that this opportunity should be availed of for taking the life of the Queen, who exercised overwhelming influence in the Court."[3]

The whole thing was to be done according to system. The Regent was made to bind himself down to the Japanese. A series of pledges was drawn up by Sugimura, and handed to the Regent, saying that this was what Miura expected of him. He, his son and his grandson "gladly assented" to the conditions and he wrote a letter guaranteeing his good faith. The Japanese Minister then resolved to carry out the plan, i.e., the attack on the palace and the murder of the Queen, by the middle of the month. A statement by the Korean War Minister that the disbandment of the Kunrentai troops was approaching caused them to hurry their plans. "It was now evident that the moment had arrived, and that no more delay should be made. Miura Goro and Fukashi Sugimura consequently determined to carry out the plot on the night of that very day."[4] The Legation drew up a detailed program of what was to happen, and orders were issued to various people. Official directions were given to the Commander of the Japanese battalion in Seoul Miura summoned some of the Japanese and asked them to collect their friends and to act as the Regent's body-guard when he entered the palace. "Miura told them that on the success of the enterprise depended the eradication of the evils that had done so much mischief in the Kingdom for the past twenty years, and instigated them to despatch the Queen when they entered the palace."[5] The head of the Japanese police force was ordered to help; and policemen off duty were to put on civilian dress, provide themselves with swords and proceed to the rendezvous. Minor men, "at the instigation of Miu-

---

3   Japanese official report.
4   Japanese official report.
5   Ibid

ra, decided to murder the Queen and took steps for collecting accomplices."[6]

The party of Japanese met at the rendezvous, to escort the Regent's palanquin. At the point of departure Okamoto (one of the Japanese Minister's two right-hand men) "assembled the whole party outside the gate of the Prine's (Regent's) residence, declaring that on entering the palace the 'fox' should be dealt with according as exigency might require, the obvious purpose of this declaration being to instigate his followers to murder Her Majesty the Queen."[7] The party proceeding towards Seoul met the Kunrentai troops outside the West Gate and then advanced more rapidly to the palace.

The Japanese Court of Preliminary Enquiries, which had Viscount Miura and his assistants before it after the murder, reported all the facts up to this point with great frankness. I have used its account solely in the above description. The Court having gone so far, then added a final finding which probably ranks as the most extraordinary statement ever presented by a responsible Court of law. "Notwithstanding these facts, there is no sufficient evidence to prove that any of the accused actually committed the crime originally meditated by them.... For these reasons the accused, each and all, are hereby discharged."

What happened after the Regent and the Japanese reached the palace? The party advanced, with the Kunrentai troops to the front. Behind them were the police, the officers in charge, and twenty-six Japanese. An inner group of these, about half of them, had special orders to find the Queen and kill her. The gates of the palace were in the hands of Japanese soldiers, so the conspirators had free admission. Most of the regular troops paraded outside, according to orders. Some went inside the grounds, accompanied by the rabble, and others moved to the sides of the palace, surrounding it to prevent any from escaping. A body of men attacked and broke down the wall near to the royal apartments.

Rumours had reached the palace that some plot was in progress, but no one seems to have taken much trouble to maintain special watch. At the first sign of the troops breaking down the walls and entering through the gates, there was general confusion. Some of the Korean body-guard tried to resist, but after a few of them were shot the others retired. The royal apartment was of the usual one-storied type, led to by a few stone steps, and with carved wooden doors and oiled-paper win-

6 Ibid
7 Ibid.

dows. The Japanese made straight for it, and, when they reached the small court-yard in front, their troops paraded up before the entrance, while the soshi broke down the doors and entered the rooms. Some caught hold of the King and presented him with a document by which he was to divorce and repudiate the Queen. Despite every threat, he refused to sign this. Others were pressing into the Queen's apart-ments. The Minister of the Household tried to stop them, but was killed on the spot. The soshi seized the terrified palace ladies, who were running away, dragged them round and round by their hair, and beat them, demanding that they should tell where the Queen was. They moaned and cried and declared that they did not know. Now the men were pressing into the side-rooms, some of them hauling-the palace ladies by their hair. Okamoto, who led the way, found a little woman hiding in a corner, grabbed her head, and asked her if she were the Queen. She denied it, freed herself, with a sudden jerk, and ran into the corridor, shouting as she ran. Her son, who was present, heard her call his name three times, but, before she could utter more, the Japanese were on her and had cut her down. Some of the female attendants were dragged up, shown the dying body, and made to recognize it, and then three of them were put to the sword.

The conspirators had brought kerosene with them. They threw a bedwrap around the Queen, probably not yet dead, and carried her to a grove of trees in the deer park not far away. There they poured the oil over her, piled faggots of wood around, and set all on fire. They fed the flames with more and more kerosene, until everything was consumed, save a few bones. Almost before the body was alight the Regent was being borne in triumph to the palace under an escort of triumphant Japanese soldiers. He at once assumed control of affairs. The King was made a pris-oner in his palace. The Regent's partizans were summoned to form a Cabinet, and orders were given that all officials known to be friendly to the Queen's party should be arrested.

The Japanese were not content with this. They did everything they could, the Regent aiding them, to blacken the memory of the murdered women. A forged Royal Decree, supposed to have been issued by the King, was officially published, denouncing Queen Min, ranking her among the lowest prostitutes, and assuming that she was not dead, but had escaped, and would again come forward. "We knew the extreme of her wickedness," said the decree, "but We were helpless and full of fear of her party, and so could not dismiss and punish her. We are convinced that she is not only unfitted and unworthy to be Queen, but also that her guilt is excessive and overflowing. With her We could not succeed to the glory of the Royal ancestors, so We hereby depose her from the rank of Queen and reduce her to the level of the lowest class."

The poor King, trembling, broken, fearful of being poisoned, remained closely confined in his palace. The foreign community, Ministers and missionaries, did their best for him, conveying him food and visiting him.

If the Japanese thought that their crime could be hushed up they were much mistaken. Some of the American missionaries' wives were the Queen's friends. A famous American newspaper man, Colonel Cockerill, of the New York *Herald*, came to Seoul, and wrote with the utmost frankness about what he learned. So much indignation was aroused that the Japanese Government promised to institute an enquiry and place the guilty on trial. Ito was then Prime Minister and declared that every unworthy son of Japan connected with the crime would be placed on trial. "Not to do so would be to condemn Japan in the eyes of all the world," he declared. "If she does not repudiate this usurpation on the part of the Tai Won Run, she must lose the respect of every civilized government on earth." Miura and his associates were, in due course, brought before a court of enquiry. But the proceedings were a farce. They were all released, Miura became a popular hero, and his friends and defenders tried openly to justify the murder.

Japan, following her usual plan of following periods of great harshness by spells of mildness, sent Count Inouye as Envoy Extraordinary, to smooth over matters. He issued a decree restoring the late Queen to full rank. She was given the posthumous title of "Guileless, revered" and a temple called "Virtuous accomplishment" was dedicated to her memory. Twenty-two officials of high rank were commissioned to write her biography. But the King was still kept a prisoner in the palace.

Then came a bolt from the blue. The Russian Minister at Seoul at this time, M. Waeber, was a man of very fine type, and he was backed by a wife as gifted and benevolent as himself. He had done his best to keep in touch with and help the King. Now a further move was made. The Russian Legation guard was increased to 160 men, and almost immediately afterwards it was announced that the King had escaped from his jailers at the palace, and had taken refuge with the Russians. A little before seven in the morning the King and Crown Prince left the palace secretly, in closed chairs, such as women use. Their escape was carefully planned. For more than a week before, the ladies of the palace had caused a number of chairs to go in and out by the several gates in order to familiarize the guards with the idea that they were paying many visits. So when, early in the morning, two women's chairs were carried out by the attendants, the guards took no special notice. The King and his son arrived at the Russian Legation very much agitated and trembling. They were expected, and were at once admitted. As it is the custom in Korea for the King to work at night and sleep in the morning, the members of the Cabinet did not discover his escape for some hours, until news was brought to them from outside that he was safe under the guardianship of his new friends.

Excitement at once spread through the city. Great crowds assembled, some armed with sticks, some with stones, some with any weapons they could lay hands on. A number of old Court dignitaries hurried to the Legation, and within an hour or two a fresh Cabinet was constituted, and the old one deposed.

The heads of the Consulates and Legations called and paid their respects to the King, the Japanese Minister being the last to do so. For him this move meant utter defeat. Later in the day, a proclamation was spread broadcast, calling on the soldiers to protect their King, to cut off the heads of the chief traitors and bring them to him. This gave final edge to the temper of the mob. Two Ministers were dragged into the street and slaughtered. Another Minister was murdered at his home. In one respect the upheaval brought peace. The people in the country districts had been on the point of rising against the Japanese, who were reported to be universally hated as oppressors. With their King in power again, they settled down peaceably.

IV
THE INDEPENDENCE CLUB

It was a double blow to Japan that the check to her plans should have been inflicted by Russia, for she now regarded Russia as the next enemy to be overthrown, and was already secretly preparing against her. Russia had succeeded in humiliating Japan by inducing France and Germany to cooperate in a demand that she should evacuate the Liaotung Peninsula, ceded to her, under the Treaty of Shimonoseki, by China. Forced to obey, Japan entered on another nine years of preparation, to enable her to cross swords with the Colossus of the North.

At the close of the nineteenth century Russia was regarded as the supreme menace to world peace. Her expansion to the south of Siberia threatened British power in India; her railway developments to the Pacific threatened Japan. She struggled for a dominating place in the councils of China and was believed to have cast an ambitious eye on Korea. Germany looked with dread on the prospect of France and Russia striking her on either side and squeezing her like a nut between the crackers. Her statesmen were eager to obtain egress to the seas of the south, through the Dardanelles, and years before it had become a part of the creed of every British schoolboy that "the Russians shall not enter Constantinople."

It was dread of what Russia might do that caused England, to the amazement of the world, to conclude an Alliance with Japan in 1902, for the maintenance of the status quo in the Far East. Japan, willing under certain conditions to forget her grievances, had first sought alliance with Russia and had sent Prince Ito on a visit to St. Petersburg for that purpose. But Russia was too proud and self-confident to contemplate any such step, and so Japan turned to Britain, and obtained a readier hearing. Under the Alliance, both Britain and Japan disclaimed any aggressive tendencies in China or Korea, but the special interests of Japan in Korea were recognized.

The Alliance was an even more important step forward for Japan in the ranks of the nations of the world than her victory against China had been, and it was the precursor of still more important developments. This, however, takes us ahead of our story.

The King of Korea, after his escape from the palace, remained for some time in the Russian Legation, conducting his Court from there. Agreements were arrived at between the Russians, Japanese and Koreans in 1896 by which the King was to return to his palace and Japan was to keep her people in Korea in stricter control. A small body of Japanese troops was to remain for a short time in Korea to guard the Japanese telegraph lines, when it was to be succeeded by some Japanese gendarmerie who were to stay "until such time as peace and order have been restored by the Government." Both countries agreed to leave to Korea the maintenance of her own national army and police.

These agreements gave the Korean monarch--who now took the title of Emperor--a final chance to save himself and his country. The Japanese campaign of aggression was checked. Russia, at the time, was behaving with considerable circumspection. A number of foreign advisers were introduced, and many reforms were initiated. Progressive statesmen were placed at the head of affairs, and the young reformer, So Jai-pil, Dr. Philip Jaisohn, was summoned from America as Adviser to the Privy Council.

It must be admitted that the results were on the whole disappointing. Certain big reforms were made. In the period between 1894 and 1904 the developments would have seemed startling to those who knew the land in the early eighties. There was a modern and well-managed railroad operating between Seoul and the port of Chemulpo, and other railroads had been planned and surveyed, work being started on some of them. Seoul had electric light, electric tramways and an electric theatre. Fine roads had been laid around the city. Many old habits of mediaeval times had been abolished. Schools and hospitals were spreading all over the land, largely as a result of missionary activity. Numbers of the people, especially in the north, had become Christians. Sanitation was improved, and the work of surveying, charting and building lighthouses for the waters around the coast begun. Many Koreans of the better classes went abroad, and young men were returning after graduation in American colleges. The police were put into modern dress and trained on modern lines; and a little modern Korean Army was launched.

Despite this, things were in an unsatisfactory state. The Emperor, whose nerve had been broken by his experiences on the night of the murder of the Queen and in the days following, was weak, uncertain and suspicious. He could not be relied on save for one thing. He was very jealous of his own prerogatives, and the belief that some of his best statesmen and advisers were trying to establish constitutional monarchy, limiting the power of the Throne, finally caused him to throw in his lot with the anti-Progressive group.

Then there was no real reform in justice. The prisons retained most of their mediaeval horrors, and every man held his life and property at the mercy of the monarch and his assistants.

Some of the foreign advisers were men of high calibre; others were unfitted for their work, and used their offices to serve their own ends and fill their own pockets. Advisers or Ministers and foreign contractors apparently agreed at times to fill their pockets at the cost of the Government. There is no other rational explanation of some of the contracts concluded, or some of the supplies received. The representatives of the European Powers and America were like one great happy family, and the life of the European and American community in Seoul was for a long time ideal. There came one jarring experience when a Government--it would be unkind to mention which--sent a Minister who was a confirmed dipsomaniac. For days after his arrival he was unable to see the Ministers of State who called on him, being in one long debauch. The members of his Legation staff had to keep close watch on him until word could be sent home, when he was promptly recalled.

The young Koreans who were given power as Ministers and Advisers after the Monarch escaped from Japanese control were anxious to promote reform and education, and to introduce some plan of popular administration. They were aided by one British official, Mr. (now Sir John) McLeavy Brown. Mr. Brown, trained in the Chinese Customs Service, was given charge of the Korean Treasury and Customs, at the instigation of the British Government. It was hoped that this appointment indicated that the British Government would take a more active interest in Korean affairs. Unfortunately Korea was far away, and the prevailing idea in England at the time was to escape any more over-seas burdens.

Mr. Brown was the terror of all men who regarded the national treasure chest as the plunder box. Even the King found his extravagance checked, and Imperial schemes were delayed and turned from mere wasteful squanderings to some good purpose. When, for example, the Emperor announced his determination to build a great new memorial palace to the late Queen, Mr. Brown pointed out that the first thing to do was to build a fine road to the spot. The road was built, to the permanent gain of the nation, and the palatial memorial waited. Old debts were paid off. The nation was making money and saving.

A national economist always arouses many foes. The popular man is the man who spends freely. Officials who found their own gains limited and the sinecure posts for their relatives cut down united against the British guardian of the purse. Just about this time Russian control was changed. M. Waeber left Seoul, to the universal regret of all who knew him, and was succeeded by M. de Speyer, who displayed the most aggressive aspects of the Russian expansionist movement. A Russian official was appointed Mr. Brown's successor and for a beginning doubled the salaries of the Korean office holders. This brought many of the Korean office holders in line against Mr. Brown. The latter held on to his office despite the appointment of the Russian, and when an active attempt was made to turn him from his office, the British Fleet appeared in Chemulpo Harbour. Mr. Brown was to be backed by all the force of England. The Russians yielded and Mr. Brown remained on at the head of the Customs, but did not retain full control over the Treasury.

Had Britain or America at this time taken a hand in the administration of Korean affairs, much future trouble would have been avoided. They would have done so as part of their Imperial task of "bearing the burden of weaker nations." Many Koreans desired and tried to obtain the intervention of America, but the United States had not then realized to the extent she was to do later that great power brings great responsibilities, not for your nation alone, but for all the world that has need of you.

During the period of active reform following the King's escape, the Progressives formed a league for the maintenance of Korean union. At their head was Dr. Philip Jaisohn, the boy General of 1884. The movement was one of considerable importance. In response to my request, Dr. Jaisohn has written the following description of what took place:

THE INDEPENDENCE CLUB

"Early in 1896 I went back to Korea after an absence of twelve years, at the urgent invitation of some Koreans who at that time held high positions in the government. When I reached Korea, I found that the Koreans who had invited me had left their government positions, either voluntarily or by force, and they were not to be seen. It seemed that some of them had to leave the country to save their lives. In those days the Korean government changed almost every month.

"At first I tried to help the Korean government in the capacity of Adviser to the Privy Council, as they offered me a five year contract to serve them in this manner. I accepted the offer and gave some advice. For the first month or two some of it was accepted by the Emperor and his Cabinet officers, but they soon found that if they carried out this advice, it would interfere with some of their private schemes and privileges. They informed the Emperor that I was not a friend of his, but a friend of the Korean people, which at that time was considered treason. My influence was decreasing every day at the Court, and my advice was ignored. I gave up the idea of helping the government officially and planned to give my services to the Korean people as a private individual.

"I started the first English newspaper, as well as the first Korean newspaper, both being known as The Independent. At first this was only published semi-weekly, but later on, every other day. The Korean edition of this paper was eagerly read by the people and the circulation increased by leaps and bounds. It was very encouraging to me and I believe it did exert considerable influence for good. It stopped the government officials from committing flagrant acts of corruption, and the people looked upon the paper as a source of appeal to their ruler. This little sheet was not only circulated in the capital and immediate vicinity, but went to the remote corners of the entire kingdom. A pathetic but interesting fact is that it was read by a subscriber, and when he had finished reading it, turned it over to his neighbours, and in this way each copy was read by at least 200 people. The reason for this was that most of the people were too poor to buy the paper, and it was also very hard to get it to the subscribers, owing to the lack of proper transportation facilities at that time.

"After the paper was running in an encouraging manner, I started a debating club, called THE INDEPENDENCE CLUB, and leased a large hall outside of the West Gate which was originally built by the government to entertain foreign envoys who visited Korea in olden times. This hall was very spacious and surrounded by considerable ground and was the best place in Korea for holding public meetings. When this club was organized there were only half a dozen members, but in the course of three months the membership increased to nearly 10,000. There were no obstacles or formalities in joining it and no dues or admission were charged. As a result, many joined, some from curiosity and some for the sake of learning the way of conducting a public meeting in Parliamentary fashion.

"The subjects discussed were mostly political and economical questions, but religion and education were not overlooked. In the beginning the Koreans were shy about standing up before an audience to make a public speech, but after a certain amount of coaching and encouragement I found that hundreds of them could make very effective speeches. I believe the Koreans have a natural talent for public speaking. Of course, all that was said in these meetings was not altogether logical or enlightening;

nevertheless, a good many new thoughts were brought out which were beneficial. Besides, the calm and orderly manner in which various subjects were debated on equal footing, produced a wonderful effect among the Korean young men and to those who were in the audience.

"In the course of a year the influence of this club was very great and the members thought it was the most marvellous institution that was ever brought to Korea. The most remarkable thing I noticed was the quick and intelligent manner in which the Korean young men grasped and mastered the intricacies of Parliamentary rule. I often noticed that some Korean raised a question of the point of order in their procedure which was well taken, worthy of expert Parliamentarians of the Western countries.

"The increasing influence of the Independence Club was feared not only by the Korean officials but by some of the foreign representatives, such as Russia and Japan, both of whom did not relish the idea of creating public opinion among the Korean people. The members of the Independence Club did not have any official status, but they enjoyed the privilege of free speech during the meeting of this club, and they did not hesitate to criticize their own officials, as well as those of the foreign nations who tried to put through certain schemes in Korea for the benefit of their selfish interests. In the course of a year and a half the opposition to this club developed in a marked degree not among the people, but among a few government officials and certain members of the foreign legations.

"The first time in Korean history that democracy made its power felt in the government was at the time Russia brought to Korea a large number of army officers to drill the Korean troops. When this question was brought up in the Independence Club debate, and the scheme was thoroughly discussed pro and con by those who took part in the debate, it was the consensus of opinion that the turning over of the Military Department to a foreign power was suicidal policy and they decided to persuade the government to stop this scheme. The next day some 10,000 or more members of the club assembled in front of the palace, and petitioned the Emperor to cancel the agreement of engaging the Russian military officers as they thought it was a dangerous procedure. The Emperor sent a messenger out several times to persuade them to disperse and explain to the people that there was no danger in engaging the Russians as military instructors. But the people did not disperse, nor did they accept the Emperor's explanation. They quietly but firmly refused to move from the palace gates unless the contract with Russia was cancelled.

"When the Russian Minister heard of this demonstration against the contract he wrote a very threatening letter to the Korean government to the effect that the Korean government must disperse the people, by force if necessary, and stop any talk imputing selfish motives on the part of the Russian government. If this was not stopped, the Russian government would withdraw all the officers from Korea at once, and Korea would have to stand the consequences. This communication was shown to the people with the explanation that if they insisted upon cancelling this contract dire consequences would result to Korea. But the people told the government they would stand the consequences, whatever they would be, but would not have Russian officers control their military establishment. The Korean government finally asked the Russian Minister to withdraw their military officers and offered to pay any damage on account of the cancellation of the contract. This was done, and the will of the people was triumphant.

"But this event made opposition to the Independence Club stronger
than ever, and the government organized an opposing organization,
known as the PEDLARS' GUILD, which was composed of all the
pedlars of the country, to counteract the influence this club
wielded in the country. In May, 1898, I left Korea for the United
States."

Dr. Jaisohn, as a naturalized American citizen, was immune from arrest by the
Korean Government, and the worst that could happen to him was dismissal. Another young man who now came to the front in the Independence movement could
claim no such immunity. Syngman Rhee, son of a good family, training in Confucian scholarship to win a literary degree and official position, heard with contempt
and dislike the tales told by his friends of foreign teachers and foreign religion. His
parents were pious Buddhists and Confucians, and he followed their faith. Finding,
however, that if he hoped to make good in official life he must know English, he
joined the Pai Chai mission school, in Seoul, under Dr. Appenzeller. He became a
member of the Independence Club, and issued a daily paper to support his cause.
Young, fiery, enthusiastic, he soon came to occupy a prominent place in the organization.

The Independents were determined to have genuine reform, and the mass of
the people were still behind them. The Conservatives, who opposed them, now
controlled practically all official actions. The Independence Club started a popular
agitation, and for months Seoul was in a ferment. Great meetings of the people
continued day after day, the shops closing that all might attend. Even the women
stirred from their retirement, and held meetings of their own to plead for change.
To counteract this movement, the Conservative party revived and called to its aid
an old secret society, the Pedlars' Guild, which had in the past been a useful agent
for reaction. The Cabinet promised fair things, and various nominal reforms were
outlined. The Independents' demands were, in the main, the absence of foreign
control, care in granting foreign concessions, public trial of important offenders,
honesty in State finance, and justice for all. In the end, another demand was added
to these--that a popular representative tribunal should be elected.

When the Pedlars' Guild had organized its forces, the King commanded the disbandment of the Independence Club. The Independents retorted by going en bloc to the police headquarters, and asking to be arrested. Early in November, 1898, seventeen of the Independent leaders were thrown into prison, and would have been put to death but for public clamour. The people rose and held a series of such angry demonstrations that, at the end of five days, the leaders were released.

The Government now, to quiet the people, gave assurances that genuine reforms would be instituted. When the mobs settled down, reform was again shelved. On one occasion, when the citizens of Seoul crowded into the main thoroughfare to renew their demands, the police were ordered to attack them with swords and destroy them. They refused to obey, and threw off their badges, saying that the cause of the people was their cause. The soldiers under foreign officers, however, had no hesitation in carrying out the Imperial commands. As a next move, many thousands of men, acting on an old national custom, went to the front of the palace and sat there in silence day and night for fourteen days. In Korea this is the most impressive of all ways of demonstrating the wrath of the nation, and it greatly embarrassed the Court.

The Pedlars' Guild was assembled in another part of the city, to make a counter demonstration. Early in the morning, when the Independents were numerically at their weakest, the Pedlars attacked them and drove them off. On attempting to return they found the way barred by police. Fight after fight occurred during the next few days between the popular party and the Conservatives, and then, to bring peace, the Emperor promised his people a general audience in front of the palace. The meeting took place amid every surrounding that could lend it solemnity. The foreign representatives and the heads of the Government were in attendance. The Emperor, who stood on a specially built platform, received the leaders of the Independents, and listened to their statement of their case. They asked that the monarch should keep some of his old promises to maintain the national integrity and do justice. The Emperor, in reply, presented them with a formal document, in which he agreed to their main demands.

The crowd, triumphant, dispersed. The organization of the reformers slackened, for they thought that victory was won. Then the Conservative party landed some of its heaviest blows. The reformers were accused of desiring to establish a republic. Dissension was created in their ranks by the promotion of a scheme to recall

Pak Yung-hio. Some of the more extreme Independents indulged in wild talk, and gave excuse for official repression. Large numbers of reform leaders were arrested on various pretexts. Meetings were dispersed at the point of the bayonet, and the reform movement was broken. The Emperor did not realize that he had, in the hour that he consented to crush the reformers, pronounced the doom of his own Imperial house, and handed his land over to an alien people.

Dr. Jaisohn maintains that foreign influence was mainly responsible for the destruction of the Independence Club. Certain Powers did not wish Korea to be strong. He adds:

> "The passing of the Independence Club was one of the most unfortunate things in the history of Korea, but there is one consolation to be derived from it, and that is, the seed of democracy was sown in Korea through this movement, and that the leaders of the present Independence Movement in Korea are mostly members of the old Independence Club, who somehow escaped with their lives from the wholesale persecution that followed the collapse of the Independence Club. Six out of the eight cabinet members elected by the people this year, (1919) were the former active members of the Independence Club."

Among the Independents arrested was Syngman Rhee. The foreign community, which in a sense stood sponsor for the more moderate of the Independents, brought influence to bear, and it was understood that in a few days the leaders would be released. Some of them were. But Rhee and a companion broke out before release, in order to stir up a revolt against the Government By a misunderstanding their friends were not on the spot to help them, and they were at once recaptured.

Rhee was now exposed to the full fury of the Emperor's wrath. He was thrown into the innermost prison, and for seven months lay one of a line of men fastened to the ground, their heads held down by heavy cangues, their feet in stocks and their hands fastened by chains so that the wrists were level with the forehead. Occasionally he was taken out to be tormented, in ancient fashion. He expected death, and rejoiced when one night he was told that he was to be executed. His death was already announced in the newspapers. But when the guard came they took, not Rhee, but the man fastened down next to him, to whom Rhee had smuggled a farewell message to be given to his father after his death. His sentence was commuted to life imprisonment.

Lying there, the mind of the young reformer went back to the messages he had heard at the mission school He turned to the Christians' God, and his first prayer was typical of the man, "O God, save my country and save my soul." To him, the dark and foetid cell became as the palace of God, for here God spoke to his soul and he found peace.

He made friends with his guards. One of them smuggled a little Testament in to him. From the faint light of the tiny window, he read passage after passage, one of the under-jailers holding the book for him--since with his bound hands he could not hold it himself--and another waiting to give warning of the approach of the chief guard. Man after man in that little cell found God, and the jailer himself was converted.

After seven months of the hell of the inner cell, Rhee was shifted to roomier quarters, where he was allowed more freedom, still, however, carrying chains around his neck and body. He organized a church in the prison, made up of his own converts. Then he obtained text-books and started a school. He did not in the least relax his own principles. He secretly wrote a book on the spirit of Independence during his imprisonment His old missionary friends sought him out and did what they could for him.

Rhee met plenty of his old friends, for the Conservatives were in the saddle now, and were arresting and imprisoning Progressives at every opportunity. Among the newcomers was a famous old Korean statesman, Yi Sang-jai, who had formerly been First Secretary to the Korean Legation at Washington. Yi incurred the Emperor's displeasure and was thrown into prison. He entered it strongly anti-Christian; before two years were over he had become a leader of the Christian band. In due course Yi was released and became Secretary of the Emperor's Cabinet. He carried his Christianity out with him, and later on, when he left office, became Religious Work leader of the Seoul Y.M.C.A. Yi was one of the most loved and honoured men in Korea. Every one who knew him spoke of him in terms of confidence and praise.

Syngman Rhee was not released from prison until 1904. He then went to America, graduated at the George Washington University, took M.A. at Harvard, and earned his Ph.D. at Princeton. He returned to Seoul as an official of the Y.M.C.A., but finding it impossible to settle down under the Japanese regime, went to Honolulu, where he became principal of the Korean School. A few years later he was chosen first President of the Republic of Korea.

When Russia leased the Liaotung Peninsula from China, after having prevented Japan from retaining it, she threw Korea as a sop to Japan. A treaty was signed by which both nations recognized the independence of Korea, but Russia definitely recognized the supreme nature of the Japanese enterprises and interests there, and promised not to impede the development of Japan's commercial and industrial Korean policy. The Russian military instructors and financial adviser were withdrawn from Seoul.

The Emperor of Korea was still in the hands of the reactionaries. His Prime Minister and favourite was Yi Yung-ik, the one-time coolie who had rescued the Queen, and was now the man at the right hand of the throne.

After a time Russia repented of her generosity. She sought to regain control in Korea. She sent M. Pavloff, an astute and charming statesman, to Seoul, and a series of intrigues began. Yi Yung-ik sided with the Russians. The end was war.

One personal recollection of these last days before the war remains stamped on my memory. I was in Seoul and had been invited to an interview with Yi Yung-ik. Squatted on the ground in his apartment we discussed matters. I urged on him the necessity of reform, if Korea was to save herself from extinction. Yi quickly retorted that Korea was safe, for her independence was guaranteed by America and Europe.

"Don't you understand," I urged, "that treaties not backed by power are useless. If you wish the treaties to be respected, you must live up to them. You must reform or perish."

"It does not matter what the other nations are doing," declared the Minister. "We have this day sent out a statement that we are neutral and asking for our neutrality to be respected."

"Why should they protect you, if you do not protect yourself?" I asked.

"We have the promise of America. She will be our friend whatever happens," the Minister insisted.

From that position he would not budge.

Three days later, the Russian ships, the Variag **and the** Korietz, lay sunken wrecks in Chemulpo Harbour, broken by the guns of the Japanese fleet, and the Japanese soldiers had seized the Korean Emperor's palace. M. Hayashi, the Japanese Minister, was dictating the terms he must accept. Korea's independence was over, in deed if not in name, and Japan was at last about to realize her centuries' old ambition to have Korea for her own.

V

THE NEW ERA

Japan was now in a position to enforce obedience. Russia could no longer interfere; England would not. A new treaty between Japan and Korea, drawn up in advance, was signed--the Emperor being ordered to assent without hesitation or alteration--and Japan began her work as the open protector of Korea. The Korean Government was to place full confidence in Japan and follow her lead; while Japan pledged herself "in a spirit of firm friendship, to secure the safety and repose" of the Imperial Korean House, and definitely guaranteed the independence and territorial integrity of the country. Japan was to be given every facility for military operations during the war.

The Japanese at first behaved with great moderation. Officials who had been hostile to them were not only left unpunished, but were, some of them, employed in the Japanese service. The troops marching northwards maintained rigid discipline and treated the people well. Food that was taken was purchased at fair prices, and the thousands of labourers who were pressed into the army service as carriers were rewarded with a liberality and promptitude that left them surprised. Mr. Hayashi did everything that he could to reassure the Korean Emperor, and repeatedly told him that Japan desired nothing but the good of Korea and the strengthening of the Korean nation. The Marquis Ito was soon afterwards sent on a special mission from the Mikado, and he repeated and emphasized the declarations of friendship and help.

All this was not without effect upon the Korean mind. The people of the north had learnt to dislike the Russians, because of their lack of discipline and want of restraint. They had been alienated in particular by occasional interference with Korean women by the Russian soldiers. I travelled largely throughout the northern regions in the early days of the war, and everywhere I heard from the people during the first few weeks nothing but expressions of friendship to the Japanese. The coolies and farmers were friendly because they hoped that Japan would modify the oppression of the native magistrates. A section of better-class people, especially those who had received some foreign training, were sympathetic, because they credited Japan's promises and had been convinced by old experience that no far-reaching reforms could come to their land without foreign aid.

As victory followed victory, however, the attitude of the Japanese grew less kindly. A large number of petty tradesmen followed the army, and these showed none of the restraint of the military. They travelled about, sword in hand, taking what they wished and doing as they pleased. Then the army cut down the rate of pay for coolies, and, from being overpaid, the native labourers were forced to toil for half their ordinary earnings. The military, too, gradually began to acquire a more domineering air.

In Seoul itself a definite line of policy was being pursued. The Korean Government had employed a number of foreign advisers. These were steadily eliminated; some of them were paid up for the full time of their engagements and sent off, and others were told that their agreements would not be renewed. Numerous Japanese advisers were brought in, and, step by step, the administration was Japanized. This process was hastened by a supplementary agreement concluded in August, when the Korean Emperor practically handed the control of administrative functions over to the Japanese. He agreed to engage a Japanese financial adviser, to reform the currency, to reduce his army, to adopt Japanese military and educational methods, and eventually to trust the foreign relations to Japan. One of the first results of this new agreement was that Mr. (now Baron) Megata was given control of the Korean finances. He quickly brought extensive and, on the whole, admirable changes into the currency. Under the old methods, Korean money was among the worst in the world. The famous gibe of a British Consul in an official report, that the Korean coins might be divided into good, good counterfeits, bad counterfeits, and counterfeits so bad that they can only be passed off in the dark, was by no means an effort of imagination. In the days before the war it was necessary, when one received any sum of money, to employ an expert to count over the coins, and put aside the worst counterfeits. The old nickels were so cumbersome that a very few pounds' worth of them formed a heavy load for a pony. Mr. Megata changed all this, and put the currency on a sound basis, naturally not without some temporary trouble, but certainly with permanent benefit to the country.

The next great step in the Japanese advance was the acquirement of the entire Korean postal and telegraph system. This was taken over, despite Korean protests. More and more Japanese gendarmes were brought in and established themselves everywhere. They started to control all political activity. Men who protested against Japanese action were arrested and imprisoned, or driven abroad. A notorious pro-Japanese society, the Il Chin Hoi, was fostered by every possible means, members receiving for a time direct payments through Japanese sources. The payment at one period was 50 sen (1s.) a day. Notices were posted in Seoul that no one could organize a political society unless the Japanese headquarters consented, and no one could hold a meeting for discussing affairs without permission, and without having it guarded by Japanese police. All letters and circulars issued by political societies were first to be submitted to the headquarters. Those who offended made themselves punishable by martial law.

Gradually the hand of Japan became heavier and heavier. Little aggravating changes were made. The Japanese military authorities decreed that Japanese time should be used for all public work, and they changed the names of the towns from Korean to Japanese. Martial law was now enforced with the utmost rigidity. Scores of thousands of Japanese coolies poured into the country, and spread abroad, acting in a most oppressive way. These coolies, who had been kept strictly under discipline in their own land, here found themselves masters of a weaker people. The Korean magistrates could not punish them, and the few Japanese residents, scattered in the provinces, would not. The coolies were poor, uneducated, strong, and with the inherited brutal traditions of generations of their ancestors who had looked upon force and strength as supreme right. They went through the country like a plague. If they wanted a thing they took it If they fancied a house, they turned the resident out.

They beat, they outraged, they murdered in a way and on a scale of which it is difficult for any white man to speak with moderation. Koreans were flogged to death for offences that did not deserve a sixpenny fine. They were shot for mere awkwardness. Men were dispossessed of their homes by every form of guile and trickery. It was my lot to hear from Koreans themselves and from white men living in the districts, hundreds upon hundreds of incidents of this time, all to the same effect. The outrages were allowed to pass unpunished and unheeded. The Korean who approached the office of a Japanese resident to complain was thrown out, as a rule, by the underlings.

One act on the part of the Japanese surprised most of those who knew them best. In Japan itself opium-smoking is prohibited under the heaviest penalties, and elaborate precautions are taken to shut opium in any of its forms out of the country. Strict anti-opium laws were also enforced in Korea under the old administration. The Japanese, however, now permitted numbers of their people to travel through the interior of Korea selling morphia to the natives. In the northwest in particular this caused quite a wave of morphia-mania.

The Japanese had evidently set themselves to acquire possession of as much Korean land as possible. The military authorities staked out large portions of the finest sites in the country, the river-lands near Seoul, the lands around Pyeng-yang, great districts to the north, and fine strips all along the railway. Hundreds of thousands of acres were thus acquired. A nominal sum was paid as compensation to the Korean Government--a sum that did not amount to one-twentieth part of the real value of the land. The people who were turned out received, in many cases, nothing at all, and, in others, one-tenth to one-twentieth of the fair value. The land was seized by the military, nominally for purposes of war. Within a few months large parts of it were being resold to Japanese builders and shopkeepers, and Japanese settlements were growing up on them. This theft of land beggared thousands of formerly prosperous people.

The Japanese Minister pushed forward, in the early days of the war, a scheme of land appropriation that would have handed two-thirds of Korea over at a blow to a Japanese concessionaire, a Mr. Nagamori, had it gone through. Under this proposal all the waste lands of Korea, which included all unworked mineral lands, were to be given to Mr. Nagamori nominally for fifty years, but really on a perpetual lease, without any payment or compensation, and with freedom from taxation for some time. Mr. Nagamori was simply a cloak for the Japanese Government in this matter. The comprehensive nature of the request stirred even the foreign representatives in Seoul to action. For the moment the Japanese had to abandon the scheme. The same scheme under another name was carried out later when the Japanese obtained fuller control.

It may be asked why the Korean people did not make vigorous protests against the appropriation of their land. They did all they could, as can be seen by the "Five Rivers" case. One part of the Japanese policy was to force loans upon the Korean Government. On one occasion it was proposed that Japan should lend Korea 2,000,000 yen. The residents in a prosperous district near Seoul, the "Five Rivers," informed the Emperor that if he wanted money, they would raise it and so save them the necessity of borrowing from foreigners. Soon afterwards these people were all served with notice to quit, as their land was wanted by the Japanese military authorities. The district contained, it was said, about 15,000 houses. The inhabitants protested and a large number of them went to Seoul, demanding to see the Minister for Home Affairs. They were met by a Japanese policeman, who was soon reenforced by about twenty others, who refused to allow them to pass. A free fight followed. Many of the Koreans were wounded, some of them severely, and finally, in spite of stubborn resistance, they were driven back. Later, a mixed force of Japanese police and soldiers went down to their district and drove them from their villages.

The Japanese brought over among their many advisers, one foreigner--an American, Mr. Stevens--who had for some time served in the Japanese Foreign Office. Mr. Stevens was nominally in the employment of the Korean Government, but really he was a more thoroughgoing servant of Japan than many Japanese themselves. Two foreigners, whose positions seemed fairly established, were greatly in the way of the new rulers. One was Dr. Allen, the American Minister at Seoul. Dr. Allen had shown himself to be an independent and impartial representative of his country. He was friendly to the Japanese, but did not think it necessary to shut his eyes to the darker sides of their administration. This led to his downfall. He took opportunity, on one or two occasions, to tell his Government some unpalatable truths. The Japanese came to know it. They suggested indirectly that he was not persona grata to them. He was summarily and somewhat discourteously recalled, his successor, Mr. E.V. Morgan, arriving at Seoul with authorization to replace him. The next victim was Mr. McLeavy Brown, the Chief Commissioner of Customs. Mr. Brown had done his utmost to work with the Japanese, but there were conflicts of authority between him and Mr. Megata. Negotiations were entered into with the

British authorities, and Mr. Brown had to go. He was too loyal and self-sacrificing to dispute the ruling, and submitted in silence.

As the summer of 1905 drew to a close it became more and more clear that the Japanese Government, despite its many promises to the contrary, intended completely to destroy the independence of Korea. Even the Court officials were at last seriously alarmed, and set about devising means to protect themselves. The Emperor had thought that because Korean independence was provided for in various treaties with Great Powers, therefore he was safe. He had yet to learn that treaty rights, unbacked by power, are worth little more than the paper upon which they are written.

The Emperor trusted in particular to the clause in the Treaty with the United States in 1882 that if other Powers dealt unjustly or oppressively with Korea, America would exert her good offices to bring about an amicable arrangement In vain did the American Minister, his old friend Dr. Allen--who had not yet gone--try to disillusion him.

Early in November the Marquis Ito arrived in Seoul on another visit, this time as Special Envoy from the Emperor of Japan. He brought with him a letter from the Mikado, saying that he hoped the Korean Emperor would follow the directions of the Marquis, and come to an agreement with him, for it was essential for the maintenance of peace in the Far East that he should do so.

Marquis Ito was received in formal audience on November 15th, and there presented a series of demands, drawn up in treaty form. These were, in the main, that the foreign relations of Korea should be placed entirely in the hands of Japan, the Korean diplomatic service brought to an end, and the Ministers recalled from foreign Courts. The Japanese Minister to Korea was to became supreme administrator of the country under the Emperor, and the Japanese Consuls in the different districts were to be made Residents, with the powers of supreme local governors. In other words, Korea was entirely to surrender her independence as a State, and was to hand over control of her internal administration to the Japanese. The Emperor met the request with a blank refusal. The conversation between the two, as reported at the time, was as follows.

The Emperor said--

"Although I have seen in the newspapers various rumours that Japan proposed to assume a protectorate over Korea, I did not believe them, as I placed faith in Japan's adherence to the promise to maintain the independence of Korea which was made by the Emperor of Japan at the beginning of the war and embodied in a treaty between Korea and Japan. When I heard you were coming to my country I was glad, as I believed your mission was to increase the friendship between our countries, and your demands have therefore taken me entirely by surprise."

To which Marquis Ito rejoined--

"These demands are not my own; I am only acting in accordance with a mandate from my Government, and if Your Majesty will agree to the demands which T have presented it will be to the benefit of both nations and peace in the East will be assured for ever. Please, therefore, consent quickly."

The Emperor replied--

"From time immemorial it has been the custom of the rulers of Korea, when confronted with questions so momentous as this, to come to no decision until all the Ministers, high and low, who hold or have held office, have been consulted, and the opinion of the scholars and the common people have been obtained, so that I cannot now settle this matter myself."

Said Marquis Ito again--

"Protests from the people can easily be disposed of, and for the sake of the friendship between the two countries Your Majesty should come to a decision at once."

To this the Emperor replied--

"Assent to your proposal would mean the ruin of my country, and I will therefore sooner die than agree to it."

The conference lasted nearly five hours, and then the Marquis had to leave, having accomplished nothing. He at once tackled the members of the Cabinet, individually and collectively. They were all summoned to the Japanese Legation on the following day, and a furious debate began, starting at three o'clock in the afternoon, and lasting till late at night. The Ministers had sworn to one another beforehand that they would not yield. In spite of threats, cajoleries, and proffered bribes, they remained steadfast The arguments used by Marquis Ito and Mr. Hayashi, apart from personal ones, were twofold. The first was that it was essential for the peace of the Far East that Japan and Korea should be united. The second appealed to racial ambition. The Japanese painted to the Koreans a picture of a great united East, with the Mongol nations all standing firm and as one against the white man, who would reduce them to submission if he could.[8] The Japanese were determined to give the Cabinet no time to regather its strength. On the 17th of November, another conference began at two in the afternoon at the Legation, but equally without result. Mr. Hayashi then advised the Ministers to go to the palace and open a Cabinet Meeting in the presence of the Emperor. This was done, the Japanese joining in.

All this time the Japanese Army had been making a great display of military force around the palace. All the Japanese troops in the district had been for days parading the streets and open places fronting the Imperial residence. The field-guns were out, and the men were fully armed. They marched, countermarched, stormed, made feint attacks, occupied the gates, put their guns in position, and did everything, short of actual violence, that they could to demonstrate to the Koreans that

---

8 As it may be questioned whether the Japanese would use such arguments, I may say that the account of the interview was given to me by one of the participating Korean Ministers, and that he dealt at great length with the pro-Asian policy suggested there. I asked him why he had not listened and accepted. He replied that he knew what such arguments meant. The unity of Asia when spoken of by Japanese meant the supreme autocracy of their country.

they were able to enforce their demands. To the Cabinet Ministers themselves, and to the Emperor, all this display had a sinister and terrible meaning. They could not forget the night in 1895, when the Japanese soldiers had paraded around another palace, and when their picked bullies had forced their way inside and murdered the Queen. Japan had done this before; why should she not do it again? Not one of those now resisting the will of Dai Nippon but saw the sword in front of his eyes, and heard in imagination a hundred times during the day the rattle of the Japanese bullets.

That evening Japanese soldiers, with fixed bayonets, entered the courtyard of the palace and stood near the apartment of the Emperor. Marquis Ito now arrived, accompanied by General Hasegawa, Commander of the Japanese Army in Korea, and a fresh attack was started on the Cabinet Ministers. The Marquis demanded an audience of the Emperor. The Emperor refused to grant it, saying that his throat was very bad, and he was in great pain. The Marquis then made his way into the Emperor's presence, and personally requested an audience. The Emperor still refused. "Please go away and discuss the matter, with the Cabinet Ministers," he said.

Thereupon Marquis Ito went outside to the Ministers. "Your Emperor has commanded you to confer with me and settle this matter," he declared. A fresh conference was opened. The presence of the soldiers, the gleaming of the bayonets outside, the harsh words of command that could be heard through the windows of the palace buildings, were not without their effect. The Ministers had fought for days and they had fought alone. No single foreign representative had offered them help or counsel. They saw submission or destruction before them. "What is the use of our resisting?" said one. "The Japanese always get their way in the end." Signs of yielding began to appear. The acting Prime Minister, Han Kew-sul, jumped to his feet and said he would go and tell the Emperor of the talk of traitors. Han Kew-sul was allowed to leave the room and then was gripped by the Japanese Secretary of the Legation, thrown into a side-room and threatened with death. Even Marquis Ito went out to him to persuade him. "Would you not yield," the Marquis said, "if your Emperor commanded you?" "No," said Han Kew-sul, "not even then!"

This was enough. The Marquis at once went to the Emperor. "Han Kew-sul is a traitor," he said. "He defies you, and declares that he will not obey your commands."

Meanwhile the remaining Ministers waited in the Cabinet Chamber. Where was their leader, the man who had urged them all to resist to death? Minute after minute passed, and still he did not return. Then a whisper went round that the Japanese had killed him. The harsh voices of the Japanese grew still more strident. Courtesy and restraint were thrown off. "Agree with us and be rich, or oppose us and perish." Pak Che-sun, the Foreign Minister, one of the best and most capable of Korean statesmen, was the last to yield. But even he finally gave way. In the early hours of the morning commands were issued that the seal of State should be brought from the Foreign Minister's apartment, and a treaty should be signed. Here another difficulty arose. The custodian of the seal had received orders in advance that, even if his master commanded, the seal was not to be surrendered for any such purpose. When telephonic orders were sent to him, he refused to bring the seal along, and special messengers had to be despatched to take it from him by force. The Emperor himself asserts to this day that he did not consent.

The news of the signing of the treaty was received by the people with horror and indignation. Han Kew-sul, once he escaped from custody, turned on his fellow-Ministers as one distraught, and bitterly reproached them. "Why have you broken your promises?" he cried. "Why have you broken your promises?" The Ministers found themselves the most hated and despised of men. There was danger lest mobs should attack them and tear them to pieces. Pak Che-sun shrank away under the storm of execration that greeted him. On December 6th, as he was entering the palace, one of the soldiers lifted his rifle and tried to shoot him, Pak Che-sun turned back, and hurried to the Japanese Legation. There he forced his way into the presence of Mr. Hayashi, and drew a knife. "It is you who have brought me to this," he cried. "You have made me a traitor to my country." He attempted to cut his own throat, but Mr. Hayashi stopped him, and he was sent to hospital for treatment. When he recovered he was chosen by the Japanese as the new Prime Minister, Han Kew-sul being exiled and disgraced. Pak did not, however, hold office for very long, being somewhat too independent to suit his new masters.

As the news spread through the country, the people of various districts assembled, particularly in the north, and started to march southwards to die in front of the palace as a protest. Thanks to the influence of the missionaries, many of them were stopped. "It is of no use your dying in that way," the missionaries told them. "You had better live and make your country better able to hold its own." A number of leading officials, including all the surviving past Prime Ministers, and over a hundred men who had previously held high office under the Crown, went to the palace, and demanded that the Emperor should openly repudiate the treaty, and execute those Ministers who had acquiesced in it. The Emperor tried to temporize with them, for he was afraid that, if he took too openly hostile an attitude, the Japanese would punish him. The memorialists sat down in the palace buildings, refusing to move, and demanding an answer. Some of their leaders were arrested by the Japanese gendarmes, only to have others, still greater men, take their place. The storekeepers of the city put up their shutters to mark their mourning.

At last a message came from the Emperor: "Although affairs now appear to you to be dangerous, there may presently result some benefit to the nation." The gendarmes descended on the petitioners and threatened them with general arrest if they remained around the palace any longer. They moved on to a shop where they tried to hold a meeting, but they were turned out of it by the police. Min Yong-whan, their leader, a former Minister for War and Special Korean Ambassador at Queen Victoria's Diamond Jubilee, went home. He wrote letters to his friends lamenting the state of his country, and then committed suicide. Several other statesmen did the same, while many others resigned. One native paper, the Whang Sung Shimbun, dared to print an exact statement of what had taken place. Its editor was promptly arrested, and thrown into prison, and the paper suppressed. Its lamentation voiced the feeling of the country:--

> "When it was recently made known the Marquis Ito would come to Korea our deluded people all said, with one voice, that he is the man who will be responsible for the maintenance of friendship between the three countries of the Far East (Japan, China, and Korea), and, believing that his visit to Korea was for the sole purpose of devising good plans for strictly maintaining the promised integrity and independence of Korea, our people, from the seacoast to the capital, united in extending to him a hearty welcome.

"But oh! How difficult is it to anticipate affairs in this world. Without warning, a proposal containing five clauses was laid before the Emperor, and we then saw how mistaken we were about the object of Marquis Ito's visit. However, the Emperor firmly refused to have anything to do with these proposals and Marquis Ito should then, properly, have abandoned his attempt and returned to his own country.

"But the Ministers of our Government, who are worse than pigs or dogs, coveting honours and advantages for themselves, and frightened by empty threats, were trembling in every limb, and were willing to become traitors to their country and betray to Japan the integrity of a nation which has stood for 4,000 years, the foundation and honour of a dynasty 500 years old, and the rights and freedom of twenty million people.

"We do not wish to too deeply blame Pak Che-sun and the other Ministers, of whom, as they are little better than brute animals, too much was not to be expected, but what can be said of the Vice-Prime Minister, the chief of the Cabinet, whose early opposition to the proposals of Marquis Ito was an empty form devised to enhance his reputation with the people?

"Can he not now repudiate the agreement or can he not rid the world of his presence? How can he again stand before the Emperor and with what face can he ever look upon any one of his twenty million compatriots?

"Is it worth while for any of us to live any longer? Our people have become the slaves of others, and the spirit of a nation which has stood for 4,000 years, since the days of Tun Kun and Ke-ja has perished in a single night. Alas! fellow-countrymen. Alas!"

Suicides, resignations, and lamentation were of no avail. The Japanese gendarmes commanded the streets, and the Japanese soldiers, behind them, were ready to back up their will by the most unanswerable of arguments--force.

Naturally, as might have been expected by those who know something of the character of the Japanese, every effort was made to show that there had been no breach of treaty promises. Korea was still an independent country, and the dignity of its Imperial house was still unimpaired. Japan had only brought a little friendly pressure on a weaker brother to assist him along the path of progress. Such talk pleased the Japanese, and helped them to reconcile the contrast between their solemn promises and their actions. It deceived no one else. Soon even, the Japanese papers made little or no more talk of Korean independence. "Korean independence is a farce," they said. And for the time they were right.

The Emperor did his utmost to induce the Powers, more particularly America, to intervene, but in vain. The story of his efforts is an interesting episode in the records of diplomacy.

Dr. Allen, the American Minister, wrote to his Secretary of State, on April 14, 1904, telling of the serious concern of the Korean Emperor over recent happenings. "He falls back in his extremity upon his old friendship with America.... The Emperor confidently expects that America will do something for him at the close of this war, or when opportunity offers, to retain for him as much of his independence as is possible. He is inclined to give a very free and favourable translation to Article I of our treaty of Jenchuan of 1882" (i.e., the pledge, "If other Powers deal unjustly or oppressively with either Government, the other will exert their good offices, on being informed of the case, to bring about an amicable arrangement, thus showing their friendly feeling").

In April, 1905, Dr. Allen transmitted to Washington copies of protests by an American missionary and certain Koreans against the conduct of Japanese subjects in Korea. Dr. Allen was shortly afterwards replaced by Mr. Edwin V. Morgan.

In October, 1905, the Emperor, determined to appeal directly to America, enlisted the services of Professor Homer B. Hulbert, editor of the Korea Review, who had been employed continuously in educational work in Seoul since 1886, and despatched him to Washington, with a letter to the President of the United States. Mr.

Hulbert informed his Minister at Seoul of his mission and started off. The Japanese learned of his departure (Mr. Hulbert suggests that the American Minister may have informed them) and used every effort to force a decision before the letter could be delivered.

On the same day that Mr. Hulbert reached Washington the Korean Cabinet were forced to sign the document giving Japan a protectorate over their land. Formal notification had not yet, however, arrived at Washington, so it was resolved not to receive Mr. Hulbert until this had come.

"I supposed that the President would be not only willing but eager to see the letter," said Mr. Hulbert in a statement presented later to the Senate; "but instead of that I received the astounding answer that the President would not receive it. I cast about in my own mind for a possible reason, but could imagine none. I went to the State Department with it, but was told that they were too busy to see me. Remember that at that very moment Korea was in her death throes; that she was in full treaty relations with us; that there was a Korean legation in Washington and an American legation in Seoul. I determined that there was something here that was more than mere carelessness. There was premeditation in the refusal. There was no other answer. They said I might come the following day. I did so and was told that they were still too busy, but might come the next day. I hurried over to the White House and asked to be admitted. A secretary came out and without any preliminary whatever told me in the lobby that they knew the contents of the letter, but that the State Department was the only place to go. I had to wait till the next day. But on that same day, the day before I was admitted, the administration, without a word to the Emperor or Government of Korea or to the Korean Legation, and knowing well the contents of the undelivered letter, accepted Japan's unsupported statement that it was all satisfactory to the Korean Government and people, cabled our legation to remove from Korea, cut off all communication with the Korean Government, and then admitted me with the letter."

On November 25th Mr. Hulbert received a message from Mr. Root that

"The letter from the Emperor of Korea which you intrusted to me has been placed in the President's hands and read by him.

"In view of the fact that the Emperor desires that the sending of the letter should remain secret, and of the fact that since intrusting it to you the Emperor has made a new agreement with Japan disposing of the whole question to which the letter relates, it seems quite impracticable that any action should be based upon it."

On the following day Mr. Hulbert received a cablegram from the Emperor, which had been despatched from Chefoo, in order not to pass over the Japanese wires:--

"I declare that the so-called treaty of protectorate recently concluded between Korea and Japan was extorted at the point of the sword and under duress and therefore is null and void. I never consented to it and never will. Transmit to American Government.
                    "THE EMPEROR OF KOREA."

Poor Emperor! Innocent simpleton to place such trust in a written bond. Mr. Root had already telegraphed to the American Minister at Seoul to withdraw from Korea and to return to the United States.

No one supposes that the Washington authorities were deceived by the statement of the Japanese authorities or that they believed for one moment that the treaty was secured in any other way than by force. To imagine so would be an insult to their intelligence. It must be remembered that Japan was at this time at the very height of her prestige. President Roosevelt was convinced, mainly through the influence of his old friend, Mr. George Kennan, that the Koreans were unfit for self-government. He was anxious to please Japan, and therefore he deliberately refused to interfere. His own explanation, given some years afterwards, was:

> "To be sure, by treaty it was solemnly covenanted that Korea should remain independent. But Korea itself was helpless to enforce the treaty, and it was out of the question to suppose that any other nation, with no interest of its own at stake, would do for the Koreans what they were utterly unable to do for themselves."

There we have the essence of international political morality.

The letter of the Emperor of Korea to the President of the United States makes interesting reading:

> "Ever since 1883 the United States and Korea have been in friendly treaty relations. Korea has received many proofs of the good will and the sympathy of the American Government and people. The American Representatives have always shown themselves to be in sympathy with the welfare and progress of Korea. Many teachers have been sent from America who have done much for the uplift of our people.

> "But we have not made the progress that we ought. This is due partly to the political machinations of foreign powers and partly to our mistakes. At the beginning of the Japan-Russia war the Japanese Government asked us to enter into an alliance with them, granting them the use of our territory, harbours, and other resources, to facilitate their military and naval operations. Japan, on her part, guaranteed to preserve the independence of Korea and the welfare and dignity of the royal house. We complied with Japan's request, loyally lived up to our obligations, and

did everything that we had stipulated. By so doing we put ourselves in such a position that if Russia had won, she could have seized Korea and annexed her to Russian territory on the ground that we were active allies of Japan.

"It is now apparent that Japan proposes to abrogate their part of this treaty and declare a protectorate over our country in direct contravention of her sworn promise in the agreement of 1904. There are several reasons why this should not be done.

"In the first place, Japan will stultify herself by such a direct breach of faith. It will injure her prestige as a power that proposes to work according to enlightened laws.

"In the second place, the actions of Japan in Korea during the past two years give no promise that our people will be handled in an enlightened manner. No adequate means have been provided whereby redress could be secured for wrongs perpetrated upon our people. The finances of the country have been gravely mishandled by Japan. Nothing has been done towards advancing the cause of education or justice. Every move on Japan's part has been manifestly selfish.

"The destruction of Korea's independence will work her a great injury, because it will intensify the contempt with which the Japanese people treat the Koreans and will make their acts all the more oppressive.

"We acknowledge that many reforms are needed in Korea. We are glad to have the help of Japanese advisers, and we are prepared loyally to carry out their suggestions. We recognize the mistakes of the past. It is not for ourselves we plead, but for the Korean people.

"At the beginning of the war our people gladly welcomed the Japanese, because this seemed to herald needed reforms and a general bettering of conditions, but soon it was seen that no genuine reforms were intended and the people had been deceived.

"One of the gravest evils that will follow a protectorate by Japan is that the Korean people will lose all incentive to improvement. No hope will remain that they can ever regain their independence. They need the spur of national feeling to make them determine upon progress and to make them persevere in it. But the extinction of nationality will bring despair, and instead of working loyally and gladly in conjunction with Japan, the old-time hatred will be intensified and suspicion and animosity will result.

"It has been said that sentiment should have no place in such affairs, but we believe, sir, that sentiment is the moving force in all human affairs, and that kindness, sympathy, and generosity are still working between nations as between individuals. We beg of you to bring to bear upon this question the same breadth of mind and the same calmness of judgment that have characterized your course hitherto, and, having weighed the matter, to render us what aid you can consistently in this our time of national danger."

[Private Seal of the Emperor of Korea.]

VI
THE RULE OF PRINCE ITO

Marquis Ito was made the first Japanese Resident-General in Korea. There could have been no better choice, and no choice more pleasing to the Korean people. He was regarded by the responsible men of the nation with a friendliness such as few other Japanese inspired. Here was a man greater than his policies. Every one who came in contact with him felt that, whatever the nature of the measures he was driven to adopt in the supposed interests of his Emperor, he yet sincerely meant well by the Korean people. The faults of his administration were the necessary accompaniments of Japanese military expansion; his virtues were his own. It was a noble act for him to take on himself the most burdensome and exacting post that Japanese diplomacy had to offer, at an age when he might well have looked for the ease and dignity of the close of an honour-sated career.

The Marquis brought with him several capable Japanese officials of high rank, and began his new rule by issuing regulations fixing the position and duties of his staff. Under these, the Resident-General became in effect supreme Administrator of Korea, with power to do what he pleased. He had authority to repeal any order or measure that he considered injurious to public interests, and he could punish to the extent of not more than a year's imprisonment or not more than a 200 yen fine. This limitation of his punitive power was purely nominal, for the country was under martial law and the courts-martial had power to inflict death. Residents and Vice-Residents, of Japanese nationality, were placed over the country, acting practically as governors. The police were placed under Japanese inspectors where they were not themselves Japanese. The various departments of affairs, agricultural, commercial, and industrial, were given Japanese directors and advisers, and the power of appointing all officials, save those of the highest rank, was finally in the hands of the Resident-General. This limitation, again, was soon put on one side. Thus, the Resident-General became dictator of Korea--a dictator, however, who still conducted certain branches of local affairs there through native officials and who had to reckon with the intrigues of a Court party which he could not as yet sweep on one side.

To Japan, Korea was chiefly of importance as a strategic position for military operations on the continent of Asia and as a field for emigration. The first steps under the new administration were in the direction of perfecting communications throughout the country, so as to enable the troops to be moved easily and rapidly from point to point. A railway had already been built from Fusan to Seoul, and another was in course of completion from Seoul to Wi-ju, thus giving a trunk line that would carry large numbers of Japanese soldiers from Japan itself to the borders of Manchuria in about thirty-six hours. A loan of 10,000,000 yen was raised on the guarantee of the Korean Customs, and a million and a half of this was spent on four main military roads, connecting some of the chief districts with the principal harbours and railway centres. Part of the cost of these was paid by the loan and part by special local taxation. It may be pointed out that these roads were military rather than industrial undertakings. The usual methods of travel and for conveying goods in the interior of Korea was by horseback and with pack-ponies. For these, the old narrow tracks served, generally speaking, very well. The new roads were finely graded, and were built in such a manner that rails could be quickly laid down on them and artillery and ammunition wagons rapidly conveyed from point to point. Another railway was built from Seoul to Gensan, on the east coast.

The old Korean "Burglar Capture Office," the native equivalent to the Bow Street Runners, or the Mulberry Street detectives, was abolished, as were the local police, and police administration was more and more put in the hands of special constables brought over from Japan. The Japanese military gendarmerie were gradually sent back and their places taken by civilian constables. This change was wholly for the good. The gendarmerie had earned a very bad reputation in country parts for harshness and arbitrary conduct. The civilian police proved themselves far better men, more conciliatory, and more just.

One real improvement instituted by the Residency-General was the closer control of Japanese immigrants. Numbers of the worst offenders were laid by the heels and sent back home. The Residency officials were increased in numbers, and in some parts at least it became easier for a Korean to obtain a hearing when he had a complaint against a Japanese. The Marquis Ito spoke constantly in favour of a policy of conciliation and friendship, and after a time he succeeded in winning over the cooeperation of some of the foreigners.

It became more and more clear, however, that the aim of the Japanese was nothing else than the entire absorption of the country and the destruction of every trace of Korean nationality. One of the most influential Japanese in Korea put this quite frankly to me in 1906. "You must understand that I am not expressing official views," he told me. "But if you ask me as an individual what is to be the outcome of our policy, I only see one end. This will take several generations, but it must come. The Korean people will be absorbed by the Japanese. They will talk our language, live our life, and be an integral part of us. There are only two ways of colonial administration. One is to rule over the people as aliens. This you British have done in India, and therefore your Empire cannot endure. India must pass out of your rule. The second way is to absorb the people. This is what we will do. We will teach them our language, establish our institutions, and make them one with us."

The policy of the new administration towards foreigners was one of gradual, but no less sure, exclusion. Everything that could be done was done to rob the white man of what prestige was yet left to him. Careful and systematic efforts were made, in particular, by the Japanese newspapers and some of the officials to make the native Christian converts turn from their American teachers, and throw in their lot with the Japanese. The native press, under Japanese editorship, systematically preached anti-white doctrines. Any one who mixed freely with the Korean people heard from them, time after time, of the principles the Japanese would fain have them learn. I was told of this by ex-Cabinet Ministers, by young students, and even by native servants. One of my own Korean "boys" put the matter in a nutshell to me one day. He raised the question of the future of Japan in Asia, and he summarized the new Japanese doctrines very succinctly. "Master," he said to me, "Japanese man wanchee all Asia be one, with Japanese man topside. All Japanese man wanchee this; some Korean man wanchee, most no wanchee; all Chinaman no wanchee."

It may be thought that the Japanese would at least have learnt from their experience in 1895 not to attempt to interfere with the dress or personal habits of the people. Nothing among all their blunders during the earlier period was more disastrous to them than the regulations compelling the men to cut off their topknots. These did Japan greater harm among the common people than even the murder of the Queen. Yet no sooner had Japan established herself again than once more sumptuary regulations were issued. The first was an order against wearing white dress in wintertime. People were to attire themselves in nothing but dark-coloured garments, and those who refused to obey were coerced in many ways. The Japanese did not at once insist on a general system of hair-cutting, but they brought the greatest pressure to bear on all in any way under their authority. Court officials, public servants, magistrates, and the like, were commanded to cut their hair. Officials were evidently instructed to make every one who came under their influence have his topknot off. The Il Chin Hoi, the pro-Japanese society, followed in the same line. European dress was forced on those connected with the Court. The national costume, like the national language, was, if possible, to die. Ladies of the Court were ordered to dress themselves in foreign style. The poor ladies in consequence found it impossible to show themselves in any public place, for they were greeted with roars of derision.

The lowered status of the white in Korea could be clearly seen by the attitude of many of the Japanese towards him. I heard stories from friends of my own, residents in the country, quiet and inoffensive people that made my blood boil. It was difficult, for instance, to restrain one's indignation when a missionary lady told you of how she was walking along the street when a Japanese soldier hustled up against her and deliberately struck her in the breast. The Roman Catholic bishop was openly insulted and struck by Japanese soldiers in his own cathedral, and nothing was done. The story of Mr. and Mrs. Weigall typifies others. Mr. Weigall is an Australian mining engineer, and was travelling up north with his wife and assistant, Mr. Taylor, and some Korean servants, in December, 1905. He had full authorizations and passports, and was going about his business in a perfectly proper manner. His party was stopped at one point by some Japanese soldiers, and treated in a fashion which it is impossible fully to describe in print. They were insulted, jabbed at with bayonets, and put under arrest. One soldier held his gun close to Mrs. Weigall and struck her full in the chest with his closed fist when she moved. The man called them by the most insulting names possible, keeping the choicest phrases for the lady. Their servants were kicked. Finally they were allowed to go away after a long delay and long exposure to bitter weather, repeated insults being hurled after them. The British authorities took up this case. There was abundant evidence, and there could be no dispute about the facts. All the satisfaction, however, that the Weigalls could obtain was a nominal apology.

Then there was the case of the Rev. Mr. McRae, a Canadian missionary living in northeastern Korea. Mr. McRae had obtained some land for a mission station, and the Japanese military authorities there wanted it. They drove stakes into part of the property, and he thereupon represented the case to the Japanese officials, and after at least twice asking them to remove their stakes, he pulled them up himself. The Japanese waited until a fellow-missionary, who lived with Mr. McRae, had gone away on a visit, and then six soldiers entered his compound and attacked him. He defended himself so well that he finally drove them off, although he received some bad injuries, especially from the blows from one of the men's rifles. Complaint was made to the chief authorities, and, in this case, the Japanese promised to punish the officer concerned. But there were dozens of instances affecting Europeans of all ranks, from consular officials to chance visitors. In most cases the complaints were met by a simple denial on the part of the Japanese. Even where the offence was admitted and punishment was promised, the Europeans would assure you that the men, whom it had been promised to imprison, came and paraded themselves outside their houses immediately afterwards in triumph. In Korea, as in Formosa, the policy was and is to humiliate the white man by any means and in any way.

Two regulations of the Japanese, apparently framed in the interests of the Koreans, proved to be a dangerous blow at their rights. New land laws were drawn up, by which fresh title-deeds were given for the old and complicated deeds of former times. As the Koreans, however, pointed out, large numbers of people held their land in such a way that it was impossible for them to prove their right by written deeds. Until the end of 1905 large numbers of Koreans went abroad to Honolulu and elsewhere as labourers. The Residency-General then framed new emigration laws, nominally to protect the natives, which have had the result of making the old systematic emigration impossible. Families who would fain have escaped the Japanese rule and establish themselves in other lands had every possible hindrance put in their way.

Act after act revealed that the Japanese considered Korea and all in it belonged to them. Did they want a thing? Then let them take it, and woe be to the man who dared to hinder them! This attitude was illustrated in an interesting fashion by a bit of vandalism on the part of Viscount Tanaka, Special Envoy from the Mikado to the Korean Emperor. When the Viscount was in Seoul, late in 1906, he was approached by a Japanese curio-dealer, who pointed out to him that there was a very famous old Pagoda in the district of P'ung-duk, a short distance from Song-do. This Pagoda was presented to Korea by the Chinese Imperial Court a thousand years ago, and the people believed that the stones of which it was constructed possessed great curative qualities. They named it the "Medicine King Pagoda" (Yakwang Top), and its fame was known throughout the country. It was a national memorial as much as the Monument near London Bridge is a national memorial for Englishmen or the Statue of Liberty for Americans. Viscount Tanaka is a great curio-collector, and when he heard of this Pagoda, he longed for it. He mentioned his desire to the Korean Minister for the Imperial Household, and the Minister told him to take it if he wanted it. A few days afterwards, Viscount Tanaka, when bidding the Emperor farewell, thanked him for the gift. The Korean Emperor looked blank, and said that he did not know what the Viscount was talking about. He had heard nothing of it.

However, before long, a party of eighty Japanese, including a number of gendarmes, well armed and ready for resistance, swooped down on Song-do. They took the Pagoda to pieces and placed the stones on carts. The people of the district gathered round them, threatened them, and tried to attack them. But the Japanese were too strong. The Pagoda was conveyed in due course to Tokyo.

Such an outrage could not go unnoticed. The story of the loss spread over the country and reached the foreign press. Defenders of the Japanese at first declared that it was an obvious and incredible lie. The Japan Mail *in particular opened the vials of its wrath and poured them upon the head of the editor of the* Korea Daily News --the English daily publication in Seoul--who had dared to tell the tale. His story was "wholly incredible." "It is impossible to imagine any educated man of ordinary intelligence foolish enough to believe such a palpable lie, unless he be totally blinded by prejudice." The Mail *discovered here again another reason for supporting its plea for the suppression of "a wholly unscrupulous and ma-*

levolent mischief-maker like the Korea Daily News." *"The Japanese should think seriously whether this kind of thing is to be tamely suffered. In allowing such charges at the door of the Mikado's Special Envoy who is also Minister of the Imperial Household, the* Korea Daily News deliberately insults the Mikado himself. There is indeed the reflection that this extravagance will not be without compensation, since it will demonstrate conclusively, if any demonstration were needed, how completely unworthy of credence have been the slanders hitherto ventilated by the Seoul journal to bring the Japanese into odium."

There were instant demands for denials, for explanations, and for proceedings against the wicked libeller. Then it turned out that the story was true, and, in the end, the Japanese officials had to admit its truth. It was said, as an excuse, that the Resident-General had not given his consent to the theft, and that Viscount Tanaka did not intend to keep the Pagoda himself, but to present it to the Mikado. The organ of the Residency-General in Seoul, the Seoul Press, made the best excuse it could. "Viscount Tanaka," it said, "is a conscientious official, liked and respected by those who know him, whether foreign or Japanese, but he is an ardent virtuoso and collector, and it appears that in this instance his collector's eagerness got the better of his sober judgment and discretion." But excuses, apologies, and regrets notwithstanding, the Pagoda was not returned.

It may be asked why the white people living in Korea did not make the full facts about Korea known at an earlier date. Some did attempt it, but the strong feeling that existed abroad in favour of the Japanese people--a feeling due to their magnificent conduct during the war--caused complaints to go unheeded. Many missionaries, while indignant at the injury done to their native neighbours, counselled patience, believing that the abuses were temporary and would soon come to an end.

At the beginning of the war every foreigner--except a small group of pro-Russians, sympathized with Japan. We had all been alienated by the follies and mistakes of the Russian Far Eastern policy. We saw Japan at her best, and we all believed that her people would act well by this weaker race. Our favourable impressions were strengthened by the first doings of the Japanese soldiers, and when scandals were whispered, and oppression began to appear, we all looked upon them as momentary disturbances due to a condition of war. We were unwilling to believe anything but the best, and it took some time to destroy our favourable prepossessions. I speak here not only for myself, but for many another white man in Korea at the time.

I might support this by many quotations. I take, for instance, Professor Hulbert, the editor of the Korea Review, to-day one of the most persistent and active critics of Japanese policy. At the opening of the war Professor Hulbert used all his influence in favour of Japan.

> "What Korea wants," he wrote, "is education, and until steps are taken in that line there is no use in hoping for a genuinely independent Korea. Now, we believe that a large majority of the best-informed Koreans realize that Japan and Japanese influence stand for education and enlightenment, and that while the paramount influence of any one outside Power is in some sense a humiliation, the paramount influence of Japan will give far less genuine cause for humiliation than has the paramount influence of Russia. Russia secured her predominance by pandering to the worst elements in Korean officialdom. Japan holds it by strength of arm, but she holds it in such a way that it gives promise of something better. The word reform never passed the Russians' lips. It is the insistent cry of Japan. The welfare of the Korean people never showed its head above the Russian horizon, but it fills the whole vision of Japan; not from altruistic motives mainly but because the prosperity of Korea and that of Japan rise and fall with the same tide."[9]

Month after month, when stories of trouble came from the interior, the Korea Review endeavoured to give the best explanation possible for them, and to reassure the public. It was not until the editor was forced thereto by consistent and sustained Japanese misgovernment that he reversed his attitude.

Foreign visitors of influence were naturally drawn to the Japanese rather than to the Koreans. They found in the officials of the Residency-General a body of capable and delightful men, who knew the Courts of Europe, and were familiar with

---

9   Korea Review, February, 1904.

world affairs. On the other hand, the Korean spokesmen had no power or skill in putting their case so as to attract European sympathy. One distinguished foreigner, who returned home and wrote a book largely given up to laudation of the Japanese and contemptuous abuse of the Koreans, admitted that he had never, during his journey, had any contact with Koreans save those his Japanese guides brought to him. Some foreign journalists were also at first blinded in the same way.

Such a state of affairs obviously could not last. Gradually the complaints of the foreign community became louder and louder, and visiting publicists began to take more notice of them. The main credit for defending the cause of the Korean people at that time must be given to a young English journalist, editor of the Korea Daily News, Mr. Bethell took up an attitude of strong hostility to the Nagamori land scheme, and came, in consequence, in sharp hostility to the Japanese officials. This naturally led to his close association with the Korean Court. The Daily News *became openly pro-Korean; its one daily edition was changed into two separate papers--one, the* Dai Han Mai Il Shinpo, printed in the Korean language, and the other, printed in English, still calling itself by the old name. Several of us thought that Mr. Bethell at first weakened his case by extreme advocacy and by his indulgence in needlessly vindictive writing. Yet it must be remembered, in common justice to him, that he was playing a very difficult part The Japanese were making his life as uncomfortable as they possibly could, and were doing everything to obstruct his work. His mails were constantly tampered with; his servants were threatened or arrested on various excuses, and his household was subjected to the closest espionage. He displayed surprising tenacity, and held on month after month without showing any sign of yielding. The complaint of extreme bitterness could not be urged against his journal to the same extent after the spring of 1907. From that time he adopted a more quiet and convincing tone. He attempted on many occasions to restrain what he considered the unwise tactics of some Korean extremists. He did his best to influence public opinion against taking up arms to fight Japan.

Failing to conciliate the editor, the Japanese sought to destroy him. In order to cut the ground from under his feet an opposition paper, printed in English, was started, with an able Japanese journalist, Mr. Zumoto, Prince Ito's leading spokesman in the press, as editor. Few could have done the work better than Mr. Zumoto, but his paper, the Seoul Press, failed to destroy the Daily News.

Diplomacy was now brought into play. During the summer of 1906, the Japanese caused the translations of a number of articles from the Dai Han Mai Il Shinpo (the Korean edition of the Daily Mail) to be submitted to the British Government, with a request that Mr. Bethell's journal might be suppressed.

On Saturday, October 12th, Mr. Bethell received a summons to appear on the following Monday at a specially appointed Consular Court, to answer the charge of adopting a course of action likely to cause a breach of the peace.

The trial took place in the Consular building, Mr. Cockburn, the very able British Consul-General, acting as Judge. The short notice made it impossible for Mr. Bethell to obtain legal aid, as there were no British lawyers nearer than Shanghai or Kobe. He had to plead his cause under great disadvantages.

Eight articles were produced in court Six were comments on or descriptions of fighting then taking place in the interior. They were no stronger, if as strong, as many of the statements published in this book.

The Consul-General's decision was as anticipated. He convicted the editor, and ordered him to enter into recognizances of L300 to be of good behaviour for six months. The Korea Daily News in commenting on the matter, said, "The effect of this judgment is that for a period of six months this newspaper will be gagged, and therefore no further reports of Japanese reverses can be published in our columns."

In June, 1908, Mr. Bethell was again prosecuted at a specially convened court at Seoul, presided over by Judge Bourne of Shanghai. The charge, made by Yagoro Miura, Secretary to the Residency-General and Resident for Seoul, was of publishing various articles calculated to excite disorder and to stir up enmity between the Government of Korea and its subjects.

Mr. Bethell was represented by counsel and applied to have the case heard before a jury. The application was refused. He was convicted, sentenced to three weeks' imprisonment and required to give security for good behaviour for six months. He did not very long survive his sentence.

The people of Korea cherish his memory, and the name of "Beth-ell," as they call him, is already becoming traditional. "We are going to build a great statue to Beth-ell some day," they say. "We will never forget the man who was our friend, and who went to prison for us."

VII
THE ABDICATION OF YI HYEUNG

The Court party was from the first the strongest opponent of the Japanese. Patriotism, tradition, and selfish interests all combined to intensify the resistance of its members. Some officials found their profits threatened, some mourned for perquisites that were cut off, some were ousted out of their places to make room for Japanese, and most felt a not unnatural anger to see men of another race quietly assume authority over their Emperor and their country. The Emperor led the opposition. Old perils had taught him cunning. He knew a hundred ways to feed the stream of discontent, without himself coming forward. Unfortunately there was a fatal strain of weakness in his character. He would support vigorous action in secret, and then, when men translated his speech into deeds, he would disavow them at the bidding of the Japanese. On one point he never wavered. All attempts to make him formally consent to the treaty of November, 1905, were in vain. "I would sooner die first!" he cried. "I would sooner take poison and end all!" In July, 1906, the Marquis Ito began to exercise stronger constraint on the personal life of the Emperor. One evening a number of Japanese police were brought into the palace. The old palace guards were withdrawn, and the Emperor was made virtually a prisoner. Police officers were posted at each gate, and no one was allowed in or out without a permit from a Japanese-nominated official. At the same time many of the old palace attendants were cleared out. The Resident-General thought that if the Emperor were isolated from his friends, and if he were constantly surrounded by enthusiastic advocates of Japan, he might be coerced or influenced into submission. Yet here Marquis Ito had struck against a vein of obstinacy and determination that he could scarce have reckoned with.

The Emperor had taken every opportunity to send messages abroad protesting against the treaty. He managed, time after time, still to hold communication with his friends, but the Japanese took good care that traitors should come to him and be loudest in their expressions of loyalty. Little that he did but was immediately known to his captors. In the early summer of 1907 the Emperor thought that he saw his chance at last of striking a blow for freedom through the Hague Conference. He was still convinced that if he could only assure the Powers that he had never consented to the treaty robbing Korea of its independence, they would then send their Ministers back to Seoul and cause Japan to relax her hand. Accordingly, amid great secrecy, three Korean delegates of high rank were provided with funds and despatched to the Hague under the guardianship of Mr. Hulbert. They reached the Hague only to be refused a hearing. The Conference would have nothing to say to them.

This action on the part of the Emperor gave the Japanese an excuse they had long been looking for. The formation of the Korean Cabinet had been altered months before in anticipation of such a crisis, and the Cabinet Ministers were now nominated not by the Emperor, but by the Resident-General. The Emperor had been deprived of administrative and executive power. The Marquis Ito had seen to it that the Ministers were wholly his tools. The time had come when his tools were to cut. The Japanese Government assumed an attitude of silent wrath. It could not allow such offences to go unpunished, its friends declared, but what punishment it would inflict it refused to say.

Proceedings were much more cleverly stage-managed than in November, 1905. Nominally, the Japanese had nothing to do with the abdication of the Emperor. Actually the Cabinet Ministers held their gathering at the Residency-General to decide on their policy, and did as they were instructed. They went to the Emperor and demanded that he should abandon the throne to save his country from being swallowed up by Japan. At first he refused, upon which their insistence grew greater. No news of sympathy or help reached him from foreign lands. Knowing the perils surrounding him, he thought that he would trick them all by a simple device. He would make his son, the Crown Prince, temporary Emperor, using a Chinese ideograph for his new title which could scarce be distinguished from the title giving him final and full authority. Here he overreached himself, for, once out, he was out for good. On July 19th, at six o'clock in the morning, after an all-night conference, the Emperor was persuaded to abdicate.

The new Emperor, feeble of intellect, could be little more than a tool in the hands of his advisers. His father, however, intended to remain by his side, and to rule through him. In less than a week the Japanese had prepared a new treaty, providing still more strictly for the absolute control of everything in the country by Japan. The six curt clauses of this measure were as far-reaching as they could possibly be made. No laws were to be acted upon or important measures taken by the Government unless the consent and approval of the Resident-General had been previously given. All officials were to hold their positions at the pleasure of the Resident-General, and the Government of Korea agreed to appoint any Japanese the Resident-General might recommend to any post. Finally, the Government of Korea was to engage no foreigner without the consent of the Japanese head.

A few days later a fresh rescript was issued in the name of the new Emperor, ordering the disbandment of the Korean Army. This was written in the most insulting language possible. "Our existing army which is composed of mercenaries, is unfit for the purposes of national defence," it declared. It was to make way "for the eventual formation of an efficient army." To add to the insult, the Korean Premier, Yi, was ordered to write a request to the Resident-General, begging him to employ the Japanese forces to prevent disturbances when the disbandment took place. It was as though the Japanese, having their heel on the neck of the enemy, slapped his face to show their contempt for him. On the morning of August 1st some of the superior officers of the Korean Army were called to the residence of the Japanese commander, General Hasegawa, and the Order was read to them. They were told that they were to assemble their men next morning, without arms, and to dismiss them after paying them gratuities, while at the same time their weapons would be secured in their absence.

One officer, Major Pak, commander of the smartest and best of the Korean battalions, returned to his barracks in despair, and committed suicide. His men learnt of what had happened and rose in mutiny. They burst upon their Japanese military instructors and nearly killed them. They then forced open the ammunition-room, secured weapons and cartridges, posted themselves behind the windows of their barracks, and fired at every Japanese they saw. News quickly reached the authorities, and Japanese companies of infantry hurried out and surrounded their barracks.

One party attacked the front with a machine-gun, and another assaulted from behind. Fighting began at half-past eight in the morning. The Koreans defended themselves until noon, and then were finally overcome by a bayonet charge from the rear. Their gallant defence excited the greatest admiration even among their enemies, and it was notable that for a few days at least the Japanese spoke with more respect of Korea and the Korean people than they had ever done before.

Only one series of incidents disgraced the day. The Japanese soldiers behaved well and treated the wounded well, but that night parties of low-class bullies emerged from the Japanese quarter, seeking victims. They beat, they stabbed and murdered any man they could find whom they suspected of being a rebel. Dozens of them would set on one helpless victim and do him to death. This was stopped as soon as the Residency-General knew what was happening, and a number of offenders were arrested.

Late in August the new Emperor of Korea was crowned amid the sullen silence of a resentful people. Of popular enthusiasm there was none. A few flags were displayed in the streets by the order of the police. In olden times a coronation had been marked by great festivities, lasting many weeks. Now there was gloom, apathy, indifference. News was coming in hourly from the provinces of uprisings and murders. The Il Chin Hoi--they call themselves reformers, but the nation has labelled them traitors--attempted to make a feast, but the people stayed away. "This is the day not for feasting but for the beginning of a year of mourning," men muttered one to the other.

The Japanese authorities who controlled the coronation ceremony did all they could to minimize it and to prevent independent outside publicity. In this they were well advised. No one who looked upon the new Emperor as he entered the hall of state, his shaking frame upborne by two officials, or as he stood later, with open mouth, fallen jaw, indifferent eyes, and face lacking even a flickering gleam of intelligent interest, could doubt that the fewer who saw this the better. Yet the ceremony, even when robbed of much of its ancient pomp and all its dignity, was unique and picturesque.

The main feature of this day was not so much the coronation itself as the cutting of the Emperor's topknot.

On the abdication of the old Emperor, the Cabinet--who were enthusiastic hair-cutters--saw their opportunity. The new Emperor was informed that his hair must be cut. He did not like it. He thought that the operation would be painful, and he was quite satisfied with his hair as it was. Then his Cabinet showed him a brilliant uniform, covered with gold lace. He was henceforth to wear that on ceremonial occasions, and not his old Korean dress. How could he put on the plumed hat of a Generalissimo with a topknot in the way? The Cabinet were determined. A few hours later a proclamation was spread through the land informing all dutiful subjects that the Emperor's topknot was coming off, and urging them to imitate him.

A new Court servant was appointed--the High Imperial Hair-cutter. He displayed his uniform in the streets around the palace, a sight for the gods. He strutted along in white breeches, voluminous white frock-coat, white shoes, and black silk hat, the centre of attention.

Early in the morning there was a great scene in the palace. The Imperial Hair-cutter was in attendance. A group of old Court officials hung around the Emperor. With blanched faces and shaking voices they implored him not to abandon the old ways. The Emperor paused, fearful. What power would be filched from him by the shearing of his locks? But there could be no hesitating now. Resolute men were behind who knew what they were going to see done. A few minutes later the great step was taken.

The Residency-General arranged the coronation ceremony in such a manner as to include as many Japanese and to exclude as many foreigners as possible. There were nearly a hundred Japanese present, including the Mayor of the Japanese settlement and the Buddhist priest. There were only six white men--five Consuls-General and Bishop Turner, chief of the Anglican Church in Korea. The Japanese came arrayed in splendid uniforms. It was part of the new Japanese policy to attire even the most minor officials in sumptuous Court dress, with much gold lace and many orders. This enabled Japan to make a brilliant show in official ceremonies, a thing not without effect in Oriental Courts.

Shortly before ten o'clock the guests assembled in the throne-room of the palace, a modern apartment with a raised dais at one end. There were Koreans to the left and Japanese to the right of the Emperor, with the Cabinet in the front line on one side and the Residency-General officials on the other. The foreigners faced the raised platform.

The new Emperor appeared, borne to the platform by the Lord Chamberlain and the Master of the Household. He was dressed in the ancient costume of his people, a flowing blue garment reaching to the ankles, with a robe of softer cream colour underneath. On his head was a quaint Korean hat, with a circle of Korean ornaments hanging from its high, outstanding horsehair brim. On his chest was a small decorative breastplate. Tall, clumsily built, awkward, and vacant-looking-- such was the Emperor.

In ancient days all would have kow-towed before him, and would have beaten their foreheads on the ground. Now no man did more than bow, save one Court herald, who knelt. Weird Korean music started in the background, the beating of drums and the playing of melancholy wind instruments. The Master of Ceremonies struck up a chant, which hidden choristers continued. Amid silence, the Prime Minister, in smart modern attire, advanced and read a paper of welcome. The Emperor stood still, apparently the least interested man in the room. He did not even look bored--simply vacant.

After this there was a pause in the proceedings. The Emperor retired and the guests went into the anterooms. Soon all were recalled, and the Emperor reappeared. There had been a quick change in the meantime. He was now wearing his new modern uniform, as Generalissimo of the Korean Army. Two high decorations--one, if I mistake not, from the Emperor of Japan--hung on his breast. He looked much more manly in his new attire. In front of him was placed his new headdress, a peaked cap with a fine plume sticking up straight in front. The music now was no longer the ancient Korean, but modern airs from the very fine European-trained band attached to the palace. The Korean players had gone, with the old dress and the old life, into limbo.

The Japanese Acting Resident-General and military commander, General Baron Hasegawa, strong and masterful-looking, stepped to the front with a message of welcome from his Emperor. He was followed by the doyen of the Consular Corps, M. Vincart, with the Consular greetings. This Consular message had been very carefully sub-edited, and all expressions implying that the Governments of the different representatives approved of the proceedings had been eliminated. Then the coronation was over.

Two figures were conspicuous by their absence. The ex-Emperor was not present According to the official explanation, he was unable to attend because "his uniform had not been finished in time," Really, as all men knew, he was sitting resentful and protesting within a few score yards of the spot where his son was crowned.

The second absent figure was the Russian Consul-General, M. de Plancon. It was announced that M. de Plancon was late, and so could not attend. Seeing that M. de Plancon lived not ten minutes' walk from the palace, and that the guests had to wait nearly an hour after the time announced before the ceremony began, he must have overslept very much indeed on that particular morning. Oddly enough, M. de Plancon is usually an early riser.

VIII
A JOURNEY TO THE "RIGHTEOUS ARMY"

It was in the autumn of 1906. The Korean Emperor had been deposed and his army disbanded. The people of Seoul, sullen, resentful, yet powerless, victims of the apathy and folly of their sires, and of their own indolence, saw their national existence filched from them, and scarce dared utter a protest. The triumphant Japanese soldiers stood at the city gates and within the palace. Princes must obey their slightest wish, even to the cutting of their hair and the fashioning of their clothes. General Hasegawa's guns commanded every street, and all men dressed in white need walk softly.

But it soon became clear that there were men who had not taken the filching of their national independence lightly. Refugees from distant villages, creeping after nightfall over the city wall, brought with them marvellous tales of the happenings in the provinces. District after district, they said, had risen against the Japanese. A "Righteous Army" had been formed, and was accomplishing amazing things. Detachments of Japanese had been annihilated and others driven back. Sometimes the Japanese, it is true, were victorious, and then they took bitter vengeance, destroying a whole countryside and slaughtering the people in wholesale fashion. So the refugees said.

How far were these stories true? I am bound to say that I, for one, regarded them with much scepticism. Familiar as I was with the offences of individual Japanese in the country, it seemed impossible that outrages could be carried on systematically by the Japanese Army under the direction of its officers. I was with a Japanese army during the war against Russia, and had marked and admired the restraint and discipline of the men of all ranks there. They neither stole nor outraged. Still more recently I had noted the action of the Japanese soldiers when repressing the uprising in Seoul itself. Yet, whether the stories of the refugees were true or false, undeniably some interesting fighting was going on.

By the first week in September it was clear that the area of trouble covered the eastern provinces from near Fusan to the north of Seoul. The rebels were evidently mainly composed of discharged soldiers and of hunters from the hills. We heard in Seoul that trained officers of the old Korean Army were drilling and organizing them into volunteer companies. The Japanese were pouring fresh troops into these centres of trouble, but the rebels, by an elaborate system of mountain-top signalling, were avoiding the troops and making their attacks on undefended spots. Reports showed that they were badly armed and lacked ammunition, and there seemed to be no effective organization for sending them weapons from the outside.

The first rallying-place of the malcontent Koreans was in a mountain district from eighty to ninety miles east of Seoul. Here lived many famous Korean tiger-hunters. These banded themselves together under the title of Eui-pyung (the "Righteous Army"). They had conflicts with small parties of Japanese troops and secured some minor successes. When considerable Japanese reinforcements arrived they retired to some mountain passes further back.

The tiger-hunters, sons of the hills, iron-nerved, and operating in their own country, were naturally awkward antagonists even for the best regular troops. They were probably amongst the boldest sportsmen in the world, and they formed the most picturesque and, romantic section of the rebels. Their only weapon was an old-fashioned percussion gun, with long barrel and a brass trigger seven to eight inches in length. Many of them fired not from the shoulder, but from the hip. They never missed. They could only fire one charge in an attack, owing to the time required to load. They were trained to stalk the tiger, to come quite close to it, and then to kill it at one shot The man who failed once died; the tiger attended to that.

Some of the stories of Korean successes reaching Seoul were at the best improbable. The tale of one fight, however, came to me through so many different and independent sources that there was reason to suspect it had substantial foundation. It recalled the doings of the people of the Tyrol in their struggle against Napoleon. A party of Japanese soldiers, forty-eight in number, were guarding a quantity of supplies from point to point. The Koreans prepared an ambuscade in a mountain valley overshadowed by precipitous hills on either side. When the troops reached the centre of the valley they were overwhelmed by a flight of great boulders rolled on them from the hilltops, and before the survivors could rally a host of Koreans rushed upon them and did them to death.

Proclamations by Koreans were smuggled into the capital. Parties of Japanese troops were constantly leaving Chinkokai, the Japanese quarter in Seoul, for the provinces. There came a public notice from General Hasegawa himself, which showed the real gravity of the rural situation. It ran as follows:--

"I, General Baron Yoshimichi Hasegawa, Commander of the Army of Occupation in Korea, make the following announcement to each and every one of the people of Korea throughout all the provinces. Taught by the natural trend of affairs in the world and impelled by the national need of political regeneration, the Government of Korea, in obedience to His Imperial Majesty's wishes, is now engaged in the task of reorganizing the various institutions of State. But those who are ignorant of the march of events in the world and who fail correctly to distinguish loyalty from treason have by wild and baseless rumours instigated people's minds and caused the rowdies in various places to rise in insurrection. These insurgents commit all sorts of horrible crimes, such as murdering peaceful people, both native and foreign, robbing their property, burning official and private buildings, and destroying means of communication. Their offences are such as are not tolerated by Heaven or earth. They affect to be loyal and patriotic and call themselves volunteers. But none the less they are lawbreakers, who oppose their Sovereign's wishes concerning political regeneration and who work the worst possible harm to their country and people.

"Unless they are promptly suppressed the trouble may assume really calamitous proportions. I am charged by His Majesty, the Emperor of Korea, with the task of rescuing you from such disasters by thoroughly stamping out the insurrection. I charge all of you, law-abiding people of Korea, to prosecute your respective peaceful avocations and be troubled with no fears. As for those who have joined the insurgents from mistaken motives, if they honestly repent and promptly surrender they will be pardoned of their offence. Any of you who will seize insurgents or will give information concerning their whereabouts will be handsomely rewarded. In case of those who wilfully join insurgents, or afford them refuge, or conceal weapons, they shall be severely punished. More than that, the villages to which such offenders belong shall be held collectively responsible and punished with rigour. I call upon each and every one of the people of Korea to understand clearly what I have herewith said to you and avoid all reprehensible action."

The Koreans in America circulated a manifesto directed against those of their countrymen who were working with Japan, under the expressive title of "explosive thunder," which breathed fury and vengeance. Groups of Koreans in the provinces issued other statements which, if not quite so picturesque, were quite forcible enough. Here is one:--

"Our numbers are twenty million, and we have over ten million strong men, excluding old, sick, and children. Now, the Japanese soldiers in Korea are not more than eight thousand, and Japanese merchants at various places are not more than some thousands. Though their weapons are sharp, how can one man kill a thousand? We beg you our brothers not to act in a foolish way and not to kill any innocent persons. We will fix the day and the hour for you to strike. Some of us, disguised as beggars and merchants, will go into Seoul. We will destroy the railway, we will kindle flames in every port, we will destroy Chinkokai, kill Ito and all the Japanese, Yi Wan-yong and his underlings, and will not leave a single rebel against our Emperor alive. Then Japan will bring out all her troops to fight us. We have no weapons at our hands,

but we will keep our own patriotism. We may not be able to fight
against the sharp weapons of the Japanese, but we will ask the
Foreign Consuls to help us with their troops, and maybe they will
assist the right persons and destroy the wicked; otherwise let us
die. Let us strike against Japan, and then, if must be, all die
together with our country and with our Emperor, for there is no
other course open to us. It is better to lose our lives now than
to live miserably a little time longer, for the Emperor and our
brothers will all surely be killed by the abominable plans of
Ito, Yi Wan-yong, and their associates. It is better to die as a
patriot than to live having abandoned one's country. Mr. Yi Chun
went to foreign lands to plead for our country, and his plans did
not carry well, so he cut his stomach asunder with a sword and
poured out his blood among the foreign nations to proclaim his
patriotism to the world. These of our twenty million people who
do not unite offend against the memory of Mr. Yi Chun. We have to
choose between destruction or the maintenance of our country.
Whether we live or die is a small thing, the great thing is that
we make up our minds at once whether we work for or against our
country."

A group of Koreans in the southern provinces petitioned Prince Ito, in the
frankest fashion:--

"You spoke much of the kindness and friendship between Japan and
Korea, but actually you have drawn away the profits from province
after province and district after district until nothing is left
wherever the hand of the Japanese falls. The Korean has been
brought to ruin, and the Japanese shall be made to follow him
downwards. We pity you very much; but you shall not enjoy the
profits of the ruin of our land. When Japan and Korea fall
together it will be a misfortune indeed for you. If you would
secure safety for yourself follow this rule: memorialize our

Majesty to impeach the traitors and put them to right punishment. Then every Korean will regard you with favour, and the Europeans will be loud in your praise. Advise the Korean authorities to carry out reforms in various directions, help them to enlarge the schools, and to select capable men for the Government service; then the three countries, Korea, China, and Japan, shall stand in the same line, strongly united and esteemed by foreign nations. If you will not do this, and if you continue to encroach on our rights, then we will be destroyed together, thanks to you.

"You thought there were no men left in Korea; you will see. We country people are resolved to destroy your railways and your settlements and your authorities. On a fixed day we shall send word to our patriots in the north, in the south, in Pyeng-yang and Kyung Sang, to rise and drive away all Japanese from the various ports, and although your soldiers are skillful with their guns it will be very hard for them to stand against our twenty million people. We will first attack the Japanese in Korea, but when we have finished them we will appeal to the Foreign Powers to assure the independence and freedom of our country. Before we send the word to our fellow-countrymen we give you this advice."

I resolved to try to see the fighting. This, I soon found, was easier attempted than done.

The first difficulty came from the Japanese authorities. They refused to grant me a passport, declaring that, owing to the disturbances, they could not guarantee my safety in the interior. An interview followed at the Residency-General, in which I was duly warned that if I travelled without a passport I would be liable, under International treaties, to "arrest at any point on the journey and punishment."

This did not trouble me very much. My real fear had been that the Japanese would consent to my going, but would insist on sending a guard of Japanese soldiers with me. It was more than doubtful if, at that time, the Japanese had any right to stop a foreigner from travelling in Korea, for the passport regulations had long been virtually obsolete. This was a point that I was prepared to argue out at leisure after my arrest and confinement in a Consular jail. So the preparations for my departure were continued.

The traveller in Korea, away from the railroads, must carry everything he wants with him, except food for his horses. He must have at least three horses or ponies: one for himself, one pack-pony, and one for his bedding and his "boy," Each pony needs its own "mafoo," or groom, to cook its food and to attend to it. So, although travelling lightly and in a hurry, I would be obliged to take two horses, one pony, and four attendants with me.

My friends in Seoul, both white and Korean, were of opinion that if I attempted the trip I would probably never return. Korean tiger-hunters and disbanded soldiers were scattered about the hills, waiting for the chance of pot-shots at passing Japanese. They would certainly in the distance take me for a Japanese, since the Japanese soldiers and leaders all wear foreign clothes, and they would make me their target before they found out their mistake. A score of suggestions were proffered as to how I should avoid this. One old servant of mine begged me to travel in a native chair, like a Korean gentleman. This chair is a kind of small box, carried by two or four bearers, in which the traveller sits all the time crouched up on his haunches. Its average speed is less than two miles an hour. I preferred the bullets. A member of the Korean Court urged me to send out messengers each night to the villages where I would be going next day, telling the people that I was "Yong guk ta-in" (Englishman) and so they must not shoot me. And so on and so forth.

This exaggerated idea of the risks of the trip unfortunately spread abroad. The horse merchant demanded specially high terms for the hire of his beasts, because he might never see them again. I needed a "boy," or native servant, and although there are plenty of "boys" in Seoul none at first was to be had.

I engaged one servant, a fine upstanding young Korean, Wo by name, who had been out on many hunting and mining expeditions. I noticed that he was looking uneasy, and I was scarcely surprised when at the end of the third day he came to me with downcast eyes. "Master," he said, "my heart is very much frightened. Please excuse me this time."

"What is there to be frightened about?" I demanded.

"Korean men will shoot you and then will kill me because my hair is cut" The rebels were reported to be killing all men not wearing topknots.

Exit Wo. Some one recommended Han, also with a great hunting record. But when Han heard the destination he promptly withdrew. Sin was a good boy out of place. Sin was sent for, but forwarded apologies for not coming.

One Korean was longing to accompany me--my old servant in the war, Kim Min-gun. But Kim was in permanent employment and could not obtain leave. "Master," he said contemptuously, when he heard of the refusals, "these men plenty much afraid," At last Kim's master very kindly gave him permission to accompany me, and the servant difficulty was surmounted.

My preparations were now almost completed, provisions bought, horses hired, and saddles overhauled. The Japanese authorities had made no sign, but they knew what was going on. It seemed likely that they would stop me when I started out.

Then fortune favoured me. A cablegram arrived for me from London. It was brief and emphatic:--

"Proceed forthwith Siberia."

My expedition was abandoned, the horses sent away, and the saddles thrown into a corner. I cabled home that I would soon be back. I made the hotel ring with my public and private complaints about this interference with my plans. I visited the shipping offices to learn of the next steamer to Vladivostock.

A few hours before I was to start I chanced to meet an old friend, who questioned me confidentially, "I suppose it is really true that you are going away, and that this is not a trick on your part?" I left him thoughtful, for his words had shown me the splendid opportunity in my hands. Early next morning, long before dawn, my ponies came back, the boys assembled, the saddles were quickly fixed and the packs adjusted, and soon we were riding as hard as we could for the mountains. The regrettable part of the affair is that many people are still convinced that the whole business of the cablegram was arranged by me in advance as a blind, and no assurances of mine will convince them to the contrary.

As in duty bound, I sent word to the acting British Consul-General, telling him of my departure. My letter was not delivered to him until after I had left. On my return I found his reply awaiting me at my hotel.

"I consider it my duty to inform you," he wrote, "that I received   a communication on the 7th inst. from the Residency-General   informing me that, in view of the disturbed conditions in the   interior, it is deemed inadvisable that foreign subjects should   be allowed to travel in the disturbed districts for the present I   would also call your attention to the stipulation in Article V.   of the treaty between Great Britain and Korea, under which   British subjects travelling in the interior of the country   without a passport are liable to arrest and to a penalty."

In Seoul no one could tell where or how the "Righteous Army" might be found. The information doled out by the Japanese authorities was fragmentary, and was obviously and naturally framed in such a manner as to minimize and discredit the disturbances. It was admitted that the Korean volunteers had a day or two earlier destroyed a small railway station on the line to Fusan. We knew that a small party of them had attacked the Japanese guard of a store of rifles, not twenty miles from the capital, and had driven them off and captured the arms and ammunition. Most of the fighting, so far as one could judge, appeared to have been around the town of Chung-ju, four days' journey from Seoul. It was for there I aimed, travelling by an indirect bridle-path in order to avoid the Japanese as far as possible.

The country in which I soon found myself presented a field of industry and of prosperity such as I had seen nowhere else in Korea. Between the somewhat desolate mountain ranges and great stretches of sandy soil we came upon innumerable thriving villages. Every possible bit of land, right up the hillsides, was carefully cultivated. Here were stretches of cotton, with bursting pods all ready for picking, and here great fields of buckwheat white with flower. The two most common crops were rice and barley, and the fields were heavy with their harvest. Near the villages were ornamental lines of chilies and beans and seed plants for oil, with occasional clusters of kowliang, fully twelve and thirteen feet high.

In the centre of the fields was a double-storied summer-house, made of straw, the centre of a system of high ropes, decked with bits of rag, running over the crops in all directions. Two lads would sit on the upper floor of each of these houses, pulling the ropes, flapping the rags, and making all kinds of harsh noises, to frighten away the birds preying on the crops.

The villages themselves were pictures of beauty and of peace. Most of them were surrounded by a high fence of wands and matting. At the entrance there sometimes stood the village "joss," although many villages had destroyed their idols. This "joss" was a thick stake of wood, six or eight feet high, with the upper part roughly carved into the shape of a very ugly human face, and crudely coloured in vermilion and green. It was supposed to frighten away the evil spirits.

The village houses, low, mud-walled, and thatch-roofed, were seen this season at their best. Gay flowers grew around. Melons and pumpkins, weighted with fruit, ran over the walls. Nearly every roof displayed a patch of vivid scarlet, for the chilies had just been gathered, and were spread out on the housetops to dry. In front of the houses were boards covered with sliced pumpkins and gherkins drying in the sun for winter use. Every courtyard had its line of black earthenware jars, four to six feet high, stored with all manner of good things, mostly preserved vegetables of many varieties, for the coming year.

I had heard much of the province of Chung-Chong-Do as the Italy of Korea, but its beauty and prosperity required seeing to be believed. It afforded an amazing contrast to the dirt and apathy of Seoul. Here every one worked. In the fields the young women were toiling in groups, weeding or harvesting. The young men were cutting bushes on the hillsides, the father of the family preparing new ground for the fresh crop, and the very children frightening off the birds. At home the housewife was busy with her children and preparing her simples and stores; and even the old men busied themselves over light tasks, such as mat-making. Every one seemed prosperous, busy, and happy. There were no signs of poverty. The uprising had not touched this district, save in the most incidental fashion.

My inquiries as to where I should find any signs of the fighting always met with the same reply--"The Japanese have been to Ichon, and have burned many villages there." So we pushed on for Ichon as hard as we could.

The chief problem that faced the traveller in Korea who ventured away from the railways in those days was how to hasten the speed of his party. "You cannot travel faster than your pack," is one of those indisputable axioms against which the impatient man fretted in vain. The pack-pony was led by a horseman, who really controlled the situation. If he sulked and determined to go slowly nothing could be done. If he hurried, the whole party must move quickly.

The Korean mafoo regards seventy li (about twenty-one miles) as a fair day's work. He prefers to average sixty li, but if you are very insistent he may go eighty.

It was imperative that I should cover from a hundred to a hundred and twenty li a day.

I tried a mixture of harsh words, praise, and liberal tips. I was up at three in the morning, setting the boys to work at cooking the animals' food, and I kept them on the road until dark. Still the record was not satisfactory. It is necessary in Korea to allow at least six hours each day for the cooking of the horses' food and feeding them. This is a time that no wise traveller attempts to cut. Including feeding-times, we were on the go from sixteen to eighteen hours a day. Notwithstanding this, the most we had reached was a hundred and ten li a day.

Then came a series of little hindrances. The pack-pony would not eat its dinner; its load was too heavy. "Hire a boy to carry part of its load," I replied. A hundred reasons would be found for halting, and still more for slow departure.

It was clear that something more must be done. I called the pack-pony leader on one side. He was a fine, broad-framed giant, a man who had in his time gone through many fights and adventures. "You and I understand one another," I said to him. "These others with their moanings and cries are but as children. Now let us make a compact. You hurry all the time and I will give you" (here I whispered a figure into his ear that sent a gratified smile over his face) "at the end of the journey. The others need know nothing. This is between men."

He nodded assent. From that moment the trouble was over. Footsore mafoos, lame horses, grumbling innkeepers--nothing mattered. "Let the fires burn quickly." "Out with the horses," The other horse-keepers, not understanding his changed attitude, toiled wearily after him. At night-time he would look up, as he led his pack-pony in at the end of a record day, and his grim smile would proclaim that he was keeping his end of the bargain.

"It is necessary for us to show these men something of the strong hand of Japan," one of the leading Japanese in Seoul, a close associate of the Prince Ito, told me shortly before I left that city. "The people of the eastern mountain districts have seen few or no Japanese soldiers, and they have no idea of our strength. We must convince them how strong we are."

As I stood on a mountain-pass, looking down on the valley leading to Ichon, I recalled these words of my friend. The "strong hand of Japan" was certainly being shown here. I beheld in front of me village after village reduced to ashes.

I rode down to the nearest heap of ruins. The place had been quite a large village, with probably seventy or eighty houses. Destruction, thorough and complete, had fallen upon it. Not a single house was left, and not a single wall of a house. Every pot with the winter stores was broken. The very earthen fireplaces were wrecked.

The villagers had come back to the ruins again, and were already rebuilding. They had put up temporary refuges of straw. The young men were out on the hills cutting wood, and every one else was toiling at house-making. The crops were ready to harvest, but there was no time to gather them in. First of all, make a shelter.

During the next few days sights like these were to be too common to arouse much emotion. But for the moment I looked around on these people, ruined and homeless, with quick pity. The old men, venerable and dignified, as Korean old men mostly are, the young wives, many with babes at their breasts, the sturdy men, had composed, if I could judge by what I saw, an exceptionally clean and peaceful community.

There was no house in which I could rest, so I sat down under a tree, and while Min-gun was cooking my dinner the village elders came around with their story. One thing especially struck me. Usually the Korean woman was shy, retiring, and afraid to open her mouth in the presence of a stranger. Here the women spoke up as freely as the men. The great calamity had broken down the barriers of their silence.

"We are glad," they said, "that a European man has come to see what has befallen us. We hope you will tell your people, so that all men may know.

"There had been some fighting on the hills beyond our village," and they pointed to the hills a mile or two further on. "The Eui-pyung" (the volunteers) "had been there, and had torn up some telegraph poles. The Eui-pyung came down from the eastern hills. They were not our men, and had nothing to do with us. The Japanese soldiers came, and there was a fight, and the Eui-pyung fell back.

"Then the Japanese soldiers marched out to our village, and to seven other villages. Look around and you can see the ruins of all. They spoke many harsh words to us. 'The Eui-pyung broke down the telegraph poles and you did not stop them,' they said. 'Therefore you are all the same as Eui-pyung. Why have you eyes if you do not watch, why have you strength if you do not prevent the Eui-pyung from doing-mischief? The Eui-pyung came to your houses and you fed them. They have gone, but we will punish you.'

"And they went from house to house, taking what they wanted and setting all alight. One old man--he had lived in his house since he was a babe suckled by his mother--saw a soldier lighting up his house. He fell on his knees and caught the foot of the soldier. 'Excuse me, excuse me,' he said, with many tears. 'Please do not burn my house. Leave it for me that I may die there. I am an old man, and near my end.'

"The soldier tried to shake him off, but the old man prayed the more. 'Excuse me, excuse me,' he moaned. Then the soldier lifted his gun and shot the old man, and we buried him.

"One who was near to her hour of child-birth was lying in a house. Alas for her! One of our young men was working in the field cutting grass. He was working and had not noticed the soldiers come. He lifted his knife, sharpening it in the sun. 'There is a Eui-pyung,' he said, and he fired and killed him. One man, seeing the fire, noticed that all his family records were burning. He rushed in to try and pull them out, but as he rushed a soldier fired, and he fell."

A man, whose appearance proclaimed him to be of a higher class than most of the villagers, then spoke in bitter tones. "We are rebuilding our houses," he said, "but of what use is it for us to do so? I was a man of family. My fathers and fathers' fathers had their record. Our family papers are destroyed. Henceforth we are a people without a name, disgraced and outcast."

I found, when I went further into the country, that this view was fairly common. The Koreans regard their family existence with peculiar veneration. The family record means everything to them. When it is destroyed, the family is wiped out It no longer exists, even though there are many members of it still living. As the province of Chung-Chong-Do prides itself on the large number of its substantial families, there could be no more effective way of striking at them than this.

I rode out of the village heavy-hearted. What struck me most about this form of punishment, however, was not the suffering of the villagers so much as the futility of the proceedings, from the Japanese point of view. In place of pacifying a people, they were turning hundreds of quiet families into rebels. During the next few days I was to see at least one town and many scores of villages treated as this one. To what end? The villagers were certainly not the people fighting the Japanese.

All they wanted to do was to look quietly after their own affairs. Japan professed a desire to conciliate Korea and to win the affection and support of her people. In one province at least the policy of house-burning had reduced a prosperous community to ruin, increased the rebel forces, and sown a crop of bitter hatred which it would take generations to root out.

We rode on through village after village and hamlet after hamlet burned to the ground. The very attitude of the people told me that the hand of Japan had struck hard there. We would come upon a boy carrying a load of wood. He would run quickly to the side of the road when he saw us, expecting he knew not what. We passed a village with a few houses left. The women flew to shelter as I drew near. Some of the stories that I heard later helped me to understand why they should run. Of course they took me for a Japanese.

All along the route I heard tales of the Japanese plundering, where they had not destroyed. At places the village elders would bring me an old man badly beaten by a Japanese soldier because he resisted being robbed. Then came darker stories. In Seoul I had laughed at them. Now, face to face with the victims, I could laugh no more.

That afternoon we rode into Ichon itself. This is quite a large town. I found it practically deserted. Most of the people had fled to the hills, to escape from the Japanese. I slept that night in a schoolhouse, now deserted and unused. There were the cartoons and animal pictures and pious mottoes around, but the children were far away. I passed through the market-place, usually a very busy spot. There was no sign of life there.

I turned to some of the Koreans.

"Where are your women? Where are your children?" I demanded. They pointed to the high and barren hills looming against the distant heavens.

"They are up there," they said. "Better for them to lie on the barren hillsides than to be outraged here."

IX
WITH THE REBELS

Day after day we travelled through a succession of burned-out villages, deserted towns, and forsaken country. The fields were covered with a rich and abundant harvest, ready to be gathered, and impossible for the invaders to destroy. But most of the farmers were hiding on the mountainsides, fearing to come down. The few courageous men who had ventured to come back were busy erecting temporary shelters for themselves before the winter cold came on, and had to let the harvest wait. Great flocks of birds hung over the crops, feasting undisturbed.

Up to Chong-ju nearly one-half of the villages on the direct line of route had been destroyed by the Japanese. At Chong-ju I struck directly across the mountains to Chee-chong, a day's journey. Four-fifths of the villages and hamlets on the main road between these two places were burned to the ground.

The few people who had returned to the ruins always disclaimed any connection with the "Righteous Army." They had taken no part in the fighting, they said. The volunteers had come down from the hills and had attacked the Japanese; the Japanese had then retaliated by punishing the local residents. The fact that the villagers had no arms, and were peaceably working at home-building, seemed at the time to show the truth of their words. Afterwards when I came up with the Korean fighters I found these statements confirmed. The rebels were mostly townsmen from Seoul, and not villagers from that district.

Between 10,000 and 20,000 people had been driven to the hills in this small district alone, either by the destruction of their homes or because of fear excited by the acts of the soldiers.

Soon after leaving Ichon I came on a village where the Red Cross was flying over one of the houses. The place was a native Anglican church. I was later on to see the Red Cross over many houses, for the people had the idea that by thus appealing to the Christians' God they made a claim on the pity and charity of the Christian nations.

In the evening, after I had settled down in the yard of the native inn, the elders of the Church came to see me, two quiet-spoken, grave, middle-aged men. They were somewhat downcast, and said that their village had suffered considerably, the parties of soldiers passing through having taken what they wanted and being guilty of some outrages. A gardener's wife had been violated by a Japanese soldier, another soldier standing guard over the house with rifle and fixed bayonet. A boy, attracted by the woman's screams, ran and fetched the husband. He came up, knife in hand. "But what could he do?" the elders asked. "There was the soldier, with rifle and bayonet, before the door."

Later on I was to hear other stories, very similar to this. These tales were confirmed on the spot, so far as confirmation was possible. In my judgment such outrages were not numerous, and were limited to exceptional parties of troops. But they produced an effect altogether disproportionate to their numbers. The Korean has high ideals about the sanctity of his women, and the fear caused by a comparatively few offences was largely responsible for the flight of multitudes to the hills.

In the burning of villages, a certain number of Korean women and children were undoubtedly killed. The Japanese troops seem in many cases to have rushed a village and to have indulged in miscellaneous wild shooting, on the chance of there being rebels around, before firing the houses. In one hamlet, where I found two houses still standing, the folk told me that these had been left because the Japanese shot the daughter of the owner of one of them, a girl of ten. "When they shot her," the villagers said, "we approached the soldiers, and said, 'Please excuse us, but since you have killed the daughter of this man you should not burn his house.' And the soldiers listened to us."

In towns like Chong-ju and Won-ju practically all the women and children and better-class families had disappeared. The shops were shut and barricaded by their owners before leaving, but many of them had been forced open and looted. The destruction in other towns paled to nothing, however, before the havoc wrought in Chee-chong. Here was a town completely destroyed.

Chee-chong was, up to the late summer of 1907, an important rural centre, containing between 2,000 and 3,000 inhabitants, and beautifully situated in a sheltered plain, surrounded by high mountains. It was a favourite resort of high officials, a Korean Bath or Cheltenham. Many of the houses were large, and some had tiled roofs--a sure evidence of wealth.

When the "Righteous Army" began operations, one portion of it occupied the hills beyond Chee-chong. The Japanese sent a small body of troops into the town. These were attacked one night on three sides, several were killed, and the others were compelled to retire. The Japanese despatched reinforcements, and after some fighting regained lost ground. They then determined to make Chee-chong an example to the countryside. The entire town was put to the torch. The soldiers carefully tended the flames, piling up everything for destruction. Nothing was left, save one image of Buddha and the magistrate's yamen. When the Koreans fled, five men, one woman, and a child, all wounded, were left behind. These disappeared in the flames.

It was a hot early autumn when I reached Chee-chong. The brilliant sunshine revealed a Japanese flag waving-over a hillock commanding the town, and glistened against the bayonet of a Japanese sentry. I dismounted and walked down the streets and over the heaps of ashes. Never have I witnessed such complete destruction. Where a month before there had been a busy and prosperous community, there was now nothing but lines of little heaps of black and gray dust and cinders. Not a whole wall, not a beam, and not an unbroken jar remained. Here and there a man might be seen poking among the ashes, seeking for aught of value. The search was vain. Chee-chong had been wiped off the map. "Where are your people?" I asked the few searchers. "They are lying on the hillsides," came the reply.

Up to this time I had not met a single rebel soldier, and very few Japanese. My chief meeting with the Japanese occurred the previous day at Chong-ju. As I approached that town, I noticed that its ancient walls were broken down. The stone arches of the city gates were left, but the gates themselves and most of the walls had gone. A Japanese sentry and a gendarme stood at the gateway, and cross-examined me as I entered. A small body of Japanese troops were stationed here, and operations in the country around were apparently directed from this centre.

I at once called upon the Japanese Colonel in charge. His room, a great apartment in the local governor's yamen, showed on all sides evidences of the thoroughness with which the Japanese were conducting this campaign. Large maps, with red marks, revealed strategic positions now occupied. A little printed pamphlet, with maps, evidently for the use of officers, lay on the table.

The Colonel received me politely, but expressed his regrets that I had come. The men he was fighting were mere robbers, he said, and there was nothing for me to see. He gave me various warnings about dangers ahead. Then he very kindly explained that the Japanese plan was to hem in the volunteers, two sections of troops operating from either side and making a circle around the seat of trouble. These would unite and gradually drive the Koreans towards a centre.

The maps which the Colonel showed me settled my movements. A glance at them made clear that the Japanese had not yet occupied the line of country between Chee-chong and Won-ju. Here, then, was the place where I must go if I would meet the Korean bands. So it was towards Won-ju that I turned our horses' heads on the following day, after gazing on the ruins of Chee-chong.

It soon became evident that I was very near to the Korean forces. At one place, not far from Chee-chong, a party of them had arrived two days before I passed, and had demanded arms. A little further on Koreans and Japanese had narrowly escaped meeting in the village street, not many hours before I stopped there. As I approached one hamlet, the inhabitants fled into the high corn, and on my arrival not a soul was to be found. They mistook me for a Japanese out on a shooting and burning expedition.

It now became more difficult to obtain carriers. Our ponies were showing signs of fatigue, for we were using them very hard over the mountainous country. It was impossible to hire fresh animals, as the Japanese had commandeered all. Up to Won-ju I had to pay double the usual rate for my carriers. From Won-ju onwards carriers absolutely refused to go further, whatever the pay.

"On the road beyond here many bad men are to be found," they told me at Won-ju. "These bad men shoot every one who passes. We will not go to be shot." My own boys were showing some uneasiness. Fortunately, I had in my personal servant Min-gun, and in the leader of the pack-pony two of the staunchest Koreans I have ever known.

The country beyond Won-ju was splendidly suited for an ambuscade, such as the people there promised me. The road was rocky and broken, and largely lay through a narrow, winding valley, with overhanging cliffs. Now we would come on a splendid gorge, evidently of volcanic origin; now we would pause to chip a bit of gold-bearing quartz from the rocks, for-this is a famous gold centre of Korea. An army might have been hidden securely around.

Twilight was just gathering as we stopped at a small village where we intended remaining for the night The people were sullen and unfriendly, a striking contrast to what I had found elsewhere. In other parts they all came and welcomed me, sometimes refusing to take payment for the accommodation they supplied. "We are glad that a white man has come," But in this village the men gruffly informed me that there was not a scrap of horse food or of rice to be had. They advised us to go on to another place, fifteen li ahead.

We started out. When we had ridden a little way from the village I chanced to glance back at some trees skirting a corn-field. A man, half-hidden by a bush, was fumbling with something in his hands, something which he held down as I turned. I took it to be the handle of a small reaping-knife, but it was growing too dark to see clearly. A minute later, however, there came a smart "ping" past my ear, followed by the thud of a bullet striking metal.

I turned, but the man had disappeared. It would have been merely foolish to blaze back with a .380 Colt at a distance of over a hundred yards, and there was no time to go back. So we continued on our way.

Before arriving at Won-ju we had been told that we would certainly find the Righteous Army around there. At Won-ju men said that it was at a place fifteen or twenty miles ahead. When we reached that distance we were directed onwards to Yan-gun. We walked into Yan-gun one afternoon, only to be again disappointed. Here, however, we learned that there had been a fight that same morning at a village fifteen miles nearer Seoul, and that the Koreans had been defeated.

Yan-gun presented a remarkable sight. A dozen red crosses waved over houses at different points. In the main street every shop was closely barricaded, and a cross was pasted on nearly every door. These crosses, roughly painted on paper in red ink, were obtained from the elder of the Roman Catholic church there. A week before some Japanese soldiers had arrived and burned a few houses. They spared one house close to them waving a Christian cross. As soon as the Japanese left nearly every one pasted a cross over his door.

At first Yan-gun seemed deserted. The people were watching me from behind the shelter of their doors. Then men and boys crept out, and gradually approached. We soon made friends. The women had fled. I settled down that afternoon in the garden of a Korean house of the better type. My boy was preparing my supper in the front courtyard, when he suddenly dropped everything to rush to me. "Master," he cried, highly excited, "the Righteous Army has come. Here are the soldiers."

In another moment half a dozen of them entered the garden, formed in line in front of me and saluted. They were all lads, from eighteen to twenty-six. One, a bright-faced, handsome youth, still wore the old uniform of the regular Korean Army. Another had a pair of military trousers. Two of them were in slight, ragged Korean dress. Not one had leather boots. Around their waists were home-made cotton cartridge belts, half full. One wore a kind of tarboosh on his head, and the others had bits of rag twisted round their hair.

I looked at the guns they were carrying. The six men had five different patterns of weapons, and none was any good. One proudly carried an old Korean sporting gun of the oldest type of muzzle-loaders known to man. Around his arm was the long piece of thin rope which he kept smouldering as touch-powder, and hanging in front of him were the powder horn and bullet bag for loading. This sporting gun was, I afterwards found, a common weapon. The ramrod, for pressing down the charge, was home-made and cut from a tree. The barrel was rust-eaten. There was only a strip of cotton as a carrying strap.

The second man had an old Korean army rifle, antiquated, and a very bad specimen of its time. The third had the same. One had a tiny sporting gun, the kind of weapon, warranted harmless, that fathers give to their fond sons at the age of ten. Another had a horse-pistol, taking a rifle cartridge. Three of the guns bore Chinese marks. They were all eaten up with ancient rust.

These were the men--think of it--who for weeks had been bidding defiance to the Japanese Army! Even now a Japanese division of regular soldiers was manoeuvring to corral them and their comrades. Three of the party in front of me were coolies. The smart young soldier who stood at the right plainly acted as sergeant, and had done his best to drill his comrades into soldierly bearing. A seventh man now came in, unarmed, a Korean of the better class, well dressed in the long robes of a gentleman, but thin, sun-stained and wearied like the others.

A pitiful group they seemed--men already doomed to certain death, fighting in an absolutely hopeless cause. But as I looked the sparkling eyes and smiles of the sergeant to the right seemed to rebuke me. Pity! Maybe my pity was misplaced. At least they were showing their countrymen an example of patriotism, however mistaken their method of displaying it might be.

They had a story to tell, for they had been in the fight that morning, and had retired before the Japanese. The Japanese had the better position, and forty Japanese soldiers had attacked two hundred of them and they had given way. But they had killed four Japanese, and the Japanese had only killed two of them and wounded three more. Such was their account.

I did not ask them why, when they had killed twice as many as the enemy, they had yet retreated. The real story of the fight I could learn later. As they talked others came to join them--two old men, one fully eighty, an old tiger-hunter, with bent back, grizzled face, and patriarchal beard. The two newcomers carried the old Korean sporting rifles. Other soldiers of the retreating force were outside. There was a growing tumult in the street. How long would it be before the triumphant Japanese, following up their victory, attacked the town?

I was not to have much peace that night. In the street outside a hundred noisy disputes were proceeding between volunteers and the townsfolk. The soldiers wanted shelter; the people, fearing the Japanese, did not wish to let them in. A party of them crowded into an empty building adjoining the house where I was, and they made the place ring with their disputes and recriminations.

Very soon the officer who had been in charge of the men during the fight that day called on me. He was a comparatively young man, dressed in the ordinary long white garments of the better-class Koreans. I asked him what precautions he had taken against a night attack, for if the Japanese knew where we were they would certainly come on us. Had he any outposts placed in positions? Was the river-way guarded? "There is no need for outposts," he replied. "Every Korean man around watches for us."

I cross-examined him about the constitution of the rebel army. How were they organized? From what he told me, it was evident that they had practically no organization at all. There were a number of separate bands held together by the loosest ties. A rich man in each place found the money. This he secretly gave to one or two open rebels, and they gathered adherents around them.

He admitted that the men were in anything but a good way. "We may have to die," he said. "Well, so let it be. It is much better to die as a free man than to live as the slave of Japan."

He had not been gone long before still another called on me, a middle-aged Korean gentleman, attended by a staff of officials. Here was a man of rank, and I soon learned that he was the Commander-in-Chief for the entire district. I was in somewhat of a predicament. I had used up all my food, and had not so much as a cigar or a glass of whiskey left to offer him. One or two flickering candles in the covered courtyard of the inn lit up his care-worn face. I apologized for the rough surroundings in which I received him, but he immediately brushed my apologies aside. He complained bitterly of the conduct of his subordinate, who had risked an engagement that morning when he had orders not to. The commander, it appeared, had been called back home for a day on some family affairs, and hurried back to the front as soon as he knew of the trouble. He had come to me for a purpose. "Our men want weapons," he said. "They are as brave as can be, but you know what their guns are like, and we have very little ammunition. We cannot buy, but you can go to and fro freely as you want. Now, you act as our agent. Buy guns for us and bring them to us. Ask what money you like, it does not matter. Five thousand dollars, ten thousand dollars, they are yours if you will have them. Only bring us guns!"

I had, of course, to tell him that I could not do anything of the kind. When he further asked me questions about the positions of the Japanese I was forced to give evasive answers. To my mind, the publicist who visits fighting forces in search of information, as I was doing, is in honour bound not to communicate what he learns to the other side. I could no more tell the rebel leader of the exposed Japanese out-posts I knew, and against which I could have sent his troops with the certainty of success, than I could on return tell the Japanese the strength of his forces.

All that night the rebels dribbled in. Several wounded men who had escaped from the fight the previous day were borne along by their comrades, and early on the following morning some soldiers came and asked me to do what I could to heal them. I went out and examined the men. One had no less than five bullet-holes in him and yet seemed remarkably cheerful. Two others had single shots of a rather more dangerous nature. I am no surgeon, and it was manifestly impossible for me to jab into their wounds with my hunting-knife in the hope of extracting the bullets. I found, however, some corrosive sublimate tabloids in my leather medicine case. These I dissolved, and bathed the wounds with the mixture to stop suppuration. I had some Listerine, and I washed their rags in it. I bound the clean rags on the wounds, bade the men lie still and eat little, and left them.

Soon after dawn the rebel regiments paraded in the streets. They reproduced on a larger scale the characteristics I had noted among the few men who came to visit me the evening before, poor weapons and little ammunition. They sent out men in advance before I departed in the morning to warn their outposts that I was an Englishman (really I am a Scots-Canadian, but to them it was all the same) who must not be injured. I left them with mutual good wishes, but I made a close inspection of my party before we marched away to see that all our weapons were in place. Some of my boys begged me to give the rebels our guns so that they might kill the Japanese!

We had not gone very far before we descended into a rocky and sandy plain by the river. Suddenly I heard one of my boys shout at the top of his voice, as he threw up his arms, "Yong guk ta-in." We all stopped, and the others took up the cry. "What does this mean?" I asked. "Some rebel soldiers are surrounding us," said Min-gun, "and they are going to fire. They think you are a Japanese." I stood against the sky-line and pointed vigorously to myself to show that they were mistaken. "Yong guk!" I shouted, with my boys. It was not dignified, but it was very necessary. Now we could see creeping, ragged figures running from rock to rock, closer and closer to us. The rifles of some were covering us while the others advanced. Then a party of a couple of dozen rose from the ground near to hand, with a young man in a European officer's uniform at their head. They ran to us, while we stood and waited. At last they saw who I was, and when they came near they apologized very gracefully for their blunder. "It was fortunate that you shouted when you did," said one ugly-faced young rebel, as he slipped his cartridge back into his pouch; "I had you nicely covered and was just going to shoot." Some of the soldiers in this band were not more than fourteen to sixteen years old. I made them stand and have their photographs taken.

By noon I arrived at the place from which the Korean soldiers had been driven on the day before. The villagers there were regarded in very unfriendly fashion by the rebels, who thought they had betrayed them to the Japanese. The villagers told me what was evidently the true story of the fight. They said that about twenty Japanese soldiers had on the previous morning marched quickly to the place and attacked two hundred rebels there. One Japanese soldier was hurt, receiving a flesh wound in the arm, and five rebels were wounded. Three of these latter got away, and these were the ones I had treated earlier in the morning. Two others were left on the field, one badly shot in the left cheek and the other in the right shoulder. To quote the words of the villagers, "As the Japanese soldiers came up to these wounded men they were too sick to speak, and they could only utter cries like animals--'Hula, hula, hula!' They had no weapons in their hands, and their blood was running on the ground. The Japanese soldiers heard their cries, and went up to them and stabbed them through and through and through again with their bayonets until they died. The men were torn very much with the bayonet stabs, and we had to take them up and bury them." The expressive faces of the villagers were more eloquent than mere description was.

Were this an isolated instance, it would scarcely be necessary to mention it. But what I heard on all sides went to show that in a large number of fights in the country the Japanese systematically killed all the wounded and all who surrendered themselves. This was not so in every case, but it certainly was in very many. The fact was confirmed by the Japanese accounts of many fights, where the figures given of Korean casualties were so many killed, with no mention of wounded or prisoners. In place after place also, the Japanese, besides burning houses, shot numbers of men whom they suspected of assisting the rebels. War is war, and one could scarcely complain at the shooting of rebels. Unfortunately much of the killing was indiscriminate, to create terror.

I returned to Seoul. The Japanese authorities evidently decided that it would not be advisable to arrest me for travelling in the interior without a passport. It was their purpose to avoid as far as possible any publicity being given to the doings of the Righteous Army, and to represent them as mere bands of disorderly characters, preying on the population. They succeeded in creating this opinion throughout the world.

But as a matter of fact the movement grew and grew. It was impossible for the

Koreans to obtain arms; they fought without arms. In June, 1908, nearly two years afterwards, a high Japanese official, giving evidence at the trial of Mr. Bethell before a specially convened British court at Seoul, said that about 20,000 troops were then engaged in putting down the disturbances, and that about one-half of the country was in a condition of armed resistance. The Koreans continued their fight until 1915, when, according to Japanese official statements, the rebellion was finally suppressed. One can only faintly imagine the hardships these mountaineers and young men of the plains, tiger hunters, and old soldiers, must have undergone. The taunts about Korean "cowardice" and "apathy" were beginning to lose their force.

X
THE LAST DAYS OF THE KOREAN EMPIRE

Prince Ito--he was made Prince after the abdication of Yi Hyeung--was Resident-General of Korea from 1906 to 1908, and was followed by Viscount Sone, who carried on his policies until 1910. Ito is still remembered as the best of the Japanese administrators.

He had an exceedingly difficult task. He had to tear up an ancient administration by the roots, and substitute a new. This could not fail to be a painful process. He had the best and the worst instincts of a nation aroused against him, the patriotism and loyalty of the Korean people, and also their obstinacy and apathy. He was hampered by the poor quality of many of the minor officials who had to carry out his orders and still more by the character of the settlers from his own land. The necessities of Japanese Imperial policy compelled the infliction of much injustice on the Korean people. The determination to plant as many Japanese on Korean soil as possible involved the expropriation of Korean interests and the harsh treatment of many small Korean landowners and tenants. The powerful and growing commercial interests of Japan were using every possible pressure to exploit Korea, to obtain concessions and to treat the land as one to be despoiled for their benefit. Ito meant well by Korea, and had vision enough to see that the ill-treatment of her people injured Japan even more than it did them. It was his misfortune to be committed to an impossible policy of Imperial absorption. He did his utmost to minimize its evils and promote reforms.

Unfortunately, all of his subordinates did not see eye to eye with him. His military chief, Hasegawa, believed in the policy of the strong hand, and practiced it. A large majority of the Japanese immigrants acted in a way fatal to the creation of a policy of good-will. The average Japanese regarded the Korean as another Ainu, a barbarian, and himself as one of the Chosen Race, who had the right to despoil and roughly treat his inferiors, as occasion served.

Some Koreans stooped to the favourite Oriental weapon of assassination.

In 1907 Mr. W.D. Stevens, Foreign Adviser to the Korean Government, was murdered by a Korean when passing through San Francisco. In October, 1909, Prince Ito, when making a journey northwards, was killed by another Korean at Harbin. Both of the murderers were nominal Christians, the first a Protestant and the second a Catholic. A deadly blow was struck at the Korean cause by the men who thus sought to serve her.

This book will probably be read by many Koreans, young men and women with hearts aflame at the sufferings of their people. I can well understand the intense anger that must fill their souls. If my people had been treated as theirs have, I would feel the same.

I hope that every man guilty of torturing, outraging or murder will eventually be brought to justice and dealt with as justice directs. But for individuals, or groups of individuals to take such punishment into their own hands is to inflict the greatest damage in their power, not on the person they attack, but on the cause they seek to serve.

Why?

In the first case, they destroy sympathy for their cause. The conscience of the world revolts at the idea of the individual or the irresponsible group of individuals taking to themselves the right of inflicting death at their will.

Next, they strengthen the cause they attack. They place themselves on or below the level of the men they seek to punish.

A third reason is that the assassins in many cases reach the wrong man. They do not know, and cannot know, because they have had no full opportunity of learning, what the other has had to say for himself. Too often, in trying to slay their victim, they injure others who have nothing to do with the business.

To attack one's victim without giving him an opportunity for defence is essentially a cowardly thing. Assassination--I prefer to give it its simpler name, murder--is wrong, whatever the supposed excuse, fundamentally wrong, wrong in principle, fatal in its outcome for those who adopt it. Have nothing to do with it.

The murder of Prince Ito was a cruel blow for Korea. It was followed by an attempt to assassinate the Korean Premier, the man who had handed his country over to Japan. For some time the military party in Japan had been clamouring for a more severe policy in the Peninsula. Now it was to have its way. General Count Terauchi was appointed Resident-General.

Count Terauchi was leader of the military party in Korea, and an avowed exponent of the policy of "thorough." A soldier from his youth up, he had risen to the General Staff, and in 1904 was Minister of War in the fight against Russia, earning his Viscountcy for brilliant services. Strong, relentless, able, he could only see one thing--Japan and the glory of Japan. He regarded the Koreans as a people to be absorbed or to be eliminated. He was generally regarded as unsympathetic to Christianity, and many of the Koreans were now Christians.

Terauchi came to Seoul in the summer of 1910, to reverse the policy of his predecessors. He was going to stamp the last traces of nationality out of existence. Where Ito had been soft, he would be hard as chilled steel. Where Ito had beaten men with whips, he would beat them with scorpions.

Every one knew ahead what was coming. The usual plan was followed. First, the official and semi-official plan was followed. The Seoul Press, now the lickspittle of the great man, gave good value for the subsidy it receives. It came out with an article hard to surpass for brutality and hypocrisy:--

> "The present requires the wielding of an iron hand rather than a gloved one in order to secure lasting peace and order in this country. There is no lack of evidence to show an intense dissatisfaction against the new state of things is fermenting at present among a section of the Koreans. It is possible that if left unchecked, it may culminate in some shocking crime. Now after carefully studying the cause and nature of the dissatisfaction just referred to, we find that it is both foolish and unreasonable....

> "Japan is in this country with the object of promoting the happiness of the masses. She has not come to Korea to please a few hundred silly youngsters or to feed a few hundred titled

loafers. It is no fault of hers that these men are dissatisfied
because of their failure to satisfy them.... She must be
prepared to sacrifice anybody who offers obstacles to her work.
Japan has hitherto dealt with Korean malcontents in a lenient
way. She has learned from experience gained during the past five
years that there are some persons who cannot be converted by
conciliatory methods. There is but one way to deal with these
people, and that is by stern and relentless methods."

The Japan Mail, as usual, echoed the same sentiments from Yokohama. "The
policy of conciliation is all very well in the hands of such a statesman as the late
Prince Ito," it declared. "But failing a successor to Prince Ito, more ordinary methods will be found safer as well as more efficacious."

Viscount Terauchi settled in the capital, and it was as though a chill had passed
over the city. He said little, in public. Callers, high and low, found him stern and
distant. "He has other things to think of than pleasant words," awed Secretaries
repeated. Things suddenly began to happen. Four Japanese papers were suspended
in a night. An item in their columns was objectionable. Let others be very careful.
The police system was reversed. The gendarmerie were to be brought back again
in full force. Every day brought its tale of arrests. Fifteen students were arrested
this morning; the old Korean President of the Railway Board had been hurried to
prison; the office of a paper in Pyeng-yang had been raided. It was as though the
new Governor-General had deliberately set himself to spread a feeling of terror.

The Korean must not so much as look awry now. Police and gendarmes were
everywhere. Spies seemed to catch men's thoughts. More troops were coming in.
Surely something was about to happen.

Yet there were some smiling. They were called to the Residency-General to
hear good news. This man was to be made a peer; he had served Japan well. This
man, if he and his kin were good, was to be suitably rewarded. Bribes for the com-
plaisant, prison for the obstinate.

Men guessed what was coming. There were mutterings, especially among the
students. But the student who spoke bravely, even behind closed doors to-day,
found himself in jail by evening. The very walls seemed to have ears.

Then it was remarked that the Ministers of State had not been seen for some days. They had shut themselves in, refusing to see all callers. They feared assassination, for they had sold their country. Policemen and troops were waiting within easy calls from their homes, lest mobs should try to burn them out, like rats out of their holes.

And then the news came. Korea had ceased to exist as an even nominally independent or separate country. Japan had swallowed it up. The Emperor--poor fool--was to step off his throne. After four thousand years, there was to be no more a throne of Korea. The Resident-General would now be Governor-General. The name of the nation was to be wiped out--henceforth it was to be Chosen, a province of Japan. Its people were to be remade into a lesser kind of Japanese, and the more adept they were in making the change, the less they would suffer. They were to have certain benefits. To mark the auspicious occasion there would be an amnesty--but a man who had tried to kill the traitor Premier would not be in it. Five per cent of taxes and all unpaid fiscal dues would be remitted. Let the people rejoice!

The Japanese expected an uprising, and were all ready for one. "Every man should be ready to fight and die in the cause of his nation's independence," they said tauntingly to the Koreans. But the people's leaders kept them in. Up on the hills, the Righteous Army was still struggling. The people must wait for better times.

One man stuck a proclamation on the West Gate, threatening death to the traitors. Man after man, scholars, old soldiers, men who loved Korea, committed suicide, after telling of their grief. "Why should we live when our land is dead?" they asked.

The Japanese sneered because the people did nothing. "We may assume, indeed, that all fear of a national uprising is now past," declared a semi-Government organ. "The nation obviously has no leaders competent to execute and direct a crusade in the cause of independence. Whether that lack is due to adroit management on the part of the Japanese or to unpatriotic apathy on the part of the Koreans we cannot pretend to judge."

The Japanese decree announcing the annexation of the country was in itself an acknowledgment that the Japanese administration so far had been a failure. Here is the opening paragraph:--

"Notwithstanding the earnest and laborious work of reforms in the administration of Korea in which the Governments of Japan and Korea have been engaged for more than four years since the conclusion of the Agreement of 1905, the existing system of government of that country has not proved entirely equal to the work of preserving public order and tranquillity, and in addition a spirit of suspicion and misgiving pervades the whole peninsula.

"In order to maintain peace and prosperity and the welfare of the Koreans and at the same time to ensure the safety and repose of foreign residents, it has been made abundantly clear that fundamental changes in the actual regime of government are actually essential."

The declaration announced various changes. It abrogated all Korean foreign treaties, and brought the subjects of foreign nations living in Korea under Japanese law. In other words, extra-territoriality was abolished. The Government agreed to maintain the old Korean tariff for ten years both for goods coming in from Japan and abroad. This was a concession to foreign importers whose trade otherwise would have been swamped. It also allowed ships under foreign registers to engage in the Korean coasting trade for ten years more.

The annexation was put in the form of a treaty between the Emperors of Japan and Korea, as though the surrender of their land had been the act of the Koreans themselves, or their ruler.

His Majesty the Emperor of Japan and His Majesty the Emperor of Korea having in view the special and close relations between their respective countries and to ensure peace in the Extreme East, and being convinced that these objects can best be attained by the annexation of Korea to the Empire of Japan have resolved to conclude a Treaty of such annexation and have for that purpose appointed as their Plenipotentiaries, that is to say,

His Majesty the Emperor of Japan, Viscount Maskata Terauchi,

His Resident General.
And His Majesty the Emperor of Korea, Ye Wan Yong, His
  Minister President of State,
Who, upon mutual conference and deliberation, have agreed to the
following articles.

Article 1. His Majesty the Emperor of Korea makes complete and
permanent cession to His Majesty the Emperor of Japan of all
rights of sovereignty over the whole of Korea.

Article 2. His Majesty the Emperor of Japan accepts the cession
mentioned in the preceding Article, and consents to the complete
annexation of Korea to the Empire of Japan.

Article 3. His Majesty the Emperor of Japan will accord to their
Majesties the Emperor and Empress of Korea and His Imperial
Highness the Crown Prince of Korea, and Their Consorts and Heirs
such titles, dignity and honour as are appropriate to their
respective rank and sufficient annual grants will be made for the
maintenance of such titles, dignity and honour.

Article 4. His Majesty the Emperor of Japan will also accord
appropriate honour and treatment to the members of the Imperial
House of Korea and their heirs, other than those mentioned in the
preceding Article and the funds necessary for the maintenance of
such honour and treatment will be granted.

Article 5. His Majesty the Emperor of Japan will confer peerages
and monetary grants upon those Koreans who, on account of
meritorious services, are regarded as deserving of such special
treatment.

Article 6. In consequence of the aforesaid annexation, the Government of Japan assumes the entire government and administration of Korea, and undertakes to afford full protection for the property and person of Koreans, obeying the laws then in force, and to promote the welfare of all such Koreans.

Article 7. The Government of Japan will, so far as circumstances permit, employ in the public service of Japan in Korea those Koreans who accept the new regime of Japan loyally and in good faith, and who are duly qualified for such service.

Article 8. This Treaty, having been approved by His Majesty the Emperor of Japan and His Majesty the Emperor of Korea shall take effect from the day of its promulgation.

Some defenders of Japan have wasted much effort in attempting to show that in destroying the Korean Empire Japan did not break her word, although she had repeatedly pledged herself to maintain and preserve the nation and the Royal House. Such arguments, under the circumstances, are merely nauseating. Japan wanted Korea; so soon as she was able, Japan took it. The only justification was

> "The good old rule ... the simple plan,
> That he shall take who has the power,
> That he shall KEEP, who can."

XI
"I WILL WHIP YOU WITH SCORPIONS"

The Japanese administration of Korea from 1910 to 1919, first under Count Terauchi and then under General Hasegawa, revealed the harshest and most relentless form of Imperial administration. When formal annexation was completed in 1910 all the hindrances which had hitherto stood in the way of the complete execution of Japanese methods were apparently swept on one side. The Governor-General had absolute power to pass what ordinances he pleased, and even to make those ordinances retroactive. Extra-territoriality was abolished, and foreign subjects in Korea were placed entirely under the Japanese laws.

Japanese statesmen were ambitious to show the world as admirable an example of efficiency in peace as Japan had already shown in war. Much thought had been given to the matter for a long time ahead. The colonial systems of other countries had been carefully studied. Service in Korea was to be a mark of distinction, re-served for the best and most highly paid. National pride and national interest were pledged to make good. Money was spent freely and some of the greatest statesmen and soldiers of Japan were placed at the head of affairs. Ito, by becoming Resident-General, had set an example for the best of the nation to follow.

Between the annexation in 1910 and the uprising of the people in 1919, much material progress was made. The old, effete administration was cleared away, sound currency maintained, railways were greatly extended, roads improved, afforesta-tion pushed forward on a great scale, agriculture developed, sanitation improved and fresh industries begun.

And yet this period of the Japanese administration in Korea ranks among the greatest failures of history, a failure greater than that of Russia in Finland or Poland or Austria-Hungary in Bosnia. America in Cuba and Japan in Korea stand out as the best and the worst examples in governing new subject peoples that the twentieth century has to show. The Japanese entered on their great task in a wrong spirit, they were hampered by fundamentally mistaken ideas, and they proved that they are not yet big enough for the job.

They began with a spirit of contempt for the Korean. Good administration is impossible without sympathy on the part of the administrators; with a blind and foolish contempt, sympathy is impossible. They started out to assimilate the Koreans, to destroy their national ideals, to root out their ancient ways, to make them over again as Japanese, but Japanese of an inferior brand, subject to disabilities from which their overlords were free. Assimilation with equality is difficult, save in the case of small, weak peoples, lacking tradition and national ideals. But assimilation with inferiority, attempted on a nation with a historic existence going back four thousand years is an absolutely impossible task. Or, to be more exact, it would only be possible by assimilating a few, the weaklings of the nation, and destroying the strong majority by persecution, direct killing and a steady course of active corruption, with drugs and vice.

The Japanese overestimated their own capacity and underestimated the Korean. They had carefully organized their claque in Europe and America, especially in America. They engaged the services of a group of paid agents--some of them holding highly responsible positions--to sing their praises and advocate their cause. They enlisted others by more subtle means, delicate flattery and social ambition. They taught diplomats and consular officials, especially of Great Britain and America, that it was a bad thing to become a persona non grata to Tokyo. They were backed by a number of people, who were sincerely won over by the finer sides of the Japanese character. In diplomatic and social intrigue, the Japanese make the rest of the world look as children. They used their forces not merely to laud themselves, but to promote the belief that the Koreans were an exhausted and good-for-nothing race.

In the end, they made the fatal mistake of believing what their sycophants and flatterers told them. Japanese civilization was the highest in the world; Japan was to be the future leader, not alone of Asia, but of all nations. The Korean was fit for nothing but to act as hewer of wood and drawer of water for his overlord.

Had Japan been wise and long-sighted enough to treat the Koreans as America treated the Cubans or England the people of the Straits Settlements, there would have been a real amalgamation--although not an assimilation--of the two peoples. The Koreans were wearied of the extravagances, abuses and follies of their old administration. But Japan in place of putting Korean interests first ruled the land for the benefit of Japan. The Japanese exploiter, the Japanese settler were the main men to be studied.

Then Japan sought to make the land a show place. Elaborate public buildings were erected, railroads opened, state maintained, far in excess of the economic strength of the nation. To pay for extravagant improvements, taxation and personal service were made to bear heavily on the people. Many of the improvements were of no possible service to the Koreans themselves. They were made to benefit Japanese or to impress strangers. And the officials forgot that even subject peoples have ideals and souls. They sought to force loyalty, to beat it into children with the stick and drill it into men by gruelling experiences in prison cells. Then they were amazed that they had bred rebels. They sought to wipe out Korean culture, and then were aggrieved because Koreans would not take kindly to Japanese learning. They treated the Koreans with open contempt, and then wondered that they did not love them.

Let us examine the administration more closely in detail.

Its outstanding feature for most of the people is (I use the present tense because as I write it still continues) the gendarmerie and police. These are established all over the country, and they have in effect, although not in name, power of life or death. They can enter into any house, without warrant, and search it. They destroy whatever they please, on the spot. Thus if a policeman searches the room of a student, and sees a book which does not please him, he can--and does--often burn it on the spot. Sometimes he takes it into the street and burns it there, to impress the neighbours.

One of the police visits most feared by many villagers is the periodical examinations to see if the houses are clean. If the policemen are not satisfied, they do not trouble to take the people to the station, but give them a flogging then and there. This house examination is frequently used by police in districts where they wish to punish the Christians, or to prevent their neighbours from becoming Christians. The Christian houses are visited and the Christians flogged, sometimes without even troubling to examine the houses at all. This method particularly prevails in parts of the Pyengyang province.

The police can arrest and search or detain any person, without warrant. This right of search is freely used on foreigners as well as Koreans. Any Korean taken to the police station can, in practice, be kept in custody as long as wanted, without trial, and then can be released without trial, or can be summarily punished without trial by the police.

The usual punishment is flogging--only Koreans and not Japanese or foreigners are liable to be flogged. This punishment can be given in such a way as to cripple, to confine the victim to his home for weeks, or to kill. While it is not supposed to be practiced on women, on men over sixty-five or on boys under fifteen, the police flog indiscriminately.

The Japanese Government passed, some years ago, regulations to prevent the abuse of flogging. These regulations are a dead letter. Here is the official statement:

"It was decided to retain it (flogging), but only for application to native offenders. In March, 1912, Regulations concerning Flogging and the Enforcing Detailed Regulations being promulgated, many improvements were made in the measures hitherto practiced. Women, boys under the age of fifteen and old men over the age of sixty are exempt from flogging, while the infliction of this punishment on sick convicts and on the insane is to be postponed for six months. The method of infliction was also improved so that by observing greater humanity, unnecessary pain in carrying out a flogging could be avoided, as far as possible,"[10]

So much for the official claim. Now for the facts.

In the last year for which returns are available, 1916-17, 82,121 offenders were handled by police summary judgment, that is, punished by the police on the spot, without trial. Two-thirds of these punishments (in the last year when actual flogging figures were published) were floggings.

The instrument used is two bamboos lashed together. The maximum legal sentence is ninety blows, thirty a day for three days in succession. To talk of this as "greater humanity" or "avoiding unnecessary pain" gives me nausea. Any experienced official who has had to do with such things will bear me out in the assertion

---

10   Annual Report of Reforms and Progress in Chosen. Keijo (Seoul), 1914.

that it is deliberately calculated to inflict the maximum of pain which the human frame can stand, and in the most long drawn out manner.

Sick men, women and boys and old men are flogged.

In the disturbances of 1919 wounded men who were being nursed in the foreign hospitals in Seoul were taken out by the police to be flogged, despite the protests of doctors and nurses. There were many cases reported of old men being flogged. The stripping and flogging of women, particularly young women, was notorious.

Here is one case of the flogging of boys.

The following letter from a missionary in Sun-chon--where there is a Presbyterian hospital,--dated May 25, 1919, was printed in the report of the Federal Council of the Churches of Christ in America. I have seen other communications from people who saw these boys, amply confirming the letter, if it requires confirmation.

Eleven Kangkei boys came here from ----. All the eleven were beaten ninety stripes--thirty each day for three days, May 16, 17 and 18, and let out May 18th. Nine came here May 22nd, and two more May 24th.

Tak Chan-kuk died about noon, May 23rd.

Kim Myungha died this evening.

Kim Hyungsun is very sick.

Kim Chungsun and Song Taksam are able to walk but are badly broken.

Kim Oosik seemed very doubtful but afterwards improved.

Choi Tungwon, Kim Changook, Kim Sungkil, and Ko Pongsu are able to be about, though the two have broken flesh.

Kim Syungha rode from ---- on his bicycle and reached here about an hour before his brother died. The first six who came into the hospital were in a dreadful fix, four days after the beating. No dressing or anything had been done for them. Dr. Sharrocks just told me that he feels doubtful about some of the others since Myungha died. It is gangrene. One of these boys is a Chun Kyoin, and another is not a Christian, but the rest are all Christians.

Mr. Lampe has photographs. The stripes were laid on to the buttocks and the flesh pounded into a pulp.

Greater humanity! Avoiding unnecessary pain! It is obvious that the method of police absolutism is open to very great abuse. In practice it works out as galling tyranny. A quotation from the Japan Chronicle illustrates one of the abuses:

"In the course of interpellations put forward by a certain member in the last session of the Diet, he remarked on the strength of a statement made by a public procurator of high rank in Korea, that it was usual for a gendarme who visits a Korean house for the purpose of searching for a criminal to violate any female inmate of the house and to take away any article that suits his fancy. And not only had the wronged Koreans no means of obtaining redress for this outrageous conduct, but the judicial authorities could take no proceedings against the offender as they must necessarily depend upon the gendarmerie for acceptable evidence of crime."

The police tyranny does not end with flogging. When a person is arrested, he is at once shut off from communication with his friends. He is not, necessarily, informed of the charge against him; his friends are not informed. He is not in the early stages allowed counsel. All that his friends know is that he has disappeared in the grip of the police, and he may remain out of sight or sound for months before being brought to trial or released.

During this period of confinement the prisoner is first in the hands of the police who are getting up the case against him. It is their work to extract a confession. To obtain this they practice torture, often of the most elaborate type. This is particularly true where the prisoners are charged with political offences. I deal with this aspect of affairs more in detail in later chapters, so that there is no need of me to bring proof at this point.

After the police have completed their case, the prisoner is brought before the procurator, whose office would, if rightly used, be a check on the police. But in many cases the police act as procurators in Korea, and in others the procurators and police work hand in hand.

When the prisoner is brought before the court he has little of the usual protection afforded in a British or American Court. It is for him to prove his innocence of the charge. His judge is the nominee of the Government-General and is its tool, who practically does what the Government-General tells him. The complaint of the most sober and experienced friends of the Koreans is that they cannot obtain justice unless it is deemed expedient by the authorities to give them justice.

Under this system crime has enormously increased. The police create it. The best evidence of this is contained in the official figures. In the autumn of 1912 Count Terauchi stated, in answer to the report that thousands of Korean Christians had been confined in jail, that he had caused enquiry to be made and there were only 287 Koreans confined in the various jails of the country (New York Sun, October 3, 1912). The Count's figures were almost certainly incorrect, or else the police released all the prisoners on the day the reckoning was taken, except the necessary few kept for effect. The actual number of convicts in Korea in 1912 was close on twelve thousand, according to the official details published later. If they were true they make the contrast with later years the more amazing.

The increase of arrests and convictions is shown in the following official return.

NUMBER OF KOREANS IMPRISONED

	Convicts	Awaiting trial	Total
1911	7,342	9,465	16,807
1912	9,652	9,842	19,494
1913	11,652	10,194	21,846
1914	12,962	11,472	24,434
1915	14,411	12,844	27,255
1916	17,577	15,259	32,836

Individual liberty is non-existent. The life of the Korean is regulated down to the smallest detail. If he is rich, he is generally required to have a Japanese steward who will supervise his expenditure. If he has money in the bank, he can only draw a small sum out at a time, unless he gives explanation why he needs it.

He has not the right of free meeting, free speech or a free press. Before a paper or book can be published it has to pass the censor. This censorship is carried to an absurd degree. It starts with school books; it goes on to every word a man may write or speak. It applies to the foreigners as well as Koreans. The very commencement day speeches of school children are censored. The Japanese journalist in Korea who dares to criticize the administration is sent to prison almost as quickly as the Korean. Japanese newspaper men have found it intolerable and have gone back to Japan, refusing to work under it. There is only one newspaper now published in Korea in the Korean language, and it is edited by a Japanese. An American missionary published a magazine, and attempted to include in it a few mild comments on current events. He was sternly bidden not to attempt it again. Old books published before the Japanese acquired control have been freely destroyed. Thus a large number of school books--not in the least partizan--prepared by Professor Hulbert were destroyed.

The most ludicrous example of censorship gone mad was experienced by Dr. Gale, one of the oldest, most learned and most esteemed of the missionaries in Korea. Dr. Gale is a British subject. For a long time he championed the Japanese cause, until the Japanese destroyed his confidence by their brutalities in 1919. But the fact that Dr. Gale was their most influential friend did not check the Japanese censors. On one occasion Dr. Gale learned that some Korean "Readers" prepared by him for use in schools had been condemned. He enquired the reason. The Censor replied that the book "contained dangerous thoughts." Still more puzzled, the doctor politely enquired if the Censor would show the passages containing "dangerous thoughts." The Censor thereupon pointed out a translation of Kipling's famous story of the elephant, which had been included in the book. "In that story," said he ominously, "the elephant refused to serve his second *master." What could be more obvious that Dr. Gale was attempting to teach Korean children, in this subtle fashion, to refuse to serve* their second master, the Japanese Emperor!

For a Korean to be a journalist has been for him to be a marked man liable to constant arrest, not for what he did or does, but for what the police suppose he may do or might have done. The natural result of this has been to drive Koreans out of regular journalism, and to lead to the creation of a secret press.

The next great group of grievances of Koreans come under the head of Exploitation. From the beginning the Japanese plan has been to take as much land as possible from the Koreans and hand it over to Japanese. Every possible trick has been used to accomplish this. In the early days of the Japanese occupation, the favourite plan was to seize large tracts of land on the plea that they were needed for the Army or Navy; to pay a pittance for them; and then to pass considerable portions of them on to Japanese. "There can be no question," admitted Mr. W.D. Stevens, the American member and supporter of Prince Ito's administration, "that at the outset the military authorities in Korea did intimate an intention of taking more land for their uses than seemed reasonable."

The first attempt of the Japanese to grab in wholesale fashion the public lands of Korea, under the so-called Nagamori scheme, aroused so much indignation that it was withdrawn. Then they set about accomplishing the same end in other ways. Much of the land of Korea was public land, held by tenants from time immemorial under a loose system of tenancy. This was taken over by the Government-General All leases were examined, and people called on to show their rights to hold their property. This worked to the same end.

The Oriental Development Company was formed for the primary purpose of developing Korea by Japanese and settling Japanese on Korean land, Japanese immigrants being given free transportation, land for settlement, implements and other assistance. This company is an immense semi-official trust of big financial interests in direct coeoperation with the Government, and is supported by an official subsidy of L50,000 a year. Working parallel to it is the Bank of Chosen, the semi-official banking institution which has been placed supreme and omnipotent in Korean finance.

How this works was explained by a writer in the New York Times (January 29, 1919). "These people declined to part with their heritage. It was here that the power of the Japanese Government was felt in a manner altogether Asiatic.... Through its branches this powerful financial institution ... called in all the specie in the country, thus making, as far as circulating-medium is concerned, the land practically valueless. In order to pay taxes and to obtain the necessaries of life, the Korean must have cash, and in order to obtain it, he must sell his land. Land values fell very rapidly, and in some instances land was purchased by the agents of the Bank of Chosen for one-fifth of its former valuation." There may be some dispute about the methods employed. There can be no doubt about the result. One-fifth of the richest land in Korea is to-day in Japanese hands.

Allied to this system of land exploitation comes the Corvee, or forced labour exacted from the country people for road making. In moderation this might be unobjectionable. As enforced by the Japanese authorities, it has been an appalling burden. The Japanese determined to have a system of fine roads. They have built them--by the Corvee.

The most convincing evidence for outsiders on this land exploitation and on the harshness of the Corvee comes from Japanese sources. Dr. Yoshino, a professor of the Imperial University of Tokyo, salaried out of the Government Treasury, made a special study of Korea. He wrote in the Taschuo-Koron of Tokyo, that the Koreans have no objection to the construction of good roads, but that the official way of carrying out the work is tyrannical. "Without consideration and mercilessly, they have resorted to laws for the expropriation of land, the Koreans concerned being compelled to part with their family property almost for nothing. On many occasions they have also been forced to work in the construction of roads without receiving any wages. To make matters worse, they must work for nothing only on the days which are convenient to the officials, however inconvenient these days may be to the unpaid workers." The result has generally been that while the roads were being built for the convenient march of the Japanese troops to suppress the builders of the roads, many families were bankrupted and starving.

"The Japanese make improvements," say the Koreans. "But they make them to benefit their own people, not us. They improve agriculture, and turn the Korean farmers out and replace them by Japanese. They pave and put sidewalks in a Seoul street, but the old Korean shopkeepers in that street have gone, and Japanese have come. They encourage commerce, Japanese commerce, but the Korean tradesman is hampered and tied down in many ways." Education has been wholly Japanized. That is to say the primary purpose of the schools is to teach Korean children to be good Japanese subjects. Teaching is mostly done in Japanese, by Japanese teachers. The whole ritual and routine is towards the glorification of Japan.

The Koreans complain, however, that, apart from this, the system of teaching established for Koreans in Korea is inferior to that established for Japanese there. Japanese and Korean children are taught in separate schools. The course of education for Koreans is four years, for Japanese six. The number of schools provided for Japanese is proportionately very much larger than for Koreans, and a much larger sum of money is spent on them. The Japanese may however claim, with some justice, that they are in the early days of the development of Korean education, and they must be given more time to develop it. Koreans bitterly complain of the ignoring of Korean history in the public schools, and the systematic efforts to destroy old sentiments. These efforts, however, have been markedly unsuccessful, and the Government school students were even more active than mission school students in the Independence movement.

It was a Japanese journalist who published the case of the Principal of a Public School for girls who roused the indignation of the girls under him during a lecture on Ethics with the syllogism, "Savages are healthy; Koreans are healthy; therefore Koreans are savages." Other teachers roused their young pupils to fury, after the death of the ex-Emperor, by employing openly of him the phrase which ordinarily indicates a low-class coolie. In the East, where honorifics and exact designations count for much, no greater insults could be imagined.

The greatest hardships of the regime of the Government-General have been the denial of justice, the destruction of liberty, the shutting out of the people from all real participation in administration, the lofty assumption and display of a spirit of insolent superiority by the Japanese, and the deliberate degradation of the people by the cultivation of vice for the purpose of personal profit. In the old days, opium was practically unknown. Today opium is being cultivated on a large scale under the direct encouragement of the Government, and the sale of morphia is carried on by large numbers of Japanese itinerant merchants. In the old days, vice hid its head. To-day the most prominent feature at night-time in Seoul, the capital, is the brilliantly lit Yoshiwara, officially created and run by Japanese, into which many Korean girls are dragged. Quarters of ill fame have been built up in many parts of the land, and Japanese panders take their gangs of diseased women on tours through smaller districts. On one occasion when I visited Sun-chon I found that the authorities had ordered some of the Christians to find accommodation in their homes for Japanese women of ill fame. Some Koreans in China sent a petition to the American Minister in Peking which dealt with some moral aspects of the Japanese rule of Korea. They said:

> "The Japanese have encouraged immorality by removing Korean marriage restrictions, and allowing marriages without formality and without regard for age. There have been marriages at as early an age as twelve. Since the annexation there have been 80,000 divorce cases in Korea. The Japanese encourage, as a source of revenue, the sale of Korean prostitutes in Chinese cities. Many of these prostitutes are only fourteen and fifteen years old. It is a part of the Japanese policy of race extermination, by which they hope to destroy all Koreans. May God regard these facts.

> "The Japanese Government has established a bureau for the sale of opium, and under the pretext that opium was to be used for medicinal purposes has caused Koreans and Formosans to engage in poppy cultivation. The opium is secretly shipped into China. Because of the Japanese encouragement of this traffic many Koreans have become users of the drug.

"The Japanese forbid any school courses for Koreans higher than the middle school and the higher schools established by missionary organizations are severely regulated. The civilization of the Far East originated in China, and was brought first to Korea and thence to Japan. The ancient books were more numerous in Korea than in Japan, but after annexation the Japanese set about destroying these books, so that Koreans should not be able to learn them. This 'burning of the books and murder of the literati' was for the purpose of debasing the Koreans and robbing them of their ancient culture....

"How can our race avoid extermination? Even if the Government of Japan were benevolent, how could the Japanese understand the aches and pains of another race of people? With her evil Government can there be anything but racial extermination for us?"

From the time of the reopening of Korea the Japanese have treated the Koreans in personal intercourse as the dust beneath their feet, or as one might imagine a crude and vixenish tempered woman of peasant birth whose husband had acquired great wealth by some freak of fortune treating an unfortunate poor gentlewoman who had come in her employment. This was bad enough in the old days; since the Japanese acquired full power in Korea it has become infinitely worse.

The Japanese coolie punches the Korean who chances to stand in his august path. The Japanese woman, wife of a little trader, spits out the one contemptuous sentence she has learned in the Korean tongue, when a Korean man draws near on the boat or on the train. The little official assumes an air of ineffable disdain and contempt. A member of the Japanese Diet was reported in the Japanese press to have said that in Korea the Japanese gendarmes were in the habit of exacting from the Korean school children the amount of deference which in Japan would be proper to the Imperial Household.

The lowest Japanese coolie practices the right to kick, beat and cuff a Korean of high birth at his pleasure, and the Korean has in effect no redress. Had the Koreans from the first have met blow with blow, a number of them no doubt would have died, but the Japanese would have been cured of the habit. The Korean dislike of fighting, until he has really some serious reason for a fight, has encouraged the Japanese bully; but it makes the bully's offence none the less.

Japanese officials in many instances seem to delight in exaggerating their contempt on those under them. This is particularly true of some of the Japanese teachers. Like all Government officials, these teachers wear swords, symbols of power. Picture the dignity of the teacher of a class of little boys who lets his sword clang to terrify the youngsters under him, or who tries to frighten the girls by displaying his weapon.

The iron rule of Terauchi was followed by the iron rule of Hasegawa, his successor. The struggle of the rebel army in the hills had died down. But men got together, wondering what steps they could take. Christians and non-Christians found a common bond of union. Their life had come to a pass where it was better to die than to live under unchecked tyranny. Thus the Independence movement came into being.

The Koreans who, despoiled of their homes or determined to submit no longer to Japan, escaped into Manchuria, escaped as a rule by the difficult and dangerous journey across the high mountain passes. What this journey means can best be understood from a report by the Rev. W.T. Cook, of the Manchuria Christian College at Moukden.

"The untold afflictions of the Korean immigrants coming into Manchuria will doubtless never be fully realized, even by those actually witnessing their distress. In the still closeness of a forty below zero climate in the dead of winter, the silent stream of white clad figures creeps over the icy mountain passes, in groups of tens, twenties and fifties, seeking a new world of subsistence, willing to take a chance of life and death in a hand-to-hand struggle with the stubborn soil of Manchuria's wooded and stony hillsides. Here, by indefatigable efforts, they seek to extract a living by applying the grub axe and hand hoe to the barren mountain sides above the Chinese fields, planting and reaping by hand between the roots the sparse yield that is often insufficient to sustain life.

"Many have died from insufficient food. Not only women and children but young men have been frozen to death. Sickness also claims its toll under these new conditions of exposure. Koreans have been seen standing barefooted on the broken ice of a riverside fording place, rolling up their baggy trousers before wading through the broad stream, two feet deep, of ice cold water, then standing on the opposite side while they hastily readjust their clothing and shoes.

"Women with insufficient clothing, and parts of their bodies exposed, carry little children on their backs, thus creating a mutual warmth in a slight degree, but it is in this way that the little ones' feet, sticking out from the binding basket, get frozen and afterwards fester till the tiny toes stick together. Old men and women, with bent backs and wrinkled faces, walk the uncomplaining miles until their old limbs refuse to call them further.

"Thus it is by households they come, old and young, weak and strong, big and little.... Babies have been born in wayside inns.

"In this way over 75,000 Koreans have entered during the past year, until the number of Koreans now living in both the north and western portions of Manchuria now totals nearly half a million."[11]

---

11   Report to the Presbyterian Board of Foreign Missions.

XII
THE MISSIONARIES

I have had occasion in previous chapters to make occasional reference to the work of the missionaries in Korea. It is necessary now to deal with them in detail, for they had become one of the great factors, and from the Japanese point of view one of the great problems, of the country.

Long before Korea was open to the outside world, missionary pioneers tried to enter it. The French Catholics forced admission as far back as the end of the eighteenth century, and made many converts, who were afterwards exterminated. Gutzaleff, a famous Protestant pioneer, landed on an island at Basil's Bay, in 1832, and remained there a month, distributing Chinese literature. Mr. Thomas, a British missionary, secured a passage on board the ill-fated General Sherman in 1866, and was killed with the rest of the crew. Dr. Ross, the Scottish Presbyterian missionary of Moukden, Manchuria, became interested in the Koreans, studied their language, talked with every Korean he could find, and built up a grammar of the language, publishing an English-Korean primer in 1876. He and a colleague, Mr. McIntyre, published Gospels in the language, and opened up a work among the Koreans on the north side of the Yalu. Those who can recall the state of that district in the days before railways were opened and order established, can best appreciate the nerve and daring needed for the task. They made converts, and one of these converts took some newly printed Christian books and set back home, reaching Seoul itself, spreading the new religion among his friends.

It was two years after the opening of Korea to the West before the first missionary arrived. In 1884 Dr. Allen, a Presbyterian physician (afterwards United States Minister to Korea), arrived at Seoul. It was very doubtful at this time how missionaries would be received, or how their converts would be treated. The law enacting death against any man who became a Christian was still unrepealed, but it was not enforced. Officialism might, however, revive it at any time. It was thought advisable, when the first converts were baptized in 1887, to perform the ceremony behind closed doors, with an earnest and athletic young American educationalist, Homer B. Hulbert, acting as guard.

Dr. Allen was soon followed by others. Dr. Underwood, brother of the famous manufacturer of typewriting machines, was the first non-medical missionary. The American and Canadian Presbyterians and Methodists undertook the main work, and the Church of England set up a bishopric. Women missionary doctors came, and at once won a place for themselves. Names like Appenzeller, Scranton, Bunker and Gale--to name a few of the pioneers--have won a permanent place in the history of missions.

The missionaries found a land almost without religion, with few temples and few monks or priests. Buddhism had been discredited by the treachery of some Japanese Buddhists during the great Japanese invasion by Hideyoshi in 1592, and no Buddhist priest was allowed inside the city of Seoul. Young men of official rank studied their Confucius diligently, but to them Confucianism was more a theory for the conduct of life and a road to high office than a religion. The main religion of the people was Shamanism, the fear of evil spirits. It darkened their souls, as the tales of a foolish nurse about goblins darken the mind of a sensitive and imaginative child. The spirits of Shamanism were evil, not good, a curse, not a blessing, bringing terror, not hope.

Christianity was very fortunate in its representatives. I have seen much of the missionaries of Manchuria and Korea. A finer, straighter lot of men I never want to meet. The magnificent climate enables them to keep at the top of form. They have initiative, daring and common sense. Those I have known are born leaders, who would have made their mark anywhere, in business or politics.

In the early days they had to be ready to set their hands to anything, to plan and build houses and churches, to open schools, to run a boat down dangerous rapids or face a dangerous mob, to overawe a haughty yang-ban or break in a dangerous horse. They were the pioneers of civilization as well as of Christianity.

Religion had to be commended by the courage of its adherents. When there came a dangerous uprising, and every one else fled, the missionary had to stay at his post. When an epidemic of cholera or yellow fever swept over a district, the missionary had to act as doctor or nurse. Sometimes the missionary died, as Dr. Heron died at Seoul and McKenzie at Sorai. Their deaths were even more effective than their lives in winning people.

Dr. Allen gained a foothold soon after his arrival by sticking to his post in Seoul during the uprising against foreigners that followed the attack by the Japanese and the reformers on the Cabinet and their seizure of the King and Queen. When Min Yung-ik, the Queen's nephew, was badly wounded, Dr. Allen attended to him and saved his life. Henceforth the King was the missionaries' friend. He built a hospital and placed Dr. Allen in charge. Women missionary doctors were appointed Court physicians to the Queen.

There were years of waiting, when the converts were few, and when it seemed that the barriers of four thousand years never would be broken down. Then came the Chino-Japanese War. Koreans were forced to see that this Western civilization, which had enabled little Japan to beat the Chinese giant, must mean something. A young man from Indiana, Samuel Moffett, with a companion, Graham Lee, had gone some time before to Pyeng-yang, reputedly the worst city in Korea. Here they had been stoned and abused. When the Chinese Army came to Pyeng-yang, and the country was devastated in the great and decisive battle between the Chinese and Japanese, these two men stayed by the Koreans in their darkest and most perilous hours. Koreans still tell how "Moksa" Moffett put on the dress of a Korean mourner and went freely around despite the Chinese, who would have almost certainly devised a specially lingering death for him, had they discovered his presence.

"There must be something in this religion," said the Koreans. Sturdy old John Newton's belief that the worst sinner makes the finest saint was borne out in the case of Pyeng-yang. It became in a few years one of the greatest scenes of missionary triumph in Asia. The harvest was ripening now. In Seoul men flung into jail for political offences turned to prayer in the darkness and despair of their torture chambers, and went to death praising God. The Secretary to the King's Cabinet preached salvation to his fellow Cabinet Ministers.

The tens of converts grew to tens of thousands. From the first, the Koreans showed themselves to be Christians of a very unusual type. They started by reforming their homes, giving their wives liberty and demanding education for their children. They took the promises and commands of the Bible literally and established a standard of conduct for church members which, if it were enforced in some older Christian communities, would cause a serious contraction of the church rolls. The first convert set out to preach to his friends. Latter converts imitated his example. From Pyeng-yang the movement spread to Sun-chon, which in a few years rivalled Pyeng-yang as a Christian centre. From here Christianity spread to the Yalu and up the Tumen River.

The Koreans themselves established Christianity in distant communities where no white man had ever been. Soon many of the missionaries were kept busy for several months each year travelling with pack-pony and mafoo, from station to station in the most remote parts of the country, fording and swimming unbridged rivers, climbing mountain passes, inspecting and examining and instructing the converts, admitting them to church membership and organizing them for still more effective work.

When I hear the cheap sneers of the obtuse stay-at-home or globe-trotter critics against missionaries and their converts, I am amused. It gives me the measure of the men, particularly of the globetrotters. When the British and American Churches seek to send out missionaries, the British and American people will have registered the sure sign of their decadence. For the Churches and nations will then cease to be alive. In travelling through the north country I employed a number of the Christian converts, I found them clean and honest, good, hard workers, men who showed their religion not by talk, but by good, straight action. It is a grief to me to know that some of these "boys" have since, because of their prominence as Christian workers, been the victims of official persecution.

Under the influence of the missionaries many schools were opened; hospitals and dispensaries were maintained, and a considerable literature, educational as well as religious, was circulated.

When the Japanese landed in Korea in 1904, the missionaries welcomed them. They knew the tyranny and abuses of the old Government, and believed that the Japanese would help to better things. The ill-treatment of helpless Koreans by Japanese soldiers and coolies caused a considerable reaction of feeling. When, however, Prince Ito became Resident-General the prevailing sentiment was that it would be better for the people to submit and to make the best of existing conditions, in the hope that the harshness and injustice of Japanese rule would pass.

Most of the Europeans and Americans in Korea at the time adopted this line. I travelled largely in the interior of Korea in 1906 and 1907. Groups of influential Koreans came to me telling their grievances and asking what to do. Sometimes big assemblies of men asked me to address them. They believed me to be their friend, and were willing to trust me. My advice was always the same. "Submit and make yourselves better men. You can do nothing now by taking up arms. Educate your children, improve your homes, better your lives. Show the Japanese by your conduct and your self-control that you are as good as they are, and fight the corruption and apathy that helped to bring your nation to its present position." Let me add that I did what I could in England, at the same time, to call attention to their grievances.

Prince Ito was openly sympathetic to the missionaries and to their medical and educational work. He once explained why, in a public gathering at Seoul. "In the early years of Japan's reformation, the senior statesmen were opposed to religious toleration, especially because of distrust of Christianity. But I fought vehemently for freedom of belief and religious propaganda, and finally triumphed. My reasoning was this: Civilization depends on morality and the highest morality upon religion. Therefore religion must be tolerated and encouraged."

Ito passed off the scene, Korea was formally annexed to Japan, and Count Terauchi became Governor-General. Terauchi was unsympathetic to Christianity and a new order of affairs began. One of the difficulties of the Christians was over the direction that children in schools and others should bow before the picture of the Japanese Emperor on feast days. The Japanese tried to maintain to the missionaries that this was only a token of respect; the Christians declared that it was an act of adoration. To the Japanese his Emperor is a divine being, the descendant of the gods.

Christians who refused to bow were carefully noted as malignants. In the famous Conspiracy Case, the official Assistant Procurator, in urging the conviction of one of the men, said: "He was head teacher of the Sin-an School, Chong-ju, and was a notorious man of anti-Japanese sentiments. He was the very obstinate member of the Society who, at a meeting on the first anniversary of the birthday of the Emperor of Japan after the annexation of Korea, refused to bow before the Imperial picture on the ground that such an act was worshipping an image." This one item was the only fact that the Assistant Procurator produced to prove the head teacher's guilt. He was convicted, and awarded seven years' penal servitude.

A strong effort was made to Japanize the Korean Churches, to make them branches of the Japanese Churches, and to make them instruments in the Japanese campaign of assimilation. The missionaries resisted this to the utmost. They declared that they would be neutral in political matters, as they were directed by their Governments to be. Having failed to win them over to their side, the Japanese authorities entered into a campaign for the breaking down of the Churches, particularly the Presbyterian Churches of the north. I am well aware that they deny this, but here is a case where actions and speeches cannot be reconciled.

Attempts were pushed to create churches of Koreans under Japanese. Son Pyung-hi, who had proved a good friend of Japan during the Chinese War, had been encouraged by the Japanese some time before to start a religious sect, the Chon-do Kyo, which it was hoped would replace Christianity, and prove a useful weapon for Japan. Here a blunder was made, for later on Son Pyung-hi flung all his influence against Japan and worked with the native Christian leaders to start the Independence movement. More important than either of these two things, however, direct persecution was begun. Several hundred Korean Christian leaders in the north were arrested, and out of them 144 were taken to Seoul, tortured, and charged with a conspiracy to murder the Governor-General. Various missionaries were named as their partners in crime. The tale of the conspiracy was a complete fabrication manufactured by the police. I describe it fully in the next chapter.

Following this came regulations aimed at the missionary schools and institutions. At the time of annexation, almost the whole of the real modern education of Korea was undertaken by the missionaries, who were maintaining 778 schools. A series of Educational Ordinances was promulgated in March, 1915, directing that no religious teaching is to be permitted in private schools, and no religious ceremonies allowed to be performed. The Japanese authorities made no secret of their intention of eventually closing all missionary schools, on the ground that even when religious teaching was excluded, pupils were influenced by their teachers, and the influence of the foreign teachers was against the Japanization of the Koreans. Mr. Komatsu, Director of the Bureau of Foreign Affairs, put this point without any attempt at concealment, in a public statement. "Our object of education is not only to develop the intellect and morality of our people, but also to foster in their minds such national spirit as will contribute to the existence and welfare of our Empire.... I sincerely hope that you will appreciate this change of the time and understand that missions should leave all affairs relating entirely to education entirely in the hands of the Government, by transferring the money and labour they have hitherto been expending on education to their proper sphere of religious propagation.... Whatever the curriculum of a school may be, it is natural that the students of that school should be influenced by the ideas and personal character of its principal and teachers. Education must be decidedly nationalistic and must not be mixed up with religion that is universal." This is a much harsher regulation against missions than prevails in Japan, where mission schools are allowed to continue their work, with freedom to carry on their religious teaching.

The Government-General agreed to allow mission schools that had already obtained Government permits to continue for ten years without having the regulations enforced. Schools that had applied for the permit but had not obtained it, owing to formal official delays, were ordered to obey or close, and police were sent to see that they closed.

The Government commanded the mission schools to cease using their own text-books and to use the officially prepared text-books. These are carefully prepared to eliminate "dangerous thoughts," i.e., anything that will promote a desire for freedom. They directly teach ancestral worship. The missionaries have protested in every way they can. The Government-General is adamant.

Before the start of the Independence movement the mission schools were being carefully watched. Dr. Arthur J. Brown gives one example of their experiences,[12] in connection with the graduating exercises at the Pyeng-yang Junior College last year.

> "Four students made addresses. The foreigners present deemed them
> void of offence, but the police declared that all the speakers
> had said things subversive of the public good. The students were
> arrested, interrogated and then released, as their previous

---

12   "The Mastery of the Far East," by Arthur Judson Brown.

records had been good. The provincial chief of gendarmes, however, summoned the students before him and again investigated the case. The president of the college was called to the office, and strictly charged to exercise greater care in the future. The matter was then reported to the Governor of the Province, and then to the Governor-General. The latter wrote to the president of the college that the indiscretion of the students was so serious that the Government was contemplating closing the school. A similar communication was sent by the Governor-General to the provincial Governor, who thereupon called the president to his office, and said that unless he was prepared to make certain changes the school would have to close. These changes were enumerated as follows: (1) Appointment of a Japanese head master; (2) dismissal of three of the boys who had spoken; relief of the fourth from certain assignments of teaching which he was doing in the academy, and promise not to repeat the oratorical program in the future; (3) secure more Japanese teachers, especially those who could understand Korean; (4) do all teaching, except the Chinese classics, Korean language and English, through the medium of the Japanese language; prepare syllabi of the subjects of instruction, so as to limit it to specified points, teachers not to deviate from them nor to speak on forbidden subjects; (6) conform to the new regulations. (That is, eliminate all Christian instruction.) When the president replied that he would do all that he could to make the first five changes desired, but that as to the sixth change, the mission preferred to continue for the present under the old permit which entitled the college to the ten year period of grace, the official was plainly disappointed, and he intimated that number six was the most important of all."

The Independence movement in 1919 enormously increased the difficulties of the missionaries, although they refrained from any direct or indirect participation in it, and the Koreans carefully avoided letting them know anything ahead about it.

The difficulties of the missionaries, and the direct action of the authorities against Christianity at that time is told later, in the chapters dealing with the movement.

The Japanese authorities will probably do two things. They will order the closing of schools under various pretexts where Christian teaching is still maintained. They will endeavour to secure the elimination of those missionaries who have shown a marked sympathy with the Korean people. They have ample powers to prosecute any missionary who is guilty of doing anything to aid disaffection. They have repeatedly searched missionary homes and missionaries themselves to find evidence of this. Save in the case of Mr. Mowry, who was convicted of sheltering some students wanted by the police, they have failed. Even in that case the original conviction has been quashed on appeal. Such evidence does not exist, because the missionaries have been really neutral. Neutrality does not satisfy Japan; she wants them to come out on her side. Unfortunately her action this year has turned many away from her who tried hard up to then to be her friends.

XIII
TORTURE A LA MODE

T he main thing, when you are tortured, is to remain calm."

The Korean spoke quietly and in a matter-of-fact way. He himself had suffered torture in its most severe form. Possibly he thought there was a chance that I, too, might have a personal experience.

"Do not struggle. Do not fight," he continued. "For instance, if you are strung up by the thumbs and you struggle and kick desperately, you may die on the spot. Keep absolutely still; it is easier to endure it in this way. Compel your mind to think of other things."

Torture! Who talks of torture in these enlightened days?

Let me tell you the tale of the Conspiracy Case, as revealed in the evidence given in open court, and then judge for yourself.

When the heads of the Terauchi administration had made up their minds that the northern Christians were inimical to the progress of the Japanese scheme of assimilation, they set their spies to work. Now the rank and file of spies are very much alike in all parts of the world. They are ignorant and often misunderstand things. When they cannot find the evidence they require, they will manufacture it.

The Japanese spies were exceptionally ignorant. First they made up their minds that the northern Christians were plotting against Japan, and then they searched for evidence. They attended church services. Here they heard many gravely suspicious things. There were hymns of war, like "Onward, Christian Soldiers" and "Soldiers of Christ Arise." What could these mean but that Christians were urged to become an army and attack the Japanese? Dangerous doctrines were openly taught in the churches and mission schools. They learned that Mr. McCune, the Sun-chon missionary, took the story of David and Goliath as the subject for a lesson, pointing out that a weak man armed with righteousness was more powerful than a mighty enemy. To the spies, this was nothing but a direct incitement to the weak Koreans to fight strong Japan. Mission premises were searched. Still more dangerous material was found there, including school essays, written by the students, on men who had rebelled against their Governments or had fought, such as George Washington and Napoleon. A native pastor had preached about the Kingdom of Heaven; this was rank treason. He was arrested and warned that "there is only one kingdom out here, and that is the kingdom of Japan."

In the autumn of 1911 wholesale arrests were made of Christian preachers, teachers, students and prominent church members, particularly in the provinces of Sun-chon and Pyeng-yang. In the Hugh O'Neill, Jr., Industrial Academy, in Sun-chon, one of the most famous educational establishments in Korea--where the principal had made the unfortunate choice of David and Goliath for one of his addresses--so many pupils and teachers were seized by the police that the school had to close. The men were hurried to jail. They were not allowed to communicate with their friends, nor to obtain the advice of counsel. They and their friends were not informed of the charge against them. This is in accordance with Japanese criminal law. Eventually 149 persons were sent to Seoul to be placed on trial. Three were reported to have died under torture or as the result of imprisonment, twenty-three were exiled without trial or released, and 123 were arraigned at the Local Court in Seoul on June 28, 1912, on a charge of conspiracy to assassinate Count Terauchi, Governor-General of Korea.

"The character of the accused men is significant," wrote Dr. Arthur Judson Brown, an authority who can scarcely be accused by his bitterest critics of unfriendliness to Japan. "Here were no criminal types, no baser elements of the population, but men of the highest standing, long and intimately known to the missionaries as Koreans of faith and purity of life, and conspicuous for their good influence over the people. Two were Congregationalists, six Methodists and eighty-nine Presbyterians. Of the Presbyterians, five were pastors of churches, eight were elders, eight deacons, ten leaders of village groups of Christians, forty-two baptized church members, and thirteen catechumens.... It is about as difficult for those who know them to believe that any such number of Christian ministers, elders and teachers had committed crime as it would be for the people of New Jersey to believe that the faculty, students and local clergy of Princeton were conspirators and assassins."

Baron Yun Chi-ho, the most conspicuous of the prisoners, had formerly been Vice Foreign Minister under the old Korean Government, and was reckoned by all who knew him as one of the most progressive and sane men in the country. He was a prominent Christian, wealthy, of high family, a keen educationalist, vice-president of the Korean Y.M.C.A., had travelled largely, spoke English fluently, and had won the confidence and good will of every European or American in Korea with whom he came in contact. Yang Ki-tak, formerly Mr. Bethell's newspaper associate, had on this account been a marked man by the Japanese police. He had been previously arrested under the Peace Preservation Act, sentenced to two years' imprisonment and pardoned under an amnesty. He had also previously been examined twice in connection with the charge against the assassin of Prince Ito, and twice on account of the attack made on Yi, the traitor Premier, but had each time been acquitted. "I am not very much concerned as to what happens to me now," he said, "but I do protest against being punished on a charge of which I am innocent."

The case for the prosecution was based on the confessions of the prisoners themselves. According to these confessions, a body of Koreans, in association with the New People's Society, headed by Baron Yun Chi-ho, plotted to murder General Terauchi, and assembled at various railway stations for that purpose, when the Governor-General was travelling northwards, more particularly at Sun-chon, on December 28, 1910. They were armed with ready revolvers, short swords or daggers, and were only prevented from carrying out their purpose by the vigilance of the gendarmerie.

A number of missionaries were named as their associates or sympathizers. Chief of these was Mr. McCune, who, according to the confessions, distributed revolvers among the conspirators and told them at Sun-chon that he would point out the right man by shaking hands with him. Dr. Moffett of Pyeng-yang, Dr. Underwood of Seoul, Bishop Harris, the Methodist Bishop for Japan and Korea who had long been conspicuous as a defender of the Japanese Administration, and a number of other prominent missionaries were implicated.

When the prisoners were faced by these confessions in the open court they arose, one after another, almost without exception, and declared either that they had been forced from them by sustained and intolerable torture, or that they had been reduced by torture to insensibility and then on recovery had been told by the Japanese police that they had made the confessions. Those who had assented under torture had in nearly every case said "Yes" to the statements put to them by the police. Now that they could speak, they stoutly denied the charges. They knew nothing of any conspiracy. The only man who admitted a murder plot in court was clearly demented.

The trial was held in a fashion which aroused immediate and wide-spread indignation. It was held, of course, in Japanese, and the official translator was openly charged in court with minimizing and altering the statements made by the prisoners. The judges acted in a way that brought disgrace on the court, bullying, mocking and browbeating the prisoners. The high Japanese officials who attended heartily backed the sallies of the bench.

The missionaries who, according to the confessions, had encouraged the conspirators were not placed on trial. The prisoners urged that they should be allowed to call them and others as witnesses, and they were eager to come. The request was refused. Under Japanese law, the judges have an absolute right to decide what witnesses shall, or shall not be called. The prosecuting counsel denied the charge of torture, and declared that all of the men had been physically examined and not one of them had even a sign of having been subjected to such ill-treatment Thereupon prisoners rose up and asked to be allowed to show the marks still on them. "I was bound up for about a month and subjected to torture," said one. "I have still marks of it upon my body." But when he asked permission to display the marks to the Court, "the Court," according to the newspaper reports, "sternly refused to allow this to be done."

The trial closed on August 30th, and judgment was delivered on September 21st. Six prisoners, including Yun Chi-ho and Yang Ki-tak, were sentenced to ten years' penal servitude; eighteen to seven years' penal servitude; forty to six years; forty-two to five years; and seventeen discharged.

The trial was widely reported, and there was a wave of indignation, particularly in America. The case was brought before the Court of Appeal, and Judge Suzuki, who heard the appeal, was given orders by the Government-General that he was to act in conciliatory fashion. The whole atmosphere of the Court of Appeal was different. There was no bullying, no browbeating. The prisoners were listened to indulgently, and were allowed considerable latitude in developing their defence. Let me add that both in the first and in subsequent trials, prominent Japanese counsel appeared for the prisoners, and defended them in a manner in accordance with the best traditions of the law.

The prisoners were now permitted in the Appeal Court to relate in detail how their "confessions" had been extracted from them by torture. Here are some typical passages from the evidence.

Chi Sang-chu was a Presbyterian, and a clerk by calling. He denied that he was guilty.

"All my confession was made under torture. I did not make these statements of my own accord. The police said they must know what information they wanted. They stripped me naked, tied my hands behind my back, and hung me up in a doorway, removing the bench on which I stood. They swung me, making me bump against a door, like a crane dancing. When I lost consciousness, I was taken down and given water, and tortured again when I came to.

"A policeman covered my mouth with my hand, and poured water into my nose. Again my thumbs were tied behind my back, one arm over and one under, and I was hung up by the cord tying them. A lighted cigarette was pressed against my body, and I was struck in my private parts. Thus I was tortured for three or four days. One evening, just after the meal, I was hung up again, and was told that I would be released if I confessed, but if not I would be tortured till I died. They were determined to make me say whatever they wanted. Leaving me hanging, the policemen went to sleep, and I fainted from the torture of hanging there.

"When I came to, I found myself lying on the floor, the police giving me water. They showed me a paper, which they said was the order of release for Yi Keun-tak and O Hak-su, who had confessed. If I wanted to be set at liberty I must do the same. Then they beat me again. I saw the paper and managed with difficulty to read it. It was to the effect that they did confess and promised never to do such things again.

"I was then introduced to Yi Keun-tak, who, they said, had confessed and been acquitted, and they urged me to follow Yi's example. I urged them to treat me as they had treated Yi. They told me what to confess, but as I had never heard of such things I refused, and they said they had better kill me.

"They resumed their tortures, and after two or three months, being unable to bear it any longer, I confessed all that is required."

Paik Yong-sok, a milk seller and a Presbyterian, with eleven in his family, said he had been a Christian for fifteen years and had determined only to follow the teachings of the Bible; he had never thought of assassination or considered establishing the independence of the country. Having to support a family of eleven, he had no time for such things.

He had made the confession recited by the Court, but it was under compulsion and false. "For a number of days I was tortured twice by day and twice by night. I was blindfolded, hung up, beaten. Often I fainted, being unable to breathe. I thought I was dying and asked the police to shoot me, so intolerable were my tortures. Driven beyond the bounds of endurance by hunger, thirst and pain, I said I would say whatever they wanted.

"The police told me that I was of no account among the twenty million Koreans, and they could kill or acquit me as they pleased.... Meanwhile five or six police dropped in and said, 'Have you repented? Did you take part in the assassination plots?' It was too much for me to say 'Yes' to this question, so I replied 'No.' Immediately they slapped my cheeks, stripped me, struck, beat and tormented me. It is quite beyond my power to describe the difficulty of enduring such pain."

The man paused and pointed to a Japanese, Watanabe by name, sitting behind the judges, "That interpreter knows all about it," he said, "He was one of the men who struck me." Watanabe was pointed out by other prisoners as a man who had been prominent in tormenting them.

Im Do-myong, a barber and a Presbyterian, also fell into the hands of experts at the game.

"At the police headquarters, I was hung up, beaten with an iron rod and tortured twice a day. Then I was taken into the presence of superiors, the interpreter (pointing out Watanabe, who was sitting: behind the judges) being present, and tortured again.

"My thumbs were tied together at my back, the right arm being put back over the shoulder and the left arm turned up from underneath. Then I was hung up by the cord that bound my thumbs. The agony was unendurable. I fainted, was taken down, was given torture, and when I came to was tortured again."

By the Court: "It would be impossible to hang you by your thumbs."

Prisoner: "My great toes scarcely touched the ground. Under such circumstances I was told to say the same thing at the Public Procurator's Office, and as I feared that I should be tortured there, too, I said 'Yes' to all questions."

Some variety was introduced into the treatment of Cho Tok-chan, a Presbyterian pastor, at Chong-ju.

"The police asked me how many men took part in the attempt at Sun-chon, saying that as I was a pastor I must know all about it. They hung, beat and struck me, saying that I had taken part in the plot and was a member of the New People's Society. At last I fainted, and afterwards was unable to eat for a number of days.

"A policeman in uniform, with one stripe, twisted my fingers with a wire, so that they were badly swollen for a long time after. Then a man with two white stripes tortured me, declaring that I had taken part in the Sun-chon affair. I said that I was too busy with Christmas preparations to go anywhere, on which the policeman severely twisted my fingers with an iron rod."

Again came one of the dramatic pauses, while the prisoner pointed out a Japanese official sitting behind the judges, Tanaka by name. "The man who interpreted at that time is sitting behind you," he declared. "He knows it very well."

They extracted his confession. But it was some time before he had been able to sign it; his fingers were hurt too severely.

It was necessary, after the police examination, for prisoners to repeat their stories or confirm them before the procurator. This might originally have been intended as a protection for the prisoners. In Korea police and procurators worked together. However, steps were taken to prevent any retraction at that point.

"When I was taken to the Public Procurator's Office," continued the Presbyterian pastor, "I did not know the nature of the place, and being put in a separate room, I feared that it might be an even more dreadful place than the police headquarters. Generally, when examined at the police headquarters, my hands were free, but here I was brought up for cross-examination with my hands and arms pinioned very firmly, so I thought it must be a harder place. Moreover, an official pulled me very hard by the cords which bound my hands, which gave me excruciating pain, seeing how they had already been treated by the police."

The next prisoner, Yi Mong-yong, a Presbyterian money lender, also pointed out the proud Tanaka. He had been describing how the police kicked and struck him to make him say what they wanted. "One of them is behind you now," said he to the judges, pointing to Tanaka.

Some of the prisoners broke down while giving their evidence. Unimas described how he had been hung, beaten, stripped and tortured by the police, and again tortured in the office of the Public Procurator. "Having got so far," the reports continue, "the prisoner began to weep and make a loud outcry, saying that he had a mother who was eighty years old at home. With this pitiful scene, the hearing ended for the day."

Yi Tai-kyong was a teacher. The police reminded him that the murderer of Prince Ito was a Christian; he was a Christian, therefore--

"They hung, beat and otherwise tormented me, until I was compelled to acknowledge all the false fabrication about the plot. The following day I was again taken into Mr. Yamana's room and again tortured with an iron rod from the stove and other things, until I had acknowledged all the false statements.

"When asked what was the party's signal, I remained silent, as I knew nothing about it. But I was tortured again, and said, 'the church bell,' that being the only thing I could think of at the time."

"I confessed to the whole prosecution story, but only as the result of torture, to which I was submitted nine times, fainting on two occasions, and being tortured again on revival," said Pak Chou-hyong. "I made my false confession under a threat that I and my whole family would be killed. I reiterated it at the Public Procurator's Office, where I was conducted by two policemen, one of them a man with a gold tooth, who boxed my ears so hard that I still feel the pain, and who told me not to vary my story.

"Fearing that my whole family would be tortured, I agreed. But when I arrived before the Public Procurator, I forgot what I had been taught to say, and wept, asking the officials to read what I had to confess. This they did, and I said, 'Yes, yes.'"

Choi Che-kiu, a petty trader, repudiated his confession of having gone with a party to Sun-chon.

"Had such a large party attempted to go to the station," he said, "they must infallibly have been arrested on the first day. Were I guilty I would be ready to die at once. The whole story was invented by officials, and I was obliged to acquiesce in it by severe torture. One night I was taken to Nanzan hill by two policemen, suspended from a pine tree and a sharp sword put to my throat. Thinking I was going to be killed, I consented to say 'Yes' to any question put to me."

"No force can make you tell such a story as this, unless you consent voluntarily," interposed the Court.

"You may well say that," replied the prisoner, grimly. "But with the blade of a sword in my face and a lighted cigarette pressed against my body, I preferred acquiescence in a story, which they told me that Kim Syong had already confessed, to death."

The prisoner paused, and the Judge looked at him with his head on one side. Suddenly the prisoner burst into a passion of weeping, with loud, incoherent cries.

In the previous trial one of the prisoners, Kim Ik-kyo, was asked why he admitted all the facts at his preliminary examination. "If the police were to go down Chong-no (one of the busiest streets in Seoul)," he replied, "and indiscriminately arrest a number of passers-by, and then examine them by putting them to torture, I am sure they would soon confess to having taken part in a plot."

The same thing was put in another way by a prisoner, Kim Eung-pong. He related a long story of torture by binding, hanging, beating and burning, continued for fifteen days, during which he was often threatened with death. Then he was taken to the "supreme enquiry" office of the police headquarters, where he was stripped naked and beaten with an iron bar from the stove. This office, he understood, had control and power of life or death over the whole peninsula, so he was compelled to confess all that they wanted. "I even would have said that I killed my father, if they put it to me," he added.

Hear the tale of An Sei-whan. As An was called up in the Appeal Court, a wave of pity passed over the white men there, for An was a miserable object, pale and emaciated. He was a consumptive and afflicted with other ills. He had been in the Christian Hospital at Pyeng-yang most of the winter, and had nearly died there. He had been walking a little for a few days, when he was arrested at the hospital in April. He had been vomiting blood.

"In this condition I was taken to the police headquarters and tortured. My thumbs were hung together and I was hung up, with my toes barely touching the ground. I was taken down nearly dead, and made to stand for hours under a chest nearly as high as my chest. Next day, when I was put under the shelf again my hair was fastened to the board, and my left leg doubled at the knee and tied. Blood came up from my lung, but fearful of the police I swallowed it. Now, I think it would have been better if I had vomited it. Then they might have had pity on me; but I did not think so then.

"Again I was hung up by the thumbs, clear of the floor this time. At the end of five minutes I was nearly dead. I asked if it would do to assent to their questions, and they took me down and took me before some superiors. When I said anything unsatisfactory I was beaten, and in this way learned what was wanted. I had no wish to deny or admit anything, only to escape further pain."

He asked that some of the missionaries who knew him might be called, to show that he was too ill to take part in any conspiracy.

One old man, Yi Chang-sik, a Presbyterian for sixteen years, had refused even under the torture to confess, and had tried to escape by suicide. "I thought that I had better commit suicide than be killed by their cruel tortures," he said. "They asked me if I had joined the conspiracy at the suggestion of Mr. McCune. I would not consent to this, so they tortured me harder. I was nearly naked, and so cold water was poured upon me. I was also beaten. Sometimes I would be tortured till the early hours of the morning.

"I longed for death to deliver me. Thanks to heaven, I found a knife one night in my room. The warder was not very careful with me. I took it secretly, intending to cut my throat--but my hand had become too weak. So I stuck it erect in the floor, and tried to cut my throat that way. Alas! At this moment the warder surprised me. When I had endured torture for over forty days, I asked them to make me guilty or innocent as quickly as possible. When I was taken to the Public Procurator's, I had pains in my ears, body and limbs. I could not stand the torture and wanted to die."

"Having got so far," wrote a spectator, "the old man broke down and began to weep, crying louder and louder. He said something as he wept, but the interpreter could not make out what it was. The Court evidently pitied him and told him to stand down. He withdrew, sobbing."

A Presbyterian student from Sun-chon, Cha Heui-syon, was arrested and kept for four months in the gendarmes office, becoming very weak. Then he was taken to the police headquarters.

"First I was hung up by my thumbs, then my hands and legs were tied, and I was made to crouch under a shelf about as high as my chest, which was intensely painful, as I could neither sit nor stand. Something was put in my mouth. I vomited blood, yet I was beaten. I was stood up on a bench and tied up so that when it was removed, I was left hanging. The interpreter who has often been in this court (Watanabe) tortured me. My arms stiffened so that I could not stretch them. As I hung I was beaten with bamboos three or four feet long and with an iron rod, which on one occasion made the hand of the official who was wielding it bleed."

At last he gave in. He was too weak to speak. They took him down and massaged his arms, which were useless. He could only nod now to the statements that they put to him. Later on they took him to the Public Procurator. Here he attempted to deny his confession. "The Public Procurator was very angry," he said. "He struck the table, getting up and sitting down again. He jerked the cord by which my hands were tied, hurting me very severely."

The case of Baron Yun Chi-ho excited special interest. The Baron being a noble of high family, the police used more care in extracting his confession. He was examined day after day for ten days, the same questions being asked and denied day after day. One day when his nerves were in shreds, they tortured another prisoner in front of his eyes, and the examiner told him that if he would not confess, he was likely to share the same fate. They told him that the others had confessed and been punished; a hundred men had admitted the facts. He did not know then that the charge against him was conspiracy to murder. He determined to make a false confession, to escape torture. He was worn out with the ceaseless questioning, and he was afraid.

The rehearing in the Court of Appeal lasted fifty-one days. In the last days many of the prisoners were allowed to speak for themselves. They made a very favourable impression. Judgment was delivered on March 20th. The original judgment was quashed in every case, and the cases reconsidered. Ninety-nine of the prisoners were found not guilty. Baron Yun Chi-ho, Yang Ki-tak and four others were convicted. Five of them were sentenced to six years' penal servitude, and one to five years. Two other appeals were made, but the only result was to increase the sentence of the sixth man to six years. Three of the men finally convicted had been members of the staff of the Dai Han Mai Il Shinpo. The Japanese do not forget or forgive readily. They had an old score to pay against the staff of that paper.

I have never yet met a man, English, American or Japanese, acquainted with the case, or who followed the circumstances, who believed that there had been any plot at all. The whole thing, from first to last, was entirely a police-created charge. The Japanese authorities showed later that they themselves did not believe it. On the coronation of the Japanese Emperor, in February, 1915, the six prisoners were released as a sign of "Imperial clemency." Baron Yun Chi-ho was appointed Secretary of the Y.M.C.A, at Seoul on his release, and Count Terauchi (whom he was supposed to have plotted to murder) thereupon gave a liberal subscription to the Y. funds.

There was one sequel to the case. The Secretary of the Korean Y.M.C.A., Mr. Gillett, having satisfied himself of the innocence of Baron Yun and his associates, while the trial was pending, sent a letter to prominent people abroad, telling the facts. The letter, by the indiscretion of one man who received it, was published in newspapers. The Japanese authorities, in consequence, succeeded in driving Mr. Gillett out of Korea. Before driving him out, they tried to get him to come over on their side. Mr. Komatsu, Director of the Bureau for Foreign Affairs, asked him and Mr. Gerdine, the President, to call on him. "The Government has met the demands of the missionary body and released ninety-nine out of the hundred and five prisoners who stood trial at the Appeal Court," said Mr. Komatsu. "It is to be expected that the missionary body will in return do something to put the Government in a strong and favourable light before the people of Japan." Mr. Komatsu added that Judge Suzuki's action was in reality the action of the Government-General, a quaint illustration of the independence of the judiciary in Korea.

The Administration made a feeble attempt to deny the tortures. Its argument was that since torture was forbidden by law, it could not take place. Let we quote the official statement:

"A word should be added in reference to the absurd rumours spread abroad concerning it (the conspiracy case) such as that the measures taken by the authorities aimed at 'wiping out the Christian movement in Korea,' since the majority of the accused were Christian converts, and that most of the accused made 'false confessions against their will,' as they were subject to 'unendurable ill-treatment or torture.' As if such imputations could be sustained for one minute, when the modern regime ruling Japan is considered!... As to torture, several provisions of the Korean criminal code indirectly recognized it, but the law was revised and those provisions were rescinded when the former Korean law courts were reformed, by appointing to them Japanese judicial staffs, in August, 1908.... According to the new criminal law (judges, procurators or police) officials are liable, if they treat accused prisoners with violence or torture, to penal servitude or to imprisonment for a period not exceeding three years. In reply to the memorial presented to the Governor-General by certain missionaries in Korea, in January, 1912, he said, 'I assure you that the entire examination of the suspected persons or witnesses is being conducted in strict compliance with the provisions of the law, and the slightest divergence from the lawful process will under no circumstances be permitted.' How then could any one imagine that it was possible for officials under him to act under any other way than in accordance with the provisions of the law."

Unfortunately for the noble indignation of the writer, the torture left its marks, and many men are living as I write still bearing them. Others only escaped from the hell of the Japanese prison in Seoul to die. They were so broken that they never recovered.

XIV
THE INDEPENDENCE MOVEMENT

The people of Korea never assented to the annexation of their country. The Japanese control of means of communication prevented their protests from being fully known by the outside world.

It was explained that the movement against the Japanese was due to the work of Koreans living outside of the land and to foreign agitators. The Japanese blamed the missionaries. They blamed foreign publicists. I understand that I was and am esteemed a special malignant. They never thought to blame themselves. As a matter of fact, missionaries and the rest of us had nothing to do with it. The real origin of the movement was among the people themselves, and it was fostered, not by outsiders, but by the iron and unjust rule of Japan.

At the same time, the Koreans living in freedom were naturally concerned over conditions at home. The large Korean communities in Manchuria and Siberia, estimated to number in all two millions, the flourishing colony in the United States and Hawaii, the Koreans in Mexico and China heard with indignation of what was happening. Young students and political prisoners released after torture, who escaped to America, fanned the flame to white heat. The Koreans living outside Korea formed a National Association, with headquarters in San Francisco, under the Presidency of Dr. David Lee, which in 1919 claimed a million and a half adherents.

The steps taken by the Japanese to suppress and prevent discontent often created and fostered it. This was specially illustrated in the schools. The new educational system, with its constant inculcation of loyalty to the Mikado, made even the little girls violently Nationalist. School children were spied upon for incipient treason as though the lisping of childish lips might overthrow the throne. The speeches of boys and girls in junior schools, at their school exercises, were carefully noted, and the child who said anything that might be construed by the Censor as "dangerous thought" would be arrested, examined and punished.

The effect of this was what might have been expected. "They compel us to learn Japanese," said one little miss, sagely. "That does not matter. We are now able to understand what they say. They cannot understand what we say. All the better for us when the hour comes." On Independence Day the children, particularly in the Government schools, were found to be banded together and organized against Japan. They had no fear in expressing their views and sought martyrdom. Some of them won it.

The Japanese hoped much from the Chon-do Kyo, a powerful movement encouraged by the authorities because they thought that it would be a valuable counteractive to Christianity. Its leader was Son Pyung-hi, an old Korean friend of Japan. As far back as 1894, when the Japanese arranged the Tong-hak Rebellion in Korea, to give them an excuse for provoking war with China, Son was one of their leading agents. He believed that Western influence and in particular Western religion was inimical to his country, and he hoped by the Tong-haks to drive them out.

As a result of his activities, he had to flee from Korea, and he did not return until 1903. He became leader of the Chon-do Kyo, the Heavenly Way Society, a body that tried to include the best of many religions and give the benefits of Christian organization and fellowship without Christianity. He had learned many things while in exile, and was now keen on reform and education. Many of his old Tong-hak friends rallied around him, and the Chon-do Kyo soon numbered considerably over a million members.

Son realized after a time that the Japanese were not the friends but the enemies of his people. He made no violent protestations. He still maintained seemingly good relations with them. But his organization was put to work. His agents went over the country. Each adherent was called on to give three spoonfuls of rice a day. Close on a million dollars was accumulated. Most of this was afterwards seized by the Japanese.

The Chon-do Kyo and the native Christian leaders came together. The Christian pastors had up to now kept their people in check. But the burden was becoming intolerable. They gave the missionaries no inkling of what was brewing. They did not wish to get them in trouble. Their real grief was that their action would, they knew, make it harder for the Churches.

Two remarkable characters took the lead among the Christians, Pastor Kil and Yi Sang-jai. Pastor Kil of Pyeng-yang was one of the oldest and most famous Christians in Korea. He had become a leader in the early days, facing death for his faith. A man of powerful brain, of fine character and with the qualities of real leadership, he was looked up to by the people as British Nonconformists a generation ago regarded Charles Spurgeon. In recent years Kil had become almost blind, but continued his work.

I have already described in an earlier chapter how Yi Sang-jai, once Secretary to the Legation at Washington, became a Christian while thrown into prison for his political views. He was now a Y.M.C.A. leader, but he was held in universal veneration by all men--Christian and non-Christian alike--as a saint, as a man who walked with God and communed with Him.

When things seemed rapidly ripening, President Wilson made his famous declaration of the rights of weaker nations. One sentence went round among the Koreans, and its effect was electrical.

"What is the task that this League of Nations is to do?

"IT IS TO PROVIDE FOR THE FREEDOM OF SMALL NATIONS, TO PREVENT THE DOMINATION OF SMALL NATIONS BY BIG ONES."

Here was the clarion call to Korea. Here was hope! Here was the promise of freedom, given by the head of the nation they had all learned to love. If any outsider was responsible for the uprising of the Korean people, that outsider was Woodrow Wilson, President of the United States of America.

"Now is the time to act," said the people. For a start, they resolved to send delegates to present their case to the Paris Conference. Three leaders in America were chosen but were refused passports. Finally another young leader, Mr. Kiusic Kimm, succeeded in landing in France. Perhaps it would not be wise to say, at this time, how he managed to get there. He soon found that his mission was in vain. The Paris Conference would not receive him. President Wilson's declaration was not to be put into full effect.

The people resolved, by open and orderly demonstration, to support their delegate in France. There were some who would have started a violent revolution. The Christians would have none of it "Let us have no violence," said they. "Let us appeal to the conscience of Japan and of the world."

There were no constitutional means for them to employ to make their case heard. But if ever there was an effort at peaceful constitutional change, this was it. Instructions were sent out, surely the most extraordinary instructions ever issued under similar circumstances:--

> "Whatever you do
> DO NOT INSULT THE JAPANESE
> DO NOT THROW STONES
> DO NOT HIT WITH YOUR FISTS.
> For these are the acts of barbarians."

It was unnecessary to tell the people not to shoot, for the Japanese had long since taken all their weapons away, even their ancient sporting blunderbusses.

A favourable moment was approaching. The old Korean Emperor lay dead. One rumour was that he had committed suicide to avoid signing a document drawn up by the Japanese for presentation to the Peace Conference, saying that he was well satisfied with the present Government of his country. Another report, still more generally believed, was that he had committed suicide to prevent the marriage of his son, Prince Kon, to the Japanese Princess Nashinoto. The engagement of this young Prince to a Korean girl had been broken off when the Japanese acquired control of the Imperial House. Royal romances always appeal to the crowd. The heart of the people turned to the old Emperor again. Men, women and children put on straw shoes, signs of national mourning, and a hundred thousand people flocked to Seoul to witness the funeral ceremonies.

The funeral was to take place on March 4th. By now the Japanese suspected something to be afoot. The astonishing thing is that the Koreans had been able to keep it from them so long. A network of organizations had been created all over the country. The Japanese hurried their preparations to prevent popular demonstrations on the day of the funeral. The leaders learned of this, and outwitted the police by a simple device. They resolved to make their demonstration not on Tuesday, March 4th, but on the previous Saturday.

Gatherings were arranged for all over the country. A Declaration of Independence was drawn up in advance and delivered to the different centres. Here it was mimeographed, and girls and boys organized themselves to ensure its distribution. Meetings, processions and demonstrations in all the big cities were planned.

Thirty-three men chose martyrdom. They were to be the original signers of the Declaration of Independence. They knew that at the best this must mean heavy punishment for them, and at the worst might well mean death. They had no delusions. Pastor Kil's son had died from the effects of Japanese torture, Yang Chun-paik and Yi Seung-hun, two of the signers, had been victims in the Conspiracy case. The first two names on the list of signers were Son Pyung-hi, leader of the Chon-do Kyo, and Pastor Kil.

On the morning of March 1st the group of thirty-two met at the Pagoda Restaurant at Seoul. Pastor Kil was the only absentee; he had been temporarily delayed on his journey from Pyeng-yang.

Some prominent Japanese had been invited to eat with the Koreans. After the meal, the Declaration was produced before their guests and read. It was despatched to the Governor-General. Then the signers rang up the Central Police Station, informed the shocked officials of what they had done, and added that they would wait in the restaurant until the police van came to arrest them.

The automobile prison van, with them inside, had to make its way to the police station through dense crowds, cheering and shouting, "Mansei! Mansei! Mansei!" It was the old national battle cry, "May Korea live ten thousand years." Old flags had been brought out, old Korean flags, with the red and blue germ on the white ground, and were being widely waved. "Mansei!" Not only Seoul but the whole country had in a few minutes broken out in open demonstration. A new kind of revolt had begun.

Pastor Kil, arriving late, hurried to the police station to take his place with his comrades.

The Declaration of Independence is a document impossible to summarize, if one is to do full justice to it. It is written in the lofty tone of the ancient prophets. It was something more than the aspiration of the Korean people. It was the cry of the New Asia, struggling to find its way out of oppression and mediaeval militarism into the promised land of liberty and peace.

THE PROCLAMATION OF KOREAN INDEPENDENCE

"We herewith proclaim the independence of Korea and the liberty of the Korean people. We tell it to the world in witness of the equality of all nations and we pass it on to our posterity as their inherent right.

"We make this proclamation, having back of us 5,000 years of history, and 20,000,000 of a united loyal people. We take this step to insure to our children for all time to come, personal liberty in accord with the awakening consciousness of this new era. This is the clear leading of God, the moving principle of the present age, the whole human race's just claim. It is something that cannot be stamped out, or stifled, or gagged, or suppressed by any means.

"Victims of an older age, when brute force and the spirit of plunder ruled, we have come after these long thousands of years to experience the agony of ten years of foreign oppression, with every loss to the right to live, every restriction of the freedom of thought, every damage done to the dignity of life, every opportunity lost for a share in the intelligent advance of the age in which we live.

"Assuredly, if the defects of the past are to be rectified, if the agony of the present is to be unloosed, if the future oppression is to be avoided, if thought is to be set free, if right of action is to be given a place, if we are to attain to any way of progress, if we are to deliver our children from the painful, shameful heritage, if we are to leave blessing and

happiness intact for those who succeed us, the first of all
necessary things is the clear-cut independence of our people.
What cannot our twenty millions do, every man with sword in
heart, in this day when human nature and conscience are making a
stand for truth and right? What barrier can we not break, what
purpose can we not accomplish?

"We have no desire to accuse Japan of breaking many solemn
treaties since 1636, nor to single out specially the teachers in
the schools or government officials who treat the heritage of our
ancestors as a colony of their own, and our people and their
civilization as a nation of savages, finding delight only in
beating us down and bringing us under their heel.

"We have no wish to find special fault with Japan's lack of
fairness or her contempt of our civilization and the principles
on which her state rests; we, who have greater cause to reprimand
ourselves, need not spend precious time in finding fault with
others; neither need we, who require so urgently to build for the
future, spend useless hours over what is past and gone. Our
urgent need to-day is the setting up of this house of ours and
not a discussion of who has broken it down, or what has caused
its ruin. Our work is to clear the future of defects in accord
with the earnest dictates of conscience. Let us not be filled
with bitterness or resentment over past agonies or past occasions
for anger.

"Our part is to influence the Japanese government, dominated as
it is by the old idea of brute force which thinks to run counter
to reason and universal law, so that it will change, act honestly
and in accord with the principles of right and truth.

"The result of annexation, brought about without any conference with the Korean people, is that the Japanese, indifferent to us, use every kind of partiality for their own, and by a false set of figures show a profit and loss account between us two peoples most untrue, digging a trench of everlasting resentment deeper and deeper the farther they go.

"Ought not the way of enlightened courage to be to correct the evils of the past by ways that are sincere, and by true sympathy and friendly feeling make a new world in which the two peoples will be equally blessed?

"To bind by force twenty millions of resentful Koreans will mean not only loss of peace forever for this part of the Far East, but also will increase the evergrowing suspicion of four hundred millions of Chinese--upon whom depends the danger or safety of the Far East--besides strengthening the hatred of Japan. From this all the rest of the East will suffer. To-day Korean independence will mean not only daily life and happiness for us, but also it would mean Japan's departure from an evil way and exaltation to the place of true protector of the East, so that China, too, even in her dreams, would put all fear of Japan aside. This thought comes from no minor resentment, but from a large hope for the future welfare and blessing of mankind.

"A new era wakes before our eyes, the old world of force is gone, and the new world of righteousness and truth is here. Out of the experience and travail of the old world arises this light on life's affairs. The insects stifled by the foe and snow of winter awake at this same time with the breezes of spring and the soft light of the sun upon them.

"It is the day of the restoration of all things on the full tide of which we set forth, without delay or fear. We desire a full measure of satisfaction in the way of liberty and the pursuit of happiness, and an opportunity to develop what is in us for the glory of our people.

"We awake now from the old world with its darkened conditions in full determination and one heart and one mind, with right on our side, along with the forces of nature, to a new life. May all the ancestors to the thousands and ten thousand generations aid us from within and all the force of the world aid us from without, and let the day we take hold be the day of our attainment. In this hope we go forward.

THREE ITEMS OF AGREEMENT

"1. This work of ours is in behalf of truth, religion and life, undertaken at the request of our people, in order to make known their desire for liberty. Let no violence be done to any one.

"2. Let those who follow us, every man, all the time, every hour, show forth with gladness this same mind.

"3. Let all things be done decently and in order, so that our behaviour to the very end may be honourable and upright."

The 4252nd year of the Kingdom of Korea 3d Month.

Representatives of the people.

The signatures attached to the document are:

Son Pyung-hi, Kil Sun Chu, Yi Pil Chu, Paik Yong Sung, Kim Won Kyu, Kim Pyung Cho, Kim Chang Choon, Kwon Dong Chin, Kwon Byung Duk, Na Yong Whan, Na In Hup, Yang Chun Paik, Yang Han Mook, Lew Yer Dai, Yi Kop Sung, Yi Mung Yong, Yi Seung Hoon, Yi Chong Hoon, Yi Chong Il, Lim Yei Whan, Pak Choon Seung, Pak Hi Do, Pak Tong Wan, Sin Hong Sik, Sin Suk Ku, Oh Sei Chang, Oh Wha Young, Chung Choon Su, Choi Sung Mo, Choi In, Han Yong Woon, Hong Byung Ki, Hong Ki Cho.

XV
THE PEOPLE SPEAK--THE TYRANTS ANSWER

On Saturday, March 1st, at two in the afternoon, in a large number of centres of population throughout the country, the Declaration of Korean Independence was solemnly read, usually to large assemblies, by representative citizens. In some places, the leaders of the Christians and the leaders of the non-Christian bodies acted in common. In other places, by mutual agreement, two gatherings were held at the same time, the one for Christians and the other for non-Christians. Then the two met in the streets, and sometimes headed by a band they marched down the street shouting "Mansei" until they were dispersed. Every detail had been thought out. Large numbers of copies of declarations of independence were ready. These were circulated, usually by boys and schoolgirls, sometimes by women, each city being mapped out in districts.

It was soon seen that every class of the community was united. Men who had been ennobled by the Japanese stood with the coolies; shopkeepers closed their stores, policemen who had worked under the Japanese took off their uniforms and joined the crowds, porters and labourers, scholars and preachers, men and women all came together.

In every other Korean demonstration, for untold centuries, only part of the nation had been included. When the yang-bans started a political revolt, in the old days, they did not recognize that such a thing as popular opinion existed and did not trouble to consult it. Korea had long known demonstrations of great family against great family, of Yis against Mins; of section against section, as when the Conservatives fought the Progressives; and of Independents against the old Court Gang. But now all were one. And with the men were the women, and even the children. Boys of six told their fathers to be firm and never to yield, as they were carried off to prison; girls of ten and twelve prepared themselves to go to jail.

The movement was a demonstration, not a riot. On the opening day and afterwards--until the Japanese drove some of the people to fury--there was no violence. The Japanese, scattered all over the country, were uninjured; the Japanese shops were left alone; when the police attacked, elders ordered the people to submit and to offer no resistance. The weak things had set themselves up to confound the strong.

At first, the Japanese authorities were so completely taken by surprise that they did not know what to do. Then the word was passed round that the movement was to be suppressed by relentless severity. And so Japan lost her last chance of winning the people of Korea and of wiping out the accentuated ill-will of centuries.

The first plan of the Japanese was to attack every gathering of people and disperse it, and to arrest every person who took part in the demonstrations or was supposed to have a hand in them. Japanese civilians were armed with clubs and swords and given carte blanche to attack any Korean they suspected of being a demonstrator. They interpreted these instructions freely. Firemen were sent out with poles with the big firemen's hooks at the end. A single pull with one of these hooks meant death or horrible mutilation for any person they struck.

The police used their swords freely. What I mean by "freely" can best be shown by one incident A little gathering of men started shouting "Mansei" in a street in Seoul. The police came after them, and they vanished. One man--it is not clear whether he called "Mansei" or was an accidental spectator--was pushed in the deep gutter by the roadside as the demonstrators rushed away. As he struggled out the police came up. There was no question of the man resisting or not resisting. He was unarmed and alone. They cut off his ears, cut them off level with his cheek, they slit up his fingers, they hacked his body, and then they left him for dead. He was carried off by some horrified spectators, and died a few hours later. A photograph of his body lies before me as I write. I showed the photograph one evening to two or three men in New York City. Next day I met the men again. "We had nightmare all night long, because of that picture," they told me.

In Seoul, when the thirty-three leaders were arrested, a demonstration was held in the Park and the Declaration read there. Then the crowd made an orderly demonstration in the streets, waving flags and hats, shouting "Mansei," parading in front of the Consulates and public buildings, and sending letters to the Consuls informing them of what they had done. There was no violence. The police, mounted and foot, tried to disperse the crowds and made numerous arrests, but the throngs were so dense that they could not scatter them.

Next day was Sunday. Here the strong Christian influences stopped demonstrations, for the Korean Christians observe the Sunday strictly. This gave the Japanese authorities time to gather their forces. Numerous arrests were made that day, not only in Seoul but all over the country. On Monday there was the funeral of the ex-Emperor. The people were quiet then. It was noticed that the school children were entirely absent from their places along the line of march. They had struck.

On Wednesday life was supposed to resume its normal aspects again. The schools reopened, but there were no pupils. The shops remained closed. The coolies in official employ did not come to work. The authorities sent police to order the shopkeepers to open. They opened while the police were by, and closed immediately they were out of sight. Finally troops were placed outside the shops to see that they remained open. The shopkeepers sat passive, and informed any chance enquirer that they did not have what he wanted. This continued for some weeks.

The authorities were specially disturbed by the refusal of the children to come to school. In one large junior school, the boys were implored to come for their Commencement exercises, and to receive their certificates. Let me tell the scene that followed, as described to me by people in the city. The boys apparently yielded, and the Commencement ceremonies were begun, in the presence of a number of official and other distinguished Japanese guests. The precious certificates were handed out to each lad. Then the head boy, a little fellow of about twelve or thirteen, came to the front to make the school speech of thanks to his teachers and to the authorities. He was the impersonation of courtesy. Every bow was given to the full; he lingered over the honorifics, as though he loved the sound of them. The distinguished guests were delighted. Then came the end. "I have only this now to say," the lad concluded. A change came over his voice. He straightened himself up, and there was a look of resolution in his eyes. He knew that the cry he was about to utter had brought death to many during the past few days. "We beg one thing more of you." He plunged one hand in his garment, pulled out the Korean flag, the possession of which is a crime. Waving the flag, he cried out, "Give us back our country.

May Korea live forever. Mansei!"

All the boys jumped up from their seats, each one pulling out a flag from under his coat and waved it, calling, "Mansei! Mansei! Mansei!" They tore up their precious certificates, in front of the now horrified guests, threw them on the ground, and trooped out.

At nine o'clock that Wednesday morning there was a great demonstration of students and high school girls around the palace. The girls had planned out their part ahead. A big crowd gathered around. Then a large force of police rushed on them, with drawn swords, knocking down, beating and arresting, lads and girls alike. The girls were treated as roughly as the men. Over four hundred, including one hundred girl students, were taken to the police station that morning. What happened to the girls there, I tell in a later chapter. Fifteen nurse-probationers of the Severance Hospital, one of the most famous missionary hospitals in the Far East, hurried out with bandages to bind up the wounded. The police took them in custody also. They were severely examined, to find if the foreigners had instigated them to take part in the demonstrations, but were released the same afternoon.

As Prince Yi was returning from the ex-Emperor's funeral that afternoon, a group of twenty literati approached his carriage and attempted to present a petition. They were stopped by the police. A petition was sent by the literati to the Governor-General; the delegates were told to take it to the police office. Here they were arrested.

Two of the most famous nobles in the land, Viscount Kim and Viscount Li, sent a dignified petition to the Governor-General, begging him to listen to the people, and deploring the severe measures taken to suppress the demonstrations. Viscount Kim was senior peer, head of the Confucian College, and had ever been a friend of Japan. As far back as 1866, he had run the risk of death by urging the King to open the country to outside nations and to conclude a treaty with Japan. The Japanese had made him one of their new Korean peerage. He was now eighty-five, feeble and bedridden. The protest of himself and his fellow senior was measured, polished, moved with a deep sympathy for the people, but with nothing in it to which the Governor-General should have taken offence.

The Japanese treatment of these two nobles was crowning proof of their incapacity to rule another people. The two were at once arrested, and with them various male members of their families. Kim was so ill that he could not be immediately moved, so a guard was placed over his house. All were brought to trial at Seoul in July. With Viscount Kim were Kim Ki-ju, his grandson, and Kim Yu-mon. With Viscount Li was his relative Li Ken-tai. The charge against them was, of violating the Peace Preservation Act. Ki-ju aggravated his position by trying to defend himself. The Japanese press reported that he was reported to "have assumed a very hostile attitude to the bench enunciating this theory and that in defence of his cause." This statement is the best condemnation of the trial. Where a prisoner is deemed to add to his guilt by attempting to defend himself, justice has disappeared.

Viscount Kim was sentenced to two years' penal servitude, and Viscount Li to eighteen months, both sentences being stayed for three years. Kim Ki-ju, Kim Yu-mon and Li Ken-tai were sentenced to hard labour for eighteen months, twelve months and six months respectively. The sentence reflected disgrace on the Government that instituted the prosecution and decreed the punishment.

The white people of Seoul were horrified by the Japanese treatment of badly wounded men who flocked to the Severance Hospital for aid. Some of these, almost fatally wounded, were put to bed. The Japanese police came and demanded that they should be delivered up to them. The doctors pointed out that it probably would be fatal to move them. The police persisted, and finally carried off three men. It was reported that one man they took off in this fashion was flogged to death.

Reports were beginning to come in from other parts. There had been demonstrations throughout the north, right up to Wiju, on the Manchurian border. At Song-chon, it was reported, thirty had been killed, a number wounded, and three hundred arrested Pyeng-yang had been the centre of a particularly impressive movement, which had been sternly repressed. From the east coast, away at Hameung, there came similar tidings. The Japanese stated that things were quiet in the south until Wednesday, when there was an outbreak at Kun-san, led by the pupils of a Christian school. The Japanese at once seized on the participation of the Christians, the press declaring that the American missionaries were at the bottom of it. A deliberate attempt was made to stir up the Japanese population against the Americans. Numbers of houses of American missionaries and leaders of philanthropic work were searched. Several of them were called to the police offices and examined; some were stopped in the streets and searched. Unable to find any evidence against the missionaries, the Japanese turned on the Korean Christians. Soon nearly every Korean Christian pastor in Seoul was in jail; and news came from many parts of the burning of churches, the arrest of leading Christians, and the flogging of their congregations. The Japanese authorities, on pressure from the American consular officials, issued statements that the missionaries had nothing to do with the uprising, but in practice they acted as though the rising were essentially a Christian movement.

In the country people were stopped by soldiers when walking along the roads, and asked, "Are you Christians?" If they answered, "Yes," they were beaten; if "No," they were allowed to go. The local gendarmes told the people in many villages that Christianity was to be wiped out and all Christians shot. "Christians are being arrested wholesale and beaten simply because they are Christians," came the reports from many parts.

Soon dreadful stories came from the prisons, not only in Seoul, but in many other parts. Men who had been released after investigation, as innocent, told of the tortures inflicted on them in the police offices, and showed their jellied and blackened flesh in proof. Some were even inconsiderate enough to die a few days after release, and on examination their bodies and heads were found horribly damaged. The treatment may be summed up in a paragraph from a statement by the Rev. A.E. Armstrong, of the Board of Foreign Missions of the Presbyterian Church of Canada, who was on a visit to Korea at the time:

> "The tortures which the Koreans suffer at the hands of the police and gendarmes are identical with those employed in the famous conspiracy trials. I read affidavits, now on their way to the United States and British Governments, which made one's blood boil, so frightful were the means used in trying to extort confessions from prisoners. And many of these had no part in the demonstrations, but were simply onlookers."

Within a fortnight, the arrests numbered thousands in Seoul alone. Every man, particularly every student, suspected of participation was jailed. But it was evident that the authorities had not secured the leaders, or else that the leaders had arranged a system by which there were men always ready to step into the place of those who were taken. The official organ, the Seoul Press, would come out with an announcement that the agitation had now died down; two or three days later there would be another great demonstration in the streets. The hundred thousand visitors who had come to Seoul for the funeral returned home to start agitations in their own districts. The authorities were particularly annoyed at their inability to discover the editors and publishers of the secret paper of the protest, the Independence News, which appeared in mimeographed form. To prevent its publication the authorities took control of mimeograph paper, and seized every mimeograph machine they could find. Time after time it was stated that the editors of the paper had been secured; the announcement was barely published before fresh editions would mysteriously appear in Seoul and in the provinces.

Despite every effort to minimize it, news of the happenings gradually crept out and were published abroad. Mr. I. Yamagata, the Director-General of Administration, was called to Tokyo for a conference with the Government. Much was hoped by many friends of Japan in America from this. It was believed that the Liberal Premier of Japan, the Hon. T. Hara, would promptly declare himself against the cruelties that had been employed. Unfortunately these hopes were disappointed. While speaking reassuringly to foreign enquirers, Mr. Hara and his Government officially determined on still harsher measures.

Mr. Yamagata's own statement, issued on his return, announced that after conference with the Premier, an audience with the Emperor and conferences with the Cabinet "decision was reached in favour of taking drastic measures by despatching more troops to the peninsula."

> "In the first stage of the trouble, the Government-General was in favour of mild measures (!), and it was hoped to quell the agitation by peaceful methods," Mr. Yamagata continued. "It is to be regretted, however, that the agitation has gradually spread to all parts of the peninsula, while the nature of the disturbance has become malignant, and it was to cope with this situation that the Government was obliged to resort to force. In spite of this, the trouble has not only continued, but has become so

uncontrollable and wide-spread that the police and military force hitherto in use has been found insufficient, necessitating the despatch of more troops and gendarmes from the mother country.... Should they (the agitators) continue the present trouble, it would be necessary to show them the full power of the military force. It is earnestly to be hoped that the trouble will be settled peacefully, before the troops are obliged to use their bayonets."

Count Hasegawa, the Governor-General, had already issued various proclamations, telling the people of the Imperial benevolence of Japan, warning them that the watchword "self-determination of races" was utterly irrevelant to Japan, and warning them of the relentless punishment that would fall on those who committed offences against the peace. Here is one of the proclamations. It may be taken as typical of all:

"When the State funeral of the late Prince Yi was on the point of being held, I issued an instruction that the people should help one another to mourn his loss in a quiet and respectful manner and avoid any rash act or disorder. Alas! I was deeply chagrined to see that, instigated by certain refractory men, people started a riot in Seoul and other places. Rumour was recently circulated that at the recent Peace Conference in Paris and other places, the independence of Chosen was recognized by foreign Powers, but the rumour is absolutely groundless. It need hardly be stated that the sovereignty of the Japanese Empire is irrevocably established in the past, and will never be broken in the future. During the ten years since annexation, the Imperial benevolence has gradually reached all parts of the country, and it is now recognized throughout the world that the country has made a marked advancement in the securing of safety to life, and property, and the development of education and industry. Those

who are trying to mislead the people by disseminating such a
rumour as cited know their own purpose, but it is certain that
the day of repentance will come to all who, discarding their
studies or vocations, take part in the mad movement. Immediate
awakening is urgently required.

"The mother country and Chosen, now merging in one body, makes a
State. Its population and strength were found adequate enough to
enter upon a League with the Powers and conduct to the promotion
of world peace and enlightenment, while at the same time the
Empire is going faithfully to discharge its duty as an Ally by
saving its neighbour from difficulty. This is the moment of time
when the bonds of unity between the Japanese and Koreans are to
be more firmly tightened and nothing will be left undone to
fulfill the mission of the Empire and to establish its prestige
on the globe. It is evident that the two peoples, which have ever
been in inseparably close relations from of old, have lately been
even more closely connected. The recent episodes are by no means
due to any antipathy between the two peoples. It will be most
unwise credulously to swallow the utterances of those refractory
people who, resident always abroad, are not well informed upon
the real conditions in the peninsula, but, nevertheless, are
attempting to mislead their brethren by spreading wild fictions
and thus disturbing the peace of the Empire, only to bring on
themselves the derision of the Powers for their indulgence in
unbridled imagination in seizing upon the watchword
'self-determination of races' which is utterly irrelevant to
Chosen, and in committing themselves to thoughtless act and
language. The Government are now doing their utmost to put an end
to such unruly behaviour and will relentlessly punish anybody
daring to commit offences against the peace. The present
excitement will soon cease to exist, but it is to be hoped that
the people on their part will do their share in restoring quiet

by rightly guarding their wards and neighbours so as to save them from any offence committing a severe penalty."[13]

The new era of relentless severity began by the enactment of various fresh laws. The regulations for Koreans going from or coming into their country were made more rigid. The Regulations Concerning Visitors and Residents had already been revised in mid-March. Under these, any person who, even as a non-commercial act, allowed a foreigner to stay in his or her house for a night or more must hereafter at once report the fact to the police or gendarmes. A fresh ordinance against agitators was published in the Official Gazette. It provided that anybody interfering or attempting to interfere in the preservation of peace and order with a view to bringing about political change would be punished by penal servitude or imprisonment for a period not exceeding ten years. The ordinance would apply to offences committed by subjects of the Empire committed outside its domains, and it was specially emphasized in the explanations of the new law given out that it would apply to foreigners as well as Japanese or Koreans.

The Government-General introduced a new principle, generally regarded by jurists of all lands as unjust and indefensible. They made the law retroactive. People who were found guilty of this offence, their acts being committed before the new law came into force, were to be sentenced under it, and not under the much milder old law. This was done.

The Koreans were quickly to learn what the new military regime meant. One of the first examples was at Cheamni, a village some miles from Suigen, on the Seoul-Fusan Railway. Various rumours reached Seoul that this place had been destroyed, and a party of Americans, including Mr. Curtice of the Consulate, Mr. Underwood, son of the famous missionary pioneer, and himself a missionary and a correspondent of the Japan Advertiser, went to investigate. After considerable enquiry they reached a place which had been a village of forty houses. They found only four or five standing. All the rest were smoking ruins.

"We passed along the path," wrote the correspondent of the Japan Advertiser, "which ran along the front of the village lengthwise, and in about the middle we came on a compound surrounded by burnt poplars, which was filled with glowing

---

13   Quoted from the Seoul Press.

ashes. It was here that we found a body frightfully burned and twisted, either of a young man or a woman. This place we found later was the Christian church, and on coming down from another direction on our return I found a second body, evidently that of a man, also badly burned, lying just outside the church compound. The odour of burned flesh in the vicinity of the church was sickening.

"We proceeded to the end of the village and climbed the hill, where we found several groups of people huddled under little straw shelters, with a few of their pitiful belongings about them. They were mostly women, some old, others young mothers with babes at breast, but all sunk in the dull apathy of abject misery and despair.

"Talking to them in their own language and with sympathy, Mr. Underwood soon won the confidence of several and got the story of what happened from different groups, and in every case these stories tallied in the essential facts. The day before we arrived, soldiers came to the village, some time in the early afternoon, and ordered all the male Christians to gather in the church. When they had so gathered, to a number estimated to be thirty by our informers, the soldiers opened fire on them with rifles and then proceeded into the church and finished them off with sword and bayonets. After this they set fire to the church, but as the direction of the wind and the central position of the church prevented the upper houses catching, soldiers fired these houses individually, and after a time left.

"As we passed down the ruined village, returning to our rikishas, we came on the last house of the village, which was standing intact, and entered in conversation with the owner, a very old man. He attributed the safety of his house to its being slightly removed, and to a vagary of the wind. He was alive because he was not a Christian and had not been called into the church. The details of his story of the occurrence tallied exactly with the others, as to what had happened."

One example will serve to show what was going on now all over the country. The following letter was written by a cultured American holding a responsible position in Korea:

"Had the authorities handled this matter in a different way, this
letter would never have been written. We are not out here to mix
in politics, and so long as it remained a purely political

problem, we had no desire to say anything on one side or the other. But the appeal of the Koreans has been met in such a way that it has been taken out of the realm of mere politics and has become a question of humanity. When it comes to weakness and helplessness being pitted against inhumanity, there can be no such thing as neutrality.

"I have seen personal friends of mine among the Koreans, educated men, middle-aged men, who up to that time had no part in the demonstrations, parts of whose bodies had been beaten to a pulp under police orders.

"A few hundred yards from where I am writing, the beating goes on, day after day. The victims are tied down on a frame and beaten on the naked body with rods till they become unconscious. Then cold water is poured on them until they revive, when the process is repeated. It is sometimes repeated many times. Reliable information comes to me that in some cases arms and legs have been broken.

"Men, women and children are shot down or bayonetted. The Christian church is specially chosen as an object of fury, and to the Christians is meted out special severity....

"A few miles from here, a band of soldiers entered a village and ordered the men to leave, the women to remain behind. But the men were afraid to leave their women, and sent the women away first. For this the men were beaten.

"A short distance from this village, this band is reported to have met a Korean woman riding in a rickshaw. She was violated by four of the soldiers and left unconscious. A Korean reported the doings of this band of soldiers to the military commander of the

district in which it occurred and the commander ordered him to be
beaten for reporting it.

"Word comes to me to-day from another province of a woman who was
stripped and strung up by the thumbs for six hours in an effort
to get her to tell the whereabouts of her husband. She probably
did not know.

"The woes of Belgium under German domination have filled our ears
for the past four years, and rightly so. The Belgian Government
has recently announced that during the more than four years that
the Germans held the country, six thousand civilians were put to
death by the Germans. Here in this land it is probably safe to
say that two thousand men, women and children, empty handed and
helpless, have been put to death in seven weeks. You may draw
your own conclusions!

"As for the Koreans, they are a marvel to us all. Even those of
us who have known them for many years, and have believed them to
be capable of great things, were surprised. Their self-restraint,
their fortitude, their endurance and their heroism have seldom
been surpassed. As an American I have been accustomed to hear, as
a boy, of the 'spirit of 76,' but I have seen it out here, and it
was under a yellow skin. More than one foreigner is saying, these
days, 'I am proud of the Koreans.'"

There were exciting scenes in Sun-chon. This city is one of the great centres
of Christianity in Korea, and its people, hardy and independent northerners, have
for long been suspected by the Japanese. Large numbers of leaders of the church
and students at the missionary academy had been arrested, confined for a very long
period and ill-treated at the time of the Conspiracy trial. They were all found to be
innocent later, on the retrial at the Appeal Court. This had not tended to promote
harmonious relations between the two peoples.

Various notices and appeals were circulated among the people. Many of them, issued by the leaders, strongly urged the people to avoid insulting behaviour, insulting language or violence towards the Japanese.

"Pray morning, noon and night, and fast on Sundays" was the notice to the Christians. Other appeals ran:

"Think, dear Korean brothers!

"What place have we or our children? Where can we speak? What has become of our land?

"Fellow countrymen, we are of one blood. Can we be indifferent? At this time, how can you Japanese show such ill feeling and such treachery? How can you injure us with guns and swords? How can your violence be so deep?

"Koreans, if in the past for small things we have suffered injuries, how much more shall we suffer to-day? Even though your flesh be torn from you, little by little, you can stand it! Think of the past. Think of the future! We stand together for those who are dying for Korea.

"We have been held in bondage. If we do not become free at this time, we shall never be able to gain freedom. Brethren, it can be done! It is possible! Do not be discouraged! Give up your business for the moment and shout for Korea. Injury to life and property are of consequence, but right and liberty are far more important. Until the news of the Peace Conference is received, do not cease. We are not wood and stones, but flesh and blood. Can we not speak out? Why go back and become discouraged? Do not fear death! Even though I die, my children and grandchildren shall enjoy the blessings of liberty. Mansei! Mansei! Mansei!"

Mr. D.V. Hudson, of the Southern Presbyterian University at Shanghai, brought the records of many outrages back with him on his return to America. From them I take the following:

> "At Maingsang, South Pyeng-yang Province, the following incident took place on March 3rd. When the uprising first broke out there were no Japanese gendarmes in the village, but Koreans only. The people there were mostly Chun-do Kyo followers, so no Christians were involved in the trouble. These Chun-do Kyo people gathered on the appointed day for the Korean Independence celebration, and held the usual speeches and shouting of 'Mansei.' The Korean gendarmes did not want to or dared not interfere, so that day was spent by the people as they pleased.

> "A few days later Japanese soldiers arrived to investigate and to put down the uprising. They found the people meeting again, ostensibly to honour one of their teachers. The soldiers immediately interfered, seized the leader of the meeting and led him away to the gendarme station. He was badly treated in the affray and the people were badly incensed. So they followed the soldiers to the station, hoping to effect the release of their leader. The soldiers tried to drive them away. Some left but others remained.

> "The police station was surrounded by a stone wall, with but one gate to the enclosure. The soldiers permitted those who insisted on following to enter, and, when they had entered, closed the door; then the soldiers deliberately set to work, shooting them down in cold blood. Only three of the fifty-six escaped death."

Let me give one other statement by a newspaper man. I might go on with tale after tale of brutality and fill another volume. Mr. William R. Giles is a Far Eastern correspondent well known for the sanity of his views and his careful statements of facts. He represents the Chicago Daily News at Peking. He visited Korea shortly after the uprising, specially to learn the truth. He remained there many weeks. Here is his deliberate verdict:

"Pekin, June 14th.--After nearly three months of travelling in Korea, in which time I journeyed from the north to the extreme south, I find that the charges of misgovernment, torture and useless slaughter by the Japanese to be substantially correct.

"In the country districts I heard stories of useless murder and crimes against women. A number of the latter cases were brought to my notice. One of the victims was a patient in a missionary hospital.

"In a valley about fifty miles from Fusan, the Japanese soldiery closed up a horseshoe-shaped valley surrounded by high hills, and then shot down the villagers who attempted to escape by climbing the steep slopes. I was informed that more than 100 persons were killed in this affray.

"In Taku, a large city midway between Seoul and Fusan, hundreds of cases of torture occurred, and many of the victims of ill-treatment were in the hospitals. In Seoul, the capital, strings of prisoners were seen daily being taken to jails which were already crowded.

"While I was in this city I spent some time in the Severance Hospital as a patient, and saw wounded men taken out by the police, one of them having been beaten to death. Two days later the hospital repeatedly was entered and the patients catechized, those in charge being unable to prevent it. Detectives even attempted in the night time secretly to enter my room while I was critically ill.

"In Seoul, Koreans were not allowed to be on the streets after dark and were not allowed to gather in groups larger than three. All the prisoners were brutally and disgustingly treated. Innocent persons were being continually arrested, kept in overcrowded prisons a month or more, and then, after being flogged, released without trial.

"Northern Korea suffered the most from the Japanese brutalities. In the Pyeng-yang and Sensan districts whole villages were destroyed and churches burned, many of which I saw and photographed.

"In Pyeng-yang I interviewed the Governor and easily saw that he was powerless, everything being in the hands of the chief of the gendarmerie. At first I was not allowed to visit the prison, but the Governor-General of Korea telegraphed his permission. I found it clean and the prisoners were well fed, but the overcrowded condition of the cells caused untold suffering.

"In one room, ten feet by six, were more than thirty prisoners. The prison governor admitted that the total normal capacity of the building was 800, but the occupants then numbered 2,100. He said he had requested the Government to enlarge the prison immediately, as otherwise epidemics would break out as soon as hot weather came.

"I visited an interior village to learn the truth in a report that the Christians had been driven from their homes. The local head official, not a Christian, admitted to me that the non-Christian villagers had driven the Christians into the mountains because the local military officials had warned him that their presence would result in the village being shot up. He said he had the most friendly feeling for the Christians but drove them out in self-protection.

"In other villages which I visited the building had been entirely destroyed and the places were destroyed. In some of the places I found only terrorized and tearful women who did not dare to speak to a foreigner because the local gendarmes would beat and torture them if they did so.

"The majority of the schools throughout the country are closed. In most places the missionaries are not allowed to hold services. Though innocent of any wrong-doing, they are under continual suspicion. It was impossible for them or others to use the telegraph and post-offices, the strictest censorship prevailing. Undoubtedly an attempt is being made to undermine Christianity and make the position of missionaries so difficult that it will be impossible for them to carry on their work.

"In the course of my investigation I was deeply impressed with the pitiful condition of the Korean people. They are allowed only a limited education and attempts are being made to cause them to forget their national history and their language.

"There is no freedom of the press or of public meeting. The people are subject to the harshest regulations and punishments without any court of appeal. They are like sheep driven to a slaughter house. Only an independent investigation can make the world understand Korea's true position. At present the groanings and sufferings of 20,000,000 people are apparently falling on deaf ear."

As these tales, and many more like them, were spread abroad, the Japanese outside of Korea tried to find some excuse for their nationals. One of the most extraordinary of these excuses was a series of instructions, said to have been issued by General Utsonomiya, commander of the military forces in Korea, to the officers and men under him. Copies of these were privately circulated by certain pro-Japanese in America among their friends, as proof of the falsity of the charges of ill-treatment. Some extracts from them were published by Bishop Herbert Welsh, of the Methodist Church, in the Christian Advocate.

"Warm sympathy should be shown to the erring Koreans, who, in spite of their offence, should be treated as unfortunate fellow countrymen, needing love and guidance.

"Use of weapons should be abstained from till the last moment of absolute necessity. Where, for instance, the demonstration is confined merely to processions and the shouting of banzai and no violence is done, efforts should be confined to the dispersal of crowds by peaceful persuasion.

"Even in case force is employed as the last resource, endeavour should be made to limit its use to the minimum extent.

"The moment the necessity therefor ceases the use of force should at once be stopped....

"Special care should be taken not to harm anybody not participating in disturbances, especially aged people, children and women. With regard to the missionaries and other foreigners, except in case of the plainest evidence, as, for instance, where they are caught in the act, all forbearance and circumspection should be used.

"You are expected to see to it that the officers and men under you (especially those detailed in small parties) will lead a clean and decent life and be modest and polite, without abating their loyalty and courage, thus exemplifying in their conduct the noble traditions of our historic Bushido."...

If a final touch were wanted to the disgrace of the Japanese administration, here it was. Brutality, especially brutality against the unarmed and against women and children, is bad enough; but when to brutality we add nauseating hypocrisy, God help us!

One of the Japanese majors who returned from Korea to Tokyo to lecture was more straightforward. "We must beat and kill the Koreans," he said. And they did.

After a time the Japanese papers began to report the punishments inflicted on the arrested Koreans. Many were released after examination and beatings. It was mentioned that up to April 13th, 2,400 of those arrested in Seoul alone had been released, "after severe admonition." The usual sentences were between six months' and four years' imprisonment.

Soon there came reports that prisoners were attempting to commit suicide in jail. Then came word that two of the original signers of the Declaration of Independence were dead in prison. Koreans everywhere mourned. For they could imagine how they had died.

During the summer the authorities published figures relating to the number of prisoners brought under the examination of Public Procurators between March 1st and June 18th, on account of the agitation. These figures do not include the large numbers released by the police after arrest, and after possibly summary punishment. Sixteen thousand one hundred and eighty-three men were brought up for examination. Of these, 8,351 were prosecuted and 5,858 set free after the Procurators' examination. One thousand seven hundred and seventy-eight were transferred from one law court to another for the purpose of thorough examination, while 178 had not yet been tried.

XVI
THE REIGN OF TERROR IN PYENG-YANG

Pyeng-Yang, the famous missionary centre in Northern Korea, has been described in previous chapters. The people here, Christians and non-Christians alike, took a prominent part in the movement. It was announced that three memorial services would be held on March 1st, in memory of the late Emperor, one in the compound of the Christian Boys' School, one in the compound of the Methodist church and the third at the headquarters of the Chun-do Kyo.

The meeting at the boys' school was typical of all. Several of the native pastors and elders of the Presbyterian churches of the city, including the Moderator of the General Assembly, were present, and the compound was crowded with fully three thousand people. After the memorial service was finished, a prominent Korean minister asked the people to keep their seats, as there was more to follow.

Then, with an air of great solemnity, the Moderator of the General Assembly read two passages from the Bible, 1 Peter 3:13-17 and Romans 9:3.

> "And who is he that will harm you, if ye be followers of that which is good.

> "But, if ye suffer for righteousness sake, happy are ye, and be not afraid of their terror, neither be troubled.

> "For I could wish that I were accurst from Christ for my brethren, my kinsmen according to the flesh."

It was the great appeal to all that was most heroic in their souls. Some of them whispered the words after the Moderator.

"Sarami doorupkei hanangusul dooru wo malmyu sodong chi malgo."

"Be not afraid of their terror."

These white-robed men knew what was before them. Terror and torture and suffering were no new things to them. Within a quarter of a century conquering and defeated armies had passed through their city time after time. They knew war, and they knew worse than war. Japan had during the past few years planted her terror among them, persecuting the Church, arresting its most prominent members on false charges, breaking them in prison by scientific torture. Many of the men knew, in that assembly, of the meaning of police flogging, the feel of police burning, the unspeakable agony of being strung up by the thumbs under the police inquisition.

"Be not afraid of their terror!" Easy to say this to Western peoples, to whom terror is known only in the form of the high explosives and dropping bombs of honourable war. But for these men it had another meaning, an inquisition awaiting them compared with which the tortures of Torquemada paled.

"Be not afraid!"

There was no tremor of fear in the voice of the college graduate who rose to his feet and came to the front. "This is the proudest and happiest day of my life," he said. "Though I die to-morrow, I cannot help but read." He had a paper in his hand. As the vast audience saw it, they gave a great cheer. Then he read the Declaration of Independence of the Korean people.

When he had finished, another man took the platform. "Nothing of an unlawful nature is to be permitted," he said. "You are all to obey orders, and make no resistance to the authorities, nor to attack the Japanese officials or people." A speech on Korean independence followed. Then some men came out of the building bearing armfuls of Korean flags, which they distributed among the people. A large Korean flag was raised on the wall behind, and the crowd rose to its feet cheering, waving flags, calling "Mansei."

There was to be a parade through the streets. But spies had already hurried off to the police station, and before the people could leave, a company of policemen arrived. "Remain quiet," the word went round. The police gathered up the flags.

In the evening a large crowd gathered in front of the police station shouting "Mansei." The police ordered the hose to be turned on them. The Korean policemen refused to obey their Japanese superiors, threw off their uniforms and joined the mob. The hose at last got to work. The mob responded by throwing stones, breaking the windows of the police station. This was the only violence. On the following day, Sunday, the churches were closed. At midnight, the police had summoned Dr. Moffett to their office and told him that no services could be allowed. Early in the morning, the leaders of the Saturday meetings were arrested, and were now in jail. "Be not afraid!"

At nine o'clock on Monday morning a company of Japanese soldiers was drilling on the campus. A number of students from the college and academy were on the top of a bank, looking on at the drill. Suddenly the soldiers, in obedience to a word of command, rushed at the students. The latter took to their heels and fled, save two or three who stood their ground. The students who had escaped cheered; and one of the men who stood his ground called "Mansei." The soldiers struck him with the butts and barrels of their rifles. Then one poked him with his rifle in his face. He was bleeding badly. Two soldiers led him off, a prisoner. The rest were dispersed with kicks and blows.

Now the Japanese started their innings. One man in plain clothes confronted a Korean who was walking quietly, slapped his face and knocked him down. A soldier joined in the sport, and after many blows with the rifle and kicks, they rolled him down an embankment into a ditch. They then ran down, pulled him out of the ditch, kicked him some more, and hauled him off to prison.

The streets were full of people now, and parties of troops were going about everywhere dispersing them. The crowds formed, shouting "Mansei"; the soldiers chased them, beating up all they could catch. There were rumours that most of the Korean policemen had deserted; they had joined the crowds; the Japanese were searching for them and arresting them; and, men whispered, they would be executed. By midday, every one had enough trouble, and the city quieted down for the rest of the day. It was not safe to go abroad now. The soldiers were beating up every one they could find, particularly women.

By Tuesday the city was full of tales of the doings of the soldiers; having tasted blood, the troops were warming to their work, "The soldiers have been chasing people to-day like they were hunters after wild beasts," wrote one foreign spectator. "Outrages have been very numerous." Still, despite the troops, the people held two or three patriotic meetings.

Let me tell the tale of Tuesday and Wednesday from two statements made by Dr. Moffett. These statements were made at the time to the officials in Pyeng-yang and in Seoul:

"On Tuesday, March 4th, I, in company with Mr. Yamada, Inspector of Schools, went into the midst of the crowds of Koreans on the college grounds, and thence went through the streets to the city.

"We saw thousands of Koreans on the streets, the shops all closed, and Japanese soldiers here and there....

"As we came back and near a police station, soldiers made a dash at some fifteen or more people in the middle of the street, and three of the soldiers dashed at some five or six men standing quietly at the side, under the eaves of the shops, hitting them with their guns. One tall young man in a very clean white coat dodged the thrust of the gun coming about five feet under the eaves when an officer thrust his sword into his back, just under the shoulder blades. The man was not more than ten feet from us in front....

"Mr. Yamada was most indignant and said, 'I shall tell Governor Kudo just what I have seen and tell him in detail.'

"I asked him if he had noticed that the man was quietly standing at the side of the road, and had given no occasion for attack. He said, 'Yes.'

"Just after that we saw thirty-four young girls and women marched along by some six or eight policemen and soldiers, the girls ahead not being more than twelve or thirteen years of age.

"Just outside the West Gate Mr. Yamada and I separated and I went towards home. As I arrived near my own compound, I saw a number of soldiers rush into the gate of the Theological Seminary professor's cottage, and saw them grab out a man, beat and kick him and lead him off. Others began clubbing a youth behind the gate and then led him out, tied him tightly and beat and kicked him.

"Then there came out three others, two youths and one man, dragged by soldiers, and then tied with rope, their hands tied behind them.

"Thinking one was my secretary, who lived in the gate house, where the men had been beaten, I moved to the junction of the road to make sure, but I recognized none of the four. When they came to the junction of the road and some of the soldiers were within ten or twelve feet of me, they all stopped, tied the ropes tighter, and then with four men tied and helpless, these twenty or more soldiers, in charge of an officer, struck the men with their fists in the face and back, hit them on the head and face with a piece of board, kicked them on the legs and back, doing these things repeatedly. The officer in a rage raised his sword over his head as he stood before a boy, and both I and the boy thought that he was to be cleft in two. The cry of terror and anguish he raised was most piercing. Then, kicking and beating these men, they led them off.

"The above I saw myself and testify to the truthfulness of my statements. In all my contact with the Koreans these five days, and in all my observation of the crowds inside and outside the city, I have witnessed no act of violence on the part of any Korean."

The Theological Seminary was due to open on March 5th. Five students from South Korea arrived and went into their dormitory on the afternoon of the 4th. They had taken no part in the demonstrations. Later in the afternoon the soldiers, searching after some people who had run away from them, burst into the seminary. They broke open the door of the dormitory, pulled the five theologues out and hauled them off to the police station. There, despite their protests, they were tied by their arms and legs to large wooden crosses, face downwards, and beaten on the naked buttocks, twenty-nine tremendous blows from a hard cane, each. Then they were dismissed.

That same night firemen were let loose on the village where many of the students lived and boarded. They dragged out the young men and beat them. The opening of the seminary had to be postponed.

The Japanese were eager to find grounds for convicting the missionaries of participation in the movement. One question was pressed on every prisoner, usually by beating and burning, "Who instigated you? Was it the foreigners?"

Dr. Moffett was a special object of Japanese hatred. The Osaka Asahi *printed a bitter attack on him on March 17th. This is the more notable because the* Asahi is a noted organ of Japanese Liberalism.

THE EVIL VILLAGE OUTSIDE THE WEST GATE IN PYENG-YANG

A Clever Crowd

"Outside the West Gate in Pyeng-yang there are some brick houses and some built after the Korean style, some high and some low. These are the homes of the foreigners. There are about a hundred of them in all, and they are Christian missionaries. In the balmy spring, strains of music can be heard from there. Outwardly they manifest love and mercy, but if their minds are fully investigated, they will be found to be filled with intrigue and greed. They pretend to be here for preaching, but they are secretly stirring up political disturbances, and foolishly keep passing on the vain talk of the Koreans, and thereby help to foster trouble. These are really the homes of devils.

"The head of the crowd is Moffett. The Christians of the place obey him as they would Jesus Himself. In the 29th year of Meiji freedom was given to any one to believe in any religion he wished, and at that time Moffett came to teach the Christian religion. He has been in Pyeng-yang for thirty years, and has brought up a great deal of land. He is really the founder of the foreign community. In this community, because of his efforts there have been established schools from the primary grade to a college and a hospital. While they are educating the Korean children and healing their diseases on the one hand, on the other there is concealed a clever shadow, and even the Koreans themselves talk of this.

"This is the centre of the present uprising. It is not in Seoul but in Pyeng-yang.

"It is impossible to know whether these statements are true or
false, but we feel certain that it is in Pyeng-yang, in the
Church schools,--in a certain college and a certain girls'
school--in the compound of these foreigners. Really this foreign
community is very vile."[14]

A veritable reign of terror was instituted. There were wholesale arrests and
the treatment of many of the people in prison was in keeping with the methods
employed by the Japanese on the Conspiracy Trial victims. The case of a little shoe
boy aroused special indignation. The Japanese thought that he knew something
about the organization of the demonstration--why they thought so, only those who
can fathom the Japanese mind would venture to say--so they beat and burned him
almost to death to make him confess. A lady missionary examined his body afterwards. There were four scars, five inches long, where the flesh had been seared
with a red-hot iron. His hands had swollen to twice their normal size from beating,
and the dead skin lay on the welts. He had been kicked and beaten until he fainted.
Then they threw water over him and gave him water to drink until he recovered
when he was again piled with questions and beaten with a bamboo rod until he
collapsed.

Some of those released from prison after they had satisfied the Japanese of their
innocence had dreadful tales to tell. Sixty people were confined in a room fourteen
by eight feet, where they had to stand up all the time, not being allowed to sit or lie
down. Eating and sleeping they stood leaning against one another. The wants of nature had to be attended to by them as they stood. The secretary of one of the mission
schools was kept for seven days in this room, as part of sixteen days' confinement,
before he was released.

A student, arrested at his house, was kept at the police station for twenty days.
Then they let him go, having found nothing against him. His bruised body when
he came out showed what he had suffered. He had been bound and a cord around
his shoulders and arms pulled tight until the breastbone was forced forward and

---

14   Osaka Asahi, quoted in the Peking and Tientsin Times, March 38,1919.

breathing almost stopped. Then he was beaten with a bamboo stick on the shoulders and arms until he lost consciousness. The bamboo stick was wrapped in paper so as to prevent the skin breaking and bleeding. He saw another man beaten ten times into unconsciousness, and ten times brought round; and a boy thrown down hard on the floor and stamped on repeatedly until he lost consciousness. Those who came out were few; what happened to those who remained within the prison must be left to the imagination.

Despite everything, the demonstrations of the people still continued. On March 7th the people of the villages of Po Paik and Kan, twenty miles north of Pyeng-yang, came out practically en masse to shout for independence. Next day four soldiers and one Korean policeman arrived, asking for the pastor of the church. They could not find him, so they seized the school-teacher, slashed his head and body with their swords and thrust a sword twice into his legs. An elder of the church stepped up to protest against such treatment, whereupon a Japanese soldier ran a sword through his side. As the soldiers left some young men threw stones at them. The soldiers replied with rifle fire, wounding four men.

Soldiers and police came again and again to find the pastor and church officers who had gone into hiding. On April 4th they seized the women and demanded where their husbands were, beating them with clubs and guns, the wife of one elder being beaten till great red bruises showed all over her body.

The police evidently made up their minds that the Christians were responsible for the demonstration, and they determined to rid the place of them. The services of some liquor sellers were enlisted to induce people to tear down the belfry of the church. On April 18th a Japanese came and addressed the crowd through an interpreter.

He told them that the Christians had been deceived by the "foreign devils," who were an ignorant, low-down lot of people, and that they should be driven out and go and live with the Americans who had corrupted them. There was nothing in the Bible about independence and "Mansei." Three thousand cavalry and three thousand infantry were coming to destroy all the Christians, and if they did not drive them out but continued to live with them, they would be shot and killed.

A number of half drunken men got together to drive out the Christians. This was done. A report was taken to the gendarmes that the Christians had been driven away, whereupon the villagers were praised. In other parts, near by, the same chief of gendarmes was ordering the families of Christians out of their homes, arresting the men and leaving the women and children to seek refuge where they might.

Word came to some other villages in the Pyeng-yang area that the police would visit them on April 27th, to inspect the house-cleaning. The Christians received warning that they must look out for a hard time. Everything was very carefully cleaned, ready for the inspection. The leader of the church sent word to all the people to gather for early worship, so as to be through before the police should come. But the police were there before them, a Japanese in charge, two Korean policemen, two secretaries and two dog killers.

The two leaders of the church were called up by the Japanese, who stepped down and ran his fingers along the floor. "Look at this dust," he said. Ordering the two men to sit down on the floor, he beat them with a flail, over the shoulders.

"Do you beat an old man, seventy years old, this way?" called the older man.

"What is seventy years, you rascal of a Christian?" came the reply.

The police took the names of the Christians from the church roll, and went round the village, picking them out and beating them all, men, women and children. They killed their dogs. The non-Christians were let alone.

On the afternoon of April 4th a cordon of police and gendarmes was suddenly picketed all around the missionary quarter in Pyeng-yang, and officials, police and detectives made an elaborate search of the houses. Some copies of an Independence newspaper, a bit of paper with a statement of the numbers killed at Anju, and a copy of the program of the memorial service were found among the papers of Dr. Moffett's secretary, and two copies of a mimeographed notice in Korean, thin paper rolled up into a thin ball and thrown away, were found in an outhouse. The secretary was arrested, bound, beaten and hauled off. Other Koreans found on the premises were treated in similar fashion. One man was knocked down, beaten and kicked on the head several times.

Dr. Moffett and the Rev. E.M. Mowry, another American Presbyterian missionary from Mansfield, Ohio, were ordered to the police office that evening, and cross-examined. Dr. Moffett convinced the authorities that he knew nothing of the independence movement and had taken no part in it (he felt bound, as a missionary, not to take part in political affairs), but Mr. Mowry was detained on the charge of sheltering Korean agitators.

Mr. Mowry had allowed five Korean students wanted by the police to remain in his house for two days early in March. Some of them were his students and one was his former secretary; Mr. Mowry was a teacher at the Union Christian College, and principal of both the boys' and girls' grammar schools at Pyeng-yang. Mr. Mowry declared that Koreans often slept at his house, and he had no knowledge that the police were trying to arrest these lads.

The missionary was kept in jail for ten days. His friends were told that he would probably be sent to Seoul for trial Then he was suddenly brought before the Pyeng-yang court, no time being given for him to obtain counsel, and was sentenced to six months' penal servitude. He was led away wearing the prisoners' cap, a wicker basket, placed over the head and face.

An appeal was at once entered, and eventually the conviction was quashed, and a new trial ordered.

XVII
GIRL MARTYRS FOR LIBERTY

The most extraordinary feature of the uprising of the Korean people is the part taken in it by the girls and women. Less than twenty years ago, a man might live in Korea for years and never come in contact with a Korean woman of the better classes, never meet her on the street, never see her in the homes of his Korean friends. I have lived for a week or two at a time, in the old days, in the house of a Korean man of high class, and have never once seen his wife or daughters. In Japan in those days--and with many families the same holds true to-day--when one was invited as a guest, the wife would receive you, bow to the guest and her lord, and then would humbly retire, not sitting to table with the men.

Christian teaching and modern ways broke down the barrier in Korea. The young Korean women took keenly to the new mode of life. The girls in the schools, particularly in the Government schools, led the way in the demand for the restoration of their national life. There were many quaint and touching incidents. In the missionary schools, the chief fear of the girls was lest they should bring trouble on their American teachers. The head mistress of one of these schools noticed for some days that her girls were unusually excited. She heard them asking one another, "Have you enrolled?" and imagined that some new girlish league was being formed. This was before the great day. One morning the head mistress came down to discover the place empty. On her desk was a paper signed by all the girls, resigning their places in the school. They thought that by this device they would show that their beloved head mistress was not responsible.

Soon there came a call from the Chief of Police. The mistress was wanted at the police office at once. All the girls from her school were demonstrating and had stirred up the whole town. Would the mistress come and disperse them?

The mistress hurried off. Sure enough, here were the girls in the street, wearing national badges, waving national flags, calling on the police to come and take them. The men had gathered and were shouting "Mansei!" also.

The worried Chief of Police, who was a much more decent kind than many of his fellows, begged the mistress to do something. "I cannot arrest them all," he said. "I have only one little cell here. It would only hold a few of them," The mistress went out to talk to the girls. They would not listen, even to her. They cheered her, and when she begged them to go home, shouted "Mansei!" all the louder.

The mistress went back to the Chief. "The only thing for you to do is to arrest me," she said.

The Chief was horrified at the idea, "I will go out and tell the girls that you are going to arrest me if they do not go," she said. "We will see what that will do. But mind you, if they do not disperse, you must arrest me."

She went out again. "Girls," she called, "the Chief of Police is going to arrest me if you do not go to your homes. I am your teacher, and it must be the fault of my teaching that you will not obey."

"No, teacher, no," the girls shouted. "It is not your fault. You have nothing to do with it. We are doing this." And some of them rushed up, as though they would rescue her by force of arms.

In the end, she persuaded the girls to go home, in order to save her. "Well," said the leaders of the girls, "it's all right now. We have done all we wanted. We have stirred up the men. They were sheep and wanted women to make a start. Now they will go on."

The police and gendarmerie generally were not so merciful as this particular Chief. The rule in many police stations was to strip and beat the girls and young women who took any part in the demonstrations, and to expose them, absolutely naked, to as many Japanese men as possible. The Korean woman is as sensitive as a white woman about the display of her person, and the Japanese, knowing this, delighted to have this means of humiliating them. In some towns, the schoolgirls arranged to go out in sections, so many one day, so many on the other. The girls who had to go out on the later days knew how those who had preceded them had been stripped and beaten. Anticipating that they would be treated in the same way, they sat up the night before sewing special undergarments on themselves, which would not be so easily removed as their ordinary clothes, hoping that they might thus avoid being stripped entirely naked.

The girls were most active of all in the city of Seoul. I have mentioned in the previous chapter the arrest of many of them. They were treated very badly indeed. Take, for instance, the case of those seized by the police on the morning of Wednesday, March 5th. They were nearly all of them pupils from the local academies. Some of them were demonstrating on Chong-no, the main street, shouting "Mansei." Others were wearing straw shoes, a sign of mourning, for the dead Emperor. Still others were arrested because the police thought that they might be on the way to demonstrate. A few of these girls were released after a spell in prison. On their release, their statements concerning their treatment were independently recorded.

They were first taken to the Chong-no Police Station, where a body of about twenty Japanese policemen kicked them with their heavy boots, slapped their cheeks or punched their heads. "They flung me against a wall with all their might, so that I was knocked senseless, and remained so for a time," said one. "They struck me such blows across the ears that my cheeks swelled up," said another. "They trampled on my feet with their heavy nailed boots till I felt as though my toes were crushed beneath them.... There was a great crowd of students, both girls and boys. They slapped the girls over the ears, kicked them, and tumbled them in the corners. Some of them they took by the hair, jerking both sides of the face. Some of the boy students they fastened down with a rope till they had their heads fastened between their legs. Then they trampled them with their heavy boots, kicking them in their faces till their eyes were swelled and blood flowed."

Seventy-five persons, forty men and thirty-five girls, were confined in a small room. The door was closed, and the atmosphere soon became dreadful. In vain they pleaded to have the door open. The girls were left until midnight without food or water. The men were removed at about ten in the evening.

During the day, the prisoners were taken one by one before police officials to be examined. Here is the narrative of one of the schoolgirls. This girl was dazed and almost unconscious from ill-treatment and the poisoned air, when she was dragged before her inquisitor.

"I was cross-questioned three times. When I went out to the place of examination they charged me with having straw shoes, and so beat me over the head with a stick. I had no sense left with which to make a reply. They asked:

"'Why did you wear straw shoes?'

"'The King had died, and whenever Koreans are in mourning they wear straw shoes,'

"'That is a lie,' said the cross-examiner. He then arose and took my mouth in his two hands and pulled it each way so that it bled. I maintained that I had told the truth and no falsehoods. 'You Christians are all liars,' he replied, taking my arm and giving it a pull.

"... The examiner then tore open my jacket and said, sneeringly, 'I congratulate you,' He then slapped my face, struck me with a stick until I was dazed and asked again, 'Who instigated you to do this? Did foreigners?'

"My answer was, 'I do not know any foreigners, but only the principal of the school. She knows nothing of this plan of ours!'

"'Lies, only lies,' said the examiner.

"Not only I, but others too, suffered every kind of punishment. One kind of torture was to make us hold a board at arm's length and hold it out by the hour. They also had a practice of twisting our legs, while they spat on our faces. When ordered to undress, one person replied, 'I am not guilty of any offence. Why should I take off my clothes before you?'

"'If you really were guilty, you would not be required to undress, but seeing you are sinless, off with your clothes,'"

He was a humorous fellow, this cross-examiner of the Chong-no Police Station. He had evidently learned something of the story of Adam and Eve in the Garden of Eden. His way was first to charge the girls--schoolgirls of good family, mind you-- with being pregnant, making every sort of filthy suggestion to them. When the girls indignantly denied, he would order them to strip.

"Since you maintain you have not sinned in any way, I see the Bible says that if there is no sin in you take off all your clothes and go before all the people naked," he told one girl. "Sinless people live naked."

Let us tell the rest of the story in the girl's own words. "The officer then came up to where I was standing, and tried to take off my clothes. I cried, and protested, and struggled, saying, 'This is not the way to treat a woman.' He desisted. When he was making these vile statements about us, he did not use the Korean interpreter, but spoke in broken Korean. The Korean interpreter seemed sorrowful while these vile things were being said by the operator. The Korean interpreter was ordered to beat me. He said he would not beat a woman; he would bite his fingers first. So the officer beat me with his fist on my shoulders, face and legs."

These examinations were continued for days. Sometimes a girl would be examined several times a day. Sometimes a couple of examiners would rush at her, beating and kicking her; sometimes they would make her hold a chair or heavy board out at full length, beating her if she let it sink in the least. Then when she was worn out they would renew their examination. The questions were all directed towards one end, to discover who inspired them, and more particularly if any foreigners or missionaries had influenced them. During this time they were kept under the worst possible conditions.

"I cannot recount all the vile things that were said to us while in the police quarters in Chong-no," declared one of the girls. "They are too obscene to be spoken, but by the kindness of the Lord I thought of how Paul had suffered in prison, and was greatly comforted. I knew that God would give the needed help, and as I bore it for my country, I did not feel the shame and misery of it." One American woman, to whom some of the girls related their experiences, said to me, "I cannot tell you, a man, all that these girls told us. I will only say this. There have been stories of girls having their arms cut off. If these girls had been daughters of mine I would rather that they had their arms cut off than that they faced what those girls endured in Chong-no."

There came a day when the girls were bound at the wrists, all fastened together, and driven in a car to the prison outside the West Gate. Some of them were crying. They were not allowed to look up or speak. The driver, a Korean, took advantage of a moment when the attention of their guard was attracted to whisper a word of encouragement. "Don't be discouraged and make your bodies weak. You are not yet condemned. This is only to break your spirits."

The prison outside the West Gate is a model Japanese jail. There were women officials here. It seemed horrible to the girls that they should be made to strip in front of men and be examined by them. Probably the men were prison doctors. But it was evidently intended to shame them as much as possible. Thus one girl relates that, after her examination, "I was told to take my clothes and go into another room. One woman went with me, about a hundred yards or more away. I wanted to put my clothes on before leaving the room, but they hurried me and pushed me. I wrapped my skirt about my body before I went out, and carried the rest of my clothes in my arms. After leaving this room, and before reaching the other, five Korean men prisoners passed us."

For the first week the girls, many of them in densely crowded cells, were kept in close confinement. After this, they were allowed out for fifteen minutes, wearing the prisoners' hat, which comes down over the head, after breakfast. Their food was beans and millet It was given to the accompaniment of jeers and insults. "You Koreans eat like dogs and cats," the wardresses told them.

The routine of life in the prison was very trying. They got up at seven. Most of the day they had to assume a haunched, kneeling position, and remain absolutely still, hour after hour. The wardresses in the corridors kept close watch, and woe to the girl who made the slightest move. "They ordered us not to move a hand or a foot but to remain perfectly still," wrote one girl. "Even the slightest movement brought down every kind of wrath. We did not dare to move even a toe-nail."

One unhappy girl, mistaking the call of an official in the corridor, "I-ri-ma sen" for a command to go to sleep, stretched out her leg to lie down. She was scolded and severely punished. Another closed her eyes in prayer. "You are sleeping," called the wardress. In vain the girl replied that she was praying. "You lie," retorted the polite Japanese lady. More punishment!

After fifteen days in the prison outside the West Gate, some of the girls were called in the office. "Go, but be very careful not to repeat your offence," they were told. "If you are caught again, you will be given a heavier punishment."

The worst happenings with the women were not in the big towns, where the presence of white people exercised some restraint, but in villages, where the new troops often behaved in almost incredible fashion, outraging freely. The police in many of these outlying parts rivalled the military in brutality. Of the many stories that reached me, the tale of Tong Chun stands out. The account was investigated by experienced white men, who shortly afterwards visited the place and saw for themselves.

The village of Tong Chun contains about 300 houses and is the site of a Christian church. The young men of the place wished to make a demonstration but the elders of the church dissuaded them for a time. However, on March 29th, market day, when there were many people in the place, some children started demonstrating, and their elders followed, a crowd of four or five hundred people marching through the streets and shouting "Mansei!" There was no violence of any kind. The police came out and arrested seventeen persons, including five women.

One of these women was a widow of thirty-one. She was taken into the police office and a policeman tore off her clothes, leaving her in her underwear. Then the police began to take off her underclothes. She protested, whereupon they struck her in the face with their hands till she was black and blue. She still clung to her clothes, so they put a wooden paddle down between her legs and tore her clothes away. Then they beat her. The beating took a long time. When it was finished the police stopped to drink tea and eat Japanese cakes, they and their companions-- there were a number of men in the room--amusing themselves by making fun of her as she sat there naked among them. She was subsequently released. For a week afterwards she had to lie down most of the time and could not walk around.

Another victim was the wife of a Christian teacher, a very bright, intelligent woman, with one child four months old, and two or three months advanced in her second pregnancy. She had taken a small part in the demonstration and then had gone to the home of the mother of another woman who had been arrested, to comfort her. Police came here, and demanded if she had shouted "Mansei." She admitted that she had. They ordered her to leave the child that she was carrying on her back and took her to the police station. As she entered the station a man kicked her forcibly from behind and she fell forward in the room. As she lay there a policeman put his foot on her neck, then raised her up and struck her again and again. She was ordered to undress. She hesitated, whereupon the policeman kicked her, and took up a paddle and a heavy stick to beat her with. "You are a teacher," he cried. "You have set the minds of the children against Japan. I will beat you to death."

He tore her underclothes off. Still clinging to them, she tried to cover her nakedness. The clothes were torn out of her hands. She tried to sit down. They forced her up. She tried by turning to the wall to conceal herself from the many men in the room. They forced her to turn round again. When she tried to shelter herself with her hands, one man twisted her arms, held them behind her back, and kept them there while the beating and kicking continued. She was so badly hurt that she would have fallen to the floor, but they held her up to continue the beating. She was then sent into another room. Later she and other women were again brought in the office. "Do you know now how wrong it is to call 'Mansei'?" the police asked. "Will you ever dare to do such a thing again?"

Gradually news of how the women were being treated spread. A crowd of five hundred people gathered next morning. The hot bloods among them were for attacking the station, to take revenge for the ill-treatment of their women. The chief Christian kept them back, and finally a deputation of two went inside the police office to make a protest. They spoke up against the stripping of the women, declaring it unlawful. The Chief of Police replied that they were mistaken. It was permitted under Japanese law. They had to strip them to search for unlawful papers. Then the men asked why only the younger women were stripped, and not the older, why they were beaten after being stripped, and why only women and not men were stripped. The Chief did not reply.

By this time the crowd was getting very ugly. "Put us in prison too, or release the prisoners," the people called. In the end the Chief agreed to release all but four of the prisoners.

Soon afterwards the prisoners emerged from the station. One woman, a widow of thirty-two who had been arrested on the previous day and very badly kicked by the police, had to be supported on either side. The wife of the Christian teacher had to be carried on a man's back. Let me quote from a description written by those on the spot:

"As they saw the women being brought out, in this condition, a wave of pity swept over the whole crowd, and with one accord they burst into tears and sobbed. Some of them cried out, 'It is better to die than to live under such savages,' and many urged that they should attack the police office with their naked hands, capture the Chief of Police, strip him and beat him to death. But the Christian elder and other wiser heads prevailed, kept the people from any acts of violence, and finally got them to disperse."

XVIII
WORLD REACTIONS

On April 23rd, at a time when the persecution was at its height, delegates, duly elected by each of the thirteen provinces of Korea, met, under the eyes of the Japanese police, in Seoul, and adopted a constitution, creating the Republic.

Dr. Syngman Rhee, the young reformer of 1894, who had suffered long imprisonment for the cause of independence, was elected the first President. Dr. Rhee was now in America, and he promptly established headquarters in Washington, from which to conduct a campaign in the interests of his people. Diplomatically, of course, the new Republican organization could not be recognized; but there are many ways in which such a body can work.

The First Ministry included several men who had taken a prominent part in reform work in the past The list was:

Prime Minister..............................Tong Hui Yee

Minister Foreign Affairs..............Yongman Park

Minister of Interior......................Tong Yung Yee

Minister of War............................Pak Yin Roe

Minister of Finance......................Si Yung Yee

Minister of Law............................Kiu Sik Cynn

Minister of Education...................Kiusic Kimm

Minister of Communications........Chang Bum Moon

Director Bureau of Labour............Chang Ho Ahn

Chief of Staff................................Tong Yul Lew

Vice Chief of Staff........................Sei Yung Lee

Vice Chief of Staff........................Nan Soo Hahn

The Provisional Constitution was essentially democratic and progressive:

PROVISIONAL CONSTITUTION

By the will of God, the people of Korea, both within and without the country, have united in a peaceful declaration of their independence, and for over one month have carried on their demonstrations in over 300 districts, and because of their faith in the movement they have by their representatives chosen a Provisional Government to carry on to completion this independence and so to preserve blessings for our children and grandchildren.

The Provisional Government, in its Council of State, has decided on a Provisional Constitution, which it now proclaims.

1. The Korean Republic shall follow republican principles.

2. All powers of State shall rest with the Provisional Council of State of the Provisional Government.

3. There shall be no class distinction among the citizens of the Korean Republic, but men and women, noble and common, rich and poor, shall have equality.

4. The citizens of the Korean Republic shall have religious liberty, freedom of speech, freedom of writing and publication, the right to hold public meetings and form social organizations and the full right to choose their dwellings or change their abode.

5. The citizens of the Korean Republic shall have the right to vote for all public officials or to be elected to public office.

6. Citizens will be subject to compulsory education and military service and payment of taxes.

7. Since by the will of God the Korean Republic has arisen in the world and has come forward as a tribute to the world peace and civilization, for this reason we wish to become a member of the League of Nations.

8. The Korean Republic will extend benevolent treatment to the former Imperial Family.

9. The death penalty, corporal punishment and public prostitution will be abolished.

10. Within one year of the recovery of our land the National Congress will be convened.

   Signed by:

      The Provisional Secretary of State,
      And the Ministers of Foreign Affairs,
            Home Affairs,
            Justice,
            Finance,
            War,
            Communications.

In the 1st Year of the Korean Republic, 4th Month.

The following are six principles of government:

1. We proclaim the equality of the people and the State.

2. The lives and property of foreigners shall be respected.

3. All political offenders shall be specially pardoned.

4. We will observe all treaties that shall be made with foreign powers.

5. We swear to stand by the independence of Korea.

6. Those who disregard the orders of the Provisional Government will be regarded as enemies of the State.

The National Council issued a statement of its aims and purpose:

April 22 1919.

We, the people of Korea, represented by thirty-three men, including Son Pyeng Heui, have already made the Declaration of Independence of Korea, found on the principle of righteousness and humanity. With a view to upholding the authority of the Declaration, solidifying the foundations of the Independence, and meeting the natural needs of humanity, we, by combining the large and small groups and the provincial representatives, have organized the Korean National Council, and hereby proclaim it to the world.

We, the people of Korea, have a history of over forty-two centuries, as a self-governing and separate state, and of special, creative civilization, and are a peace-loving race. We claim a right to be sharers in the world's enlightenment, and contributors in the evolution of mankind. With a distinctive and world-wide glorious past, and with our healthy national spirit, we should never be subjected to inhuman and unnatural oppression, nor assimilation by another race; and still less could we submit to the materialistic subjugation by the Japanese, whose spiritual civilization is 2,000 years behind ours.

The world knows that Japan has violated the sworn treaties of the past and is robbing us of the right of existence. We, however, are not discussing the wrongs done us by the Japanese in the past, nor considering their accumulated sins; but, in order to guarantee our rights of existence, extend liberty and equality, safeguard righteousness and humanity, maintain the peace of the Orient, and respect the equitable welfare of the whole world, do claim the independence of Korea. This is truly the will of God, motivation of truth, just claim, and legitimate action. By this the world's verdict is to be won, and the repentance of Japan hastened.

At this time, when the militarism which once threatened the peace of the world is brought to submission, and when the world is being reconstructed for a lasting peace, will Japan refuse self-reflection and self-awakening? Obstinate clinging to the errors, which have gone contrary to the times and nature, will result in nothing but the diminution of the happiness of the two peoples and endangering of the peace of the world. This council demands with all earnestness that the government of Japan abandon as early as possible the inhuman policy of aggression and firmly safeguard the tripodic relationship of the Far East, and further duly warn the people of Japan.

Can it be that the conscience of mankind will calmly witness the cruel atrocities visited upon us by the barbarous, military power of Japan for our actions in behalf of the rights of life founded upon civilization? The devotion and blood of our 20,000,000 will never cease nor dry under this unrighteous oppression. If Japan does not repent and mend her ways for herself, our race will be obliged to take the final action, to the limit of the last man and the last minute, which will secure the complete independence of Korea. What enemy will withstand when our race marches forward with righteousness and humanity? With our utmost devotion and best labour we demand before the world our national independence and racial autonomy.

THE KOREAN NATIONAL COUNCIL

Representatives of the thirteen Provinces:

Yee Man Jik   Kim Hyung Sun
Yee Nai Su   Yu Keun
Pak Han Yung   Kang Ji Yung
Pak Chang Ho   Chang Seung
Yee Yeng Jun   Kim Heyen Chun
Choi Chun Koo Kim Ryu
Yee Yong Kiu   Kim Sig
Yu Sik Kiu   Chu Ik
Yu Jang Wuk   Hong Seung Wuk
Song Ji Hun   Chang Chun
Yee Tong Wuk   Chung Tam Kio
Kim Taik   Pak Tak
Kang Hoon

RESOLUTIONS

That a Provisional Government shall be organized.

That a demand be made of the Government of Japan to withdraw the administrative and military organs from Korea.

That a delegation shall be appointed to the Paris Peace Conference. That the Koreans in the employ of the Japanese Government shall withdraw.

That the people shall refuse to pay taxes to the Japanese Government.

That the people shall not bring petitions or litigations before the Japanese Government.

*   *   *   *   *

It was expected in Korea that there would be an immediate agitation in America to secure redress. The American churches were for some weeks strangely silent. There is no reason why the full reasons should not be made public.

The missionary organizations mainly represented in Korea are also strongly represented in Japan. Their officials at their headquarters are almost forced to adopt what can be politely described as a statesmanlike attitude over matters of controversy between different countries. When Mr. Armstrong, of the Presbyterian Board of Missions of Canada, arrived in America, burning with indignation over what he had seen, he found among the American leaders a spirit of great caution. They did not want to offend Japan, nor to injure Christianity there. And there was a feeling--a quite honest feeling,--that they might accomplish more by appealing to the better side of Japan than by frankly proclaiming the truth. The whole matter was referred, by the Presbyterian and Methodist Boards, to the Commission on Relations with the Orient of the Federal Council of the Churches, a body representing the Churches as a whole.

The Secretary of that Commission is the Rev. Sydney Gulick, the most active defender of Japanese interests of any European or American to-day. Mr. Gulick lived a long time in Japan; he sees things, inevitably, from a Japanese point of view. He at once acted as though he were resolved to keep the matter from the public gaze. This was the course recommended by the Japanese Consul-General Yada at New York. Private pressure was brought on the Japanese authorities, and the preparation of a report was begun in very leisurely fashion.

Every influence that Mr. Gulick possessed was exercised to prevent premature publicity. The report of the Federal Council was not issued until between four and five months after the atrocities began. A Presbyterian organization, The New Era Movement, issued a stinging report on its own account, a few days before. The report of the Federated Council was preceded by a cablegram from Mr. Hara, the Japanese Premier, declaring that the report of abuses committed by agents of the Japanese Government in Korea had been engaging his most serious attention. "I am fully prepared to look squarely at actual facts."

The report itself, apart from a brief, strongly pro-Japanese introduction, consisted of a series of statements by missionaries and others in Korea, and was as outspoken and frank as any one could desire. The only regret was that it had not been issued immediately. Here was a situation that called for the pressure of world public opinion. In keeping this back as long as possible Mr. Gulick, I am convinced, did the cause of Korean Christianity a grave injury, and helped to prevent earlier redress being obtained.

"No neutrality for brutality" was the motto adopted by many of the missionaries of Korea. It is a good one for the Churches as a whole. There are times when the open expression of a little honest indignation is better than all the "ecclesiastical statesmanship" that can be employed.

In Japan itself, every effort was made by the authorities to keep back details of what was happening. Mr. Hara, the Progressive Premier, was in none too strong a position. The military party, and the forces of reaction typified by Prince Yamagata, had too much power for him to do as much as he himself perhaps would. He consented to the adoption of still more drastic methods in April, and while redress was promised in certain particular instances, as in the Suigen outrage, there was no desire displayed to meet the situation fully. Taxed in Parliament, he tried to wriggle out of admissions that anything was wrong.

The attitude of the people of Japan at first was frankly disappointing to those who hoped that the anti-militarist party there would really act. One American-Japanese paper, the Japan Advertiser, sent a special correspondent to Korea and his reports were of the utmost value. The Japan Chronicle, the English owned paper at Kobe, was equally outspoken. The Japanese press as a whole had very little to say; it had been officially "requested" not to say anything about Korea.

The Japanese Constitutional Party sent Mr. Konosuke Morya to investigate the situation on the spot. He issued a report declaring that the disturbances were due to the discriminatory treatment of Koreans, complicated and impracticable administrative measures, extreme censorship of public speeches, forcible adoption of the assimilation system, and the spread of the spirit of self-determination. Of the assimilation system he said, "It is a great mistake of colonial policy to attempt to enforce upon the Koreans, with a 2,000-year history, the same spiritual and mental training as the Japanese people."

By this time the Japanese Churches were beginning to stir. The Federation of Churches in Japan sent Dr. Ishizaka, Secretary of the Mission Board of the Japan Methodist Church, to enquire. Dr. Ishizaka's findings were published in the Go-kyo. I am indebted for a summary of them to an article by Mr. R.S. Spencer, in the Christian Advocate of New York:

"Dr. Ishizaka first showed, on the authority of officials, missionaries and others, that the missionaries could in no just way be looked upon as the cause of the disturbances. Many Koreans and most of the missionaries had looked hopefully to Japanese control as offering a cure for many ills of the old regime, but in the ten years of occupation feeling had undergone a complete revulsion and practically all were against the Japanese governing system. The reasons he then sketches as follows: (1) The much-vaunted educational system established by the Governor-General makes it practically impossible for a Korean to go higher than the middle schools (roughly equivalent to an American high school) or a technical school. Even when educated Koreans were universally discriminated against. In the same office, at the same work, Koreans receive less pay than Japanese.

(The quotations are from the translation of the Japan Advertiser.) 'A Korean student in Aoyama Gakuin, who stayed at Bishop Honda's home, became the head officer of the Taikyu district office. That was before the annexation.... That officer is not in Taikyu now. He is serving in some petty office in the country. The Noko Bank, in Keijo (Seoul) is the only place where the Japanese and Koreans are treated equally, but there, also, the equality is only an outward form.' (2) The depredations of the Oriental Improvement Co., the protege of the government, resulted in the eviction of hundreds of Korean farmers, who fled to Manchuria and Siberia, many dying miserably. The wonderful roads are mentioned, it being shown that they are built and cared for by forced labour of the Koreans. That most galling and obnoxious of all bureaucratic methods, carried to the nth power in Japan--the making out of endless reports and forms--has created dissatisfaction. Dr. Ishizaka relates how an underling official required a Korean of education to rewrite a notice of change of residence six times because he omitted a dot in one of those atrocious Chinese characters, which are a hobble on the development of Japan. This last opinion is mine, not the doctor's. (3) The gendarmerie, or military police system, is mentioned, 13,000 strong, of whom about 8,000 are renegade Koreans. Admittedly a rough lot, these men are endowed with absolute power of search, personal or domiciliary, detention, arrest (and judging from the reports, I would say torture) without warrant. Bribery is, of course, rampant among them. (4) Associated closely with the police system, indeed controlling it and the civil administration and everything else, is the military government. The Governor-General must be a military officer. Dr. Ishizaka says: 'Militarism means tyranny; it never acts in open daylight, but seeks to cover up its intentions. The teachers in primary schools and even in girls' schools, that is, the men teachers, wear swords.' (5) Lastly, Dr. Ishizaka speaks of the method, which we can easily recognize as to source, of trying to 'assimilate' the Koreans by prohibiting the language, discarding Korean history from the schools, repressing customs, etc.

"In conclusion Dr. Ishizaka points out that not alone must these errors be righted, but that the only hope lies in the assumption on the part of Japanese, public and private, of an attitude of Christian brotherhood towards the Koreans. He announces a campaign to raise money among Japanese Christians for the benefit of Koreans and their churches."

The Japanese Government at last came to see that something must be done. Count Hasegawa, the Governor-General and Mr. Yamagata, Director-General of Administration, were recalled and Admiral Baron Saito and Mr. Midzuno were appointed to succeed them. Numerous other changes in personnel were also made. An Imperial Rescript was issued late in August announcing that the Government of Korea was to be reformed, and Mr. Hara in a statement issued at the same time announced that the gendarmerie were to be replaced by a force of police, under the control of the local governors, except in districts where conditions make their immediate elimination advisable, and that "It is the ultimate purpose of the Japanese Government in due course to treat Korea as in all respects on the same footing as Japan." Admiral Saito, in interviews, promised the inauguration of a liberal regime on the Peninsula.

The change unfortunately does not touch the fundamental needs of the situation. No doubt there will be an attempt to lessen some abuses. This there could not fail to be, if Japan is to hold its place longer among the civilized Powers. But Mr. Hara's explanation of the new program showed that the policy of assimilation is to be maintained, and with it, the policy of exploitation can hardly fail to be joined.

These two things spell renewed failure.

XIX
WHAT CAN WE DO?

W hat do you want us to do?" men ask me. "Do you seriously suggest that America or Great Britain should risk a breach of good relations or even a war with Japan to help Korea? If not, what is the use of saying anything? You only make the Japanese harden their hearts still more."

What can we do? Everything!

I appeal first to the Christian Churches of the United States, Canada and Britain. I have seen what your representatives, more particularly the agents of the American and Canadian Churches, have accomplished in Korea itself. They have built wisely and well, and have launched the most hopeful and flourishing Christian movement in Asia. Their converts have established congregations that are themselves missionary churches, sending out and supporting their own teachers and preachers to China. A great light has been lit in Asia. Shall it be extinguished? For, make no mistake, the work is threatened with destruction. Many of the church buildings have been burned; many of the native leaders have been tortured and imprisoned; many of their followers, men, women and children, have been flogged, or clubbed, or shot.

You, the Christians of the United States and of Canada, are largely responsible for these people. The teachers you sent and supported taught them the faith that led them to hunger for freedom. They taught them the dignity of their bodies and awakened their minds. They brought them a Book whose commands made them object to worship the picture of Emperor--even of Japanese Emperor--made them righteously angry when they were ordered to put part of their Christian homes apart for the diseased outcasts of the Yoshiwara to conduct their foul business, made them resent having the trade of the opium seller or the morphia agent introduced among them.

Your teaching has brought them floggings, tortures unspeakable, death. I do not mourn for them, for they have found something to which the blows of the lashed twin bamboos and the sizzling of the hot iron as it sears their flesh are small indeed. But I would mourn for you, if you were willing to leave them unhelped, to shut your ears to their calls, to deny them your practical sympathy.

What can we do? you ask. You can exercise the powers that democratic government has given you to translate your indignation into action. You can hold public meetings, towns meetings and church meetings, and declare, formally and with all the weight of your communities behind you, where you stand in this matter. You can make your sentiments known to your own Government and to the Imperial Japanese Government.

Then you can extend practical support to the victims of this outbreak of cruelty. There could be no more effective rebuke than for the Churches of the English-speaking nations to say to their fellow Christians of Korea, "We are standing by you. We cannot share your bodily sufferings, but we will try to show our sympathy in other ways. We will rebuild some of your churches that have been burned down; we will support the widows or orphans of Christians who have been unjustly slain, or will help to support the families of those now imprisoned for their faith and for freedom. We will show, by deeds, not words, that Christian brotherhood is a reality and not a sham."

In doing so, you will supply an example that will not be forgotten so long as Asia endures. Men say--and say rightly--that Korea is the key-land of Northeastern Asia, so far as domination of that part of the lands of the Pacific is concerned. Korea is still more the key-land of Asia for Western civilization and Christian ideals. Let Christianity be throttled here, and it will have received a set-back in Asia from which it will take generations to recover.

"The Koreans are a degenerate people, not fit for self-government," says the man whose mind has been poisoned by subtle Japanese propaganda. Korea has only been a very few years in contact with Western civilization, but it has already indicated that this charge is a lie. Its old Government was corrupt, and deserved to fall. But its people, wherever they have had a chance, have demonstrated their capacity. In Manchuria hundreds of thousands of them, mostly fled from Japanese oppression, are industrious and prosperous farmers. In the Hawaiian Islands, there are five thousand Koreans, mainly labourers, and their families, working on the sugar plantations. They have built twenty-eight schools for their children, and raise among themselves $20 a head a year for the education of their children; they have sixteen churches; they bought $80,000 worth of Liberty bonds during the war, and subscribed liberally to the Red Cross. Some of these Hawaiian Koreans--210 in all--volunteered to serve in the war. A large number of Manchurian Koreans--their total has been placed as high as thirty thousand--joined the Russian forces, fought under General Lin, and later, in conjunction with the Czecho-Slovak prisoners, fought the rearmed German prisoners and the Bolsheviks.

In America the Koreans who were fortunate enough to escape have brought the culture of rice into California, and are a prosperous community there. Young Koreans have won prominent place in American colleges and in American business. One big business in Philadelphia was created and is conducted by a Korean. Give these people a chance, and they soon show what they can do.

A word with the statesmen.

Japan is a young country, so far as Western civilization is concerned. She is the youngest of the Great Powers. She desires the good will of the world, and is willing to do much to win it. Be frank with her. You owe it to her to deal faithfully with her.

When you ask me if I would risk a war over Korea, I answer this: Firm action to-day might provoke conflict, but the risk is very small. Act weakly now, however, and you make a great war in the Far East almost certain within a generation. The main burden of the Western nations in such a war will be borne by America.

To the Japanese themselves, I venture to repeat words that I wrote over eleven years ago. They are even more true now than when they were written:

"The future of Japan, the future of the East, and, to some extent, the future of the world, lies in the answer to the question whether the militarists or the party of peaceful expansion gain the upper hand in the immediate future (in Japan). If the one, then we shall have harsher rule in Korea, steadily increasing aggression in Manchuria, growing interference with China, and, in the end, a titanic conflict, the end of which none can see. Under the other, Japan will enter into an inheritance, wider, more glorious and more assured than any Asiatic Power has attained for many centuries.... Japan has it in her to be, not the Mistress of the East, reigning, sword in hand, over subject races--for that she can never permanently be--but the bringer of peace to, and the teacher of, the East. Will she choose the nobler end?"

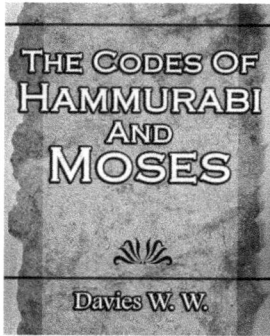

The Codes Of Hammurabi And Moses
W. W. Davies

QTY

The discovery of the Hammurabi Code is one of the greatest achievements of archaeology, and is of paramount interest, not only to the student of the Bible, but also to all those interested in ancient history...

Religion   **ISBN:** *1-59462-338-4*   **Pages:132**
MSRP $12.95

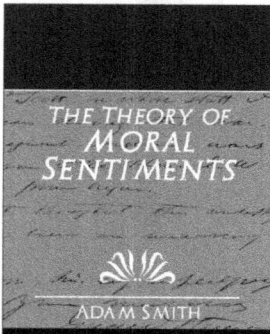

The Theory of Moral Sentiments
Adam Smith

QTY

This work from 1749. contains original theories of conscience amd moral judgment and it is the foundation for systemof morals.

Philosophy **ISBN:** *1-59462-777-0*   **Pages:536**
MSRP $19.95

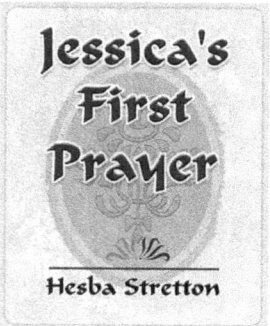

Jessica's First Prayer
Hesba Stretton

QTY

In a screened and secluded corner of one of the many railway-bridges which span the streets of London there could be seen a few years ago, from five o'clock every morning until half past eight, a tidily set-out coffee-stall, consisting of a trestle and board, upon which stood two large tin cans, with a small fire of charcoal burning under each so as to keep the coffee boiling during the early hours of the morning when the work-people were thronging into the city on their way to their daily toil...

Pages:84

Childrens   **ISBN:** *1-59462-373-2*   *MSRP $9.95*

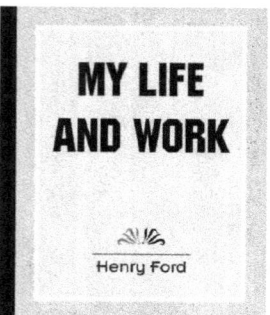

My Life and Work
Henry Ford

QTY

Henry Ford revolutionized the world with his implementation of mass production for the Model T automobile. Gain valuable business insight into his life and work with his own auto-biography... "We have only started on our development of our country we have not as yet, with all our talk of wonderful progress, done more than scratch the surface. The progress has been wonderful enough but..."

Pages:300

Biographies/   **ISBN:** *1-59462-198-5*   *MSRP $21.95*

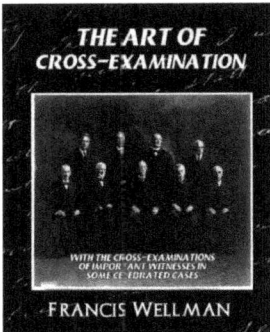

The Art of Cross-Examination
Francis Wellman

QTY

I presume it is the experience of every author, after his first book is published upon an important subject, to be almost overwhelmed with a wealth of ideas and illustrations which could readily have been included in his book, and which to his own mind, at least, seem to make a second edition inevitable. Such certainly was the case with me; and when the first edition had reached its sixth impression in five months, I rejoiced to learn that it seemed to my publishers that the book had met with a sufficiently favorable reception to justify a second and considerably enlarged edition. ..

Pages:412

Reference   ISBN: *1-59462-647-2*   *MSRP $19.95*

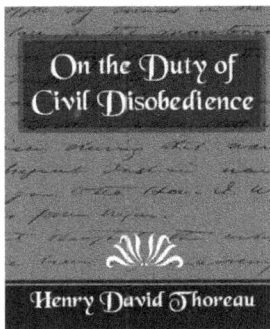

On the Duty of Civil Disobedience
Henry David Thoreau

QTY

Thoreau wrote his famous essay, On the Duty of Civil Disobedience, as a protest against an unjust but popular war and the immoral but popular institution of slave-owning. He did more than write—he declined to pay his taxes, and was hauled off to gaol in consequence. Who can say how much this refusal of his hastened the end of the war and of slavery ?

Law   ISBN: *1-59462-747-9*   **Pages:48**
                                                  MSRP $7.45

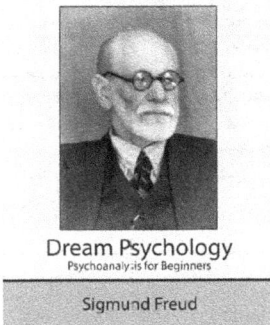

Dream Psychology Psychoanalysis for Beginners
Sigmund Freud

QTY

Sigmund Freud, born Sigismund Schlomo Freud (May 6, 1856 - September 23, 1939), was a Jewish-Austrian neurologist and psychiatrist who co-founded the psychoanalytic school of psychology. Freud is best known for his theories of the unconscious mind, especially involving the mechanism of repression; his redefinition of sexual desire as mobile and directed towards a wide variety of objects; and his therapeutic techniques, especially his understanding of transference in the therapeutic relationship and the presumed value of dreams as sources of insight into unconscious desires.

Pages:196

Psychology   ISBN: *1-59462-905-6*   *MSRP $15.45*

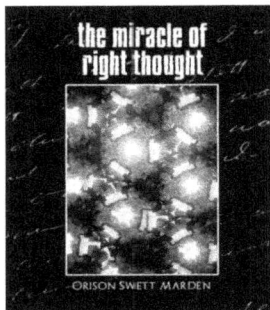

The Miracle of Right Thought
Orison Swett Marden

QTY

Believe with all of your heart that you will do what you were made to do. When the mind has once formed the habit of holding cheerful, happy, prosperous pictures, it will not be easy to form the opposite habit. It does not matter how improbable or how far away this realization may see, or how dark the prospects may be, if we visualize them as best we can, as vividly as possible, hold tenaciously to them and vigorously struggle to attain them, they will gradually become actualized, realized in the life. But a desire, a longing without endeavor, a yearning abandoned or held indifferently will vanish without realization.

Pages:360

Self Help   ISBN: *1-59462-644-8*   *MSRP $25.45*

www.bookjungle.com *email: sales@bookjungle.com fax: 630-214-0564 mail: Book Jungle PO Box 2226 Champaign, IL 61825*

QTY

☐ **The Rosicrucian Cosmo-Conception Mystic Christianity** *by Max Heindel* ISBN: *1-59462-188-8* **$38.95**
The Rosicrucian Cosmo-conception is not dogmatic, neither does it appeal to any other authority than the reason of the student. It is: not controversial, but is: sent forth in the, hope that it may help to clear... *New Age/Religion Pages 646*

☐ **Abandonment To Divine Providence** *by Jean-Pierre de Caussade* ISBN: *1-59462-228-0* **$25.95**
"The Rev. Jean Pierre de Caussade was one of the most remarkable spiritual writers of the Society of Jesus in France in the 18th Century. His death took place at Toulouse in 1751. His works have gone through many editions and have been republished... *Inspirational/Religion Pages 400*

☐ **Mental Chemistry** *by Charles Haanel* ISBN: *1-59462-192-6* **$23.95**
Mental Chemistry allows the change of material conditions by combining and appropriately utilizing the power of the mind. Much like applied chemistry creates something new and unique out of careful combinations of chemicals the mastery of mental chemistry... *New Age Pages 354*

☐ **The Letters of Robert Browning and Elizabeth Barret Barrett 1845-1846 vol II** ISBN: *1-59462-193-4* **$35.95**
by Robert Browning and Elizabeth Barrett *Biographies Pages 596*

☐ **Gleanings In Genesis (volume I)** *by Arthur W. Pink* ISBN: *1-59462-130-6* **$27.45**
Appropriately has Genesis been termed "the seed plot of the Bible" for in it we have, in germ form, almost all of the great doctrines which are afterwards fully developed in the books of Scripture which follow... *Religion/Inspirational Pages 420*

☐ **The Master Key** *by L. W. de Laurence* ISBN: *1-59462-001-6* **$30.95**
In no branch of human knowledge has there been a more lively increase of the spirit of research during the past few years than in the study of Psychology, Concentration and Mental Discipline. The requests for authentic lessons in Thought Control, Mental Discipline and... *New Age/Business Pages 422*

☐ **The Lesser Key Of Solomon Goetia** *by L. W. de Laurence* ISBN: *1-59462-092-X* **$9.95**
This translation of the first book of the "Lemegton" which is now for the first time made accessible to students of Talismanic Magic was done, after careful collation and edition, from numerous Ancient Manuscripts in Hebrew, Latin, and French... *New Age/Occult Pages 92*

☐ **Rubaiyat Of Omar Khayyam** *by Edward Fitzgerald* ISBN:*1-59462-332-5* **$13.95**
Edward Fitzgerald, whom the world has already learned, in spite of his own efforts to remain within the shadow of anonymity, to look upon as one of the rarest poets of the century, was born at Bredfield, in Suffolk, on the 31st of March, 1809. He was the third son of John Purcell... *Music Pages 172*

☐ **Ancient Law** *by Henry Maine* ISBN: *1-59462-128-4* **$29.95**
The chief object of the following pages is to indicate some of the earliest ideas of mankind, as they are reflected in Ancient Law, and to point out the relation of those ideas to modern thought. *Religion/History Pages 452*

☐ **Far-Away Stories** *by William J. Locke* ISBN: *1-59462-129-2* **$19.45**
"Good wine needs no bush, but a collection of mixed vintages does. And this book is just such a collection. Some of the stories I do not want to remain buried for ever in the museum files of dead magazine-numbers an author's not unpardonable vanity..." *Fiction Pages 272*

☐ **Life of David Crockett** *by David Crockett* ISBN: *1-59462-250-7* **$27.45**
"Colonel David Crockett was one of the most remarkable men of the times in which he lived. Born in humble life, but gifted with a strong will, an indomitable courage, and unremitting perseverance... *Biographies/New Age Pages 424*

☐ **Lip-Reading** *by Edward Nitchie* ISBN: *1-59462-206-X* **$25.95**
Edward B. Nitchie, founder of the New York School for the Hard of Hearing, now the Nitchie School of Lip-Reading, Inc, wrote "LIP-READING Principles and Practice". The development and perfecting of this meritorious work on lip-reading was an undertaking... *How-to Pages 400*

☐ **A Handbook of Suggestive Therapeutics, Applied Hypnotism, Psychic Science** ISBN: *1-59462-214-0* **$24.95**
by Henry Munro *Health/New Age/Health/Self-help Pages 376*

☐ **A Doll's House: and Two Other Plays** *by Henrik Ibsen* ISBN: *1-59462-112-8* **$19.95**
Henrik Ibsen created this classic when in revolutionary 1848 Rome. Introducing some striking concepts in playwriting for the realist genre, this play has been studied the world over. *Fiction/Classics/Plays 308*

☐ **The Light of Asia** *by sir Edwin Arnold* ISBN: *1-59462-204-3* **$13.95**
In this poetic masterpiece, Edwin Arnold describes the life and teachings of Buddha. The man who was to become known as Buddha to the world was born as Prince Gautama of India but he rejected the worldly riches and abandoned the reigns of power when... *Religion/History/Biographies Pages 170*

☐ **The Complete Works of Guy de Maupassant** *by Guy de Maupassant* ISBN: *1-59462-157-8* **$16.95**
"For days and days, nights and nights, I had dreamed of that first kiss which was to consecrate our engagement, and I knew not on what spot I should put my lips..." *Fiction/Classics Pages 240*

☐ **The Art of Cross-Examination** *by Francis L. Wellman* ISBN: *1-59462-309-0* **$26.95**
Written by a renowned trial lawyer, Wellman imparts his experience and uses case studies to explain how to use psychology to extract desired information through questioning. *How-to/Science/Reference Pages 408*

☐ **Answered or Unanswered?** *by Louisa Vaughan* ISBN: *1-59462-248-5* **$10.95**
Miracles of Faith in China *Religion Pages 112*

☐ **The Edinburgh Lectures on Mental Science (1909)** *by Thomas* ISBN: *1-59462-008-3* **$11.95**
This book contains the substance of a course of lectures recently given by the writer in the Queen Street Hall, Edinburgh. Its purpose is to indicate the Natural Principles governing the relation between Mental Action and Material Conditions... *New Age/Psychology Pages 148*

☐ **Ayesha** *by H. Rider Haggard* ISBN: *1-59462-301-5* **$24.95**
Verily and indeed it is the unexpected that happens! Probably if there was one person upon the earth from whom the Editor of this, and of a certain previous history, did not expect to hear again... *Classics Pages 380*

☐ **Ayala's Angel** *by Anthony Trollope* ISBN: *1-59462-352-X* **$29.95**
The two girls were both pretty, but Lucy who was twenty-one who supposed to be simple and comparatively unattractive, whereas Ayala was credited, as her Bombwhat romantic name might show, with poetic charm and a taste for romance. Ayala when her father died was nineteen... *Fiction Pages 484*

☐ **The American Commonwealth** *by James Bryce* ISBN: *1-59462-286-8* **$34.45**
An interpretation of American democratic political theory. It examines political mechanics and society from the perspective of Scotsman James Bryce *Politics Pages 572*

☐ **Stories of the Pilgrims** *by Margaret P. Pumphrey* ISBN: *1-59462-116-0* **$17.95**
This book explores pilgrims religious oppression in England as well as their escape to Holland and eventual crossing to America on the Mayflower, and their early days in New England... *History Pages 268*

www.bookjungle.com *email: sales@bookjungle.com fax: 630-214-0564 mail: Book Jungle PO Box 2226 Champaign, IL 61825*

QTY

The Fasting Cure *by Sinclair Upton*   ISBN: *1-59462-222-1* **$13.95**
In the Cosmopolitan Magazine for May, 1910, and in the Contemporary Review (London) for April, 1910, I published an article dealing with my experiences in fasting. I have written a great many magazine articles, but never one which attracted so much attention... New Age/Self Help/Health Pages 164

Hebrew Astrology *by Sepharial*   ISBN: *1-59462-308-2* **$13.45**
In these days of advanced thinking it is a matter of common observation that we have left many of the old landmarks behind and that we are now pressing forward to greater heights and to a wider horizon than that which represented the mind-content of our progenitors... Astrology Pages 144

Thought Vibration or The Law of Attraction in the Thought World   ISBN: *1-59462-127-6* **$12.95**

by William Walker Atkinson   *Psychology/Religion Pages 144*

Optimism *by Helen Keller*   ISBN: *1-59462-108-X* **$15.95**
Helen Keller was blind, deaf, and mute since 19 months old, yet famously learned how to overcome these handicaps, communicate with the world, and spread her lectures promoting optimism. An inspiring read for everyone... Biographies/Inspirational Pages 84

Sara Crewe *by Frances Burnett*   ISBN: *1-59462-360-0* **$9.45**
In the first place, Miss Minchin lived in London. Her home was a large, dull, tall one, in a large, dull square, where all the houses were alike, and all the sparrows were alike, and where all the door-knockers made the same heavy sound... Childrens/Classic Pages 88

The Autobiography of Benjamin Franklin *by Benjamin Franklin*   ISBN: *1-59462-135-7* **$24.95**
The Autobiography of Benjamin Franklin has probably been more extensively read than any other American historical work, and no other book of its kind has had such ups and downs of fortune. Franklin lived for many years in England, where he was agent... Biographies/History Pages 332

Name	
Email	
Telephone	
Address	
City, State ZIP	

☐ **Credit Card**   ☐ **Check / Money Order**

Credit Card Number	
Expiration Date	
Signature	

Please Mail to: *Book Jungle*
PO Box 2226
Champaign, IL 61825
or Fax to: *630-214-0564*

ORDERING INFORMATION

web: *www.bookjungle.com*
email: *sales@bookjungle.com*
fax: *630-214-0564*
mail: *Book Jungle PO Box 2226 Champaign, IL 61825*
or PayPal *to sales@bookjungle.com*

Please contact us for bulk discounts

DIRECT-ORDER TERMS

**20% Discount if You Order
Two or More Books**
Free Domestic Shipping!
Accepted: Master Card, Visa,
Discover, American Express

www.ingramcontent.com/pod-product-compliance
Lightning Source LLC
Chambersburg PA
CBHW081148270326
41930CB00014B/3080